Born to be a Footballer

Born to be a Footballer: My Autobiography

Liam Brady

First published by Eriu
An imprint of Black & White Publishing Group
A Bonnier Books UK company

4th Floor, Victoria House,
Bloomsbury Square,
London, WC1B 4DA

Owned by Bonnier Books
Sveavägen 56, Stockholm, Sweden

Twitter – @eriu_books
Instagram – @eriubooks

Hardback – 978-1-80418-468-4
Hardback (Ireland only) – 978-1-80418-079-2
Ebook – 978-1-80418-358-8

A CIP catalogue of this book is available from the British Library.

Printed and bound by Clays Ltd, Elcograf S.p.A

1 3 5 7 9 10 8 6 4 2

Eriu is an imprint of Bonnier Books UK
www.bonnierbooks.co.uk

Thanks to my wife Sarah, my family and friends for the love, support and friendship down through the years.

Contents

Foreword

I FIRST MET LIAM in February 1974, when Arsenal came to play Leeds at Elland Road. He wasn't yet 18, but I'd heard all about him. We won 3–1, though he was brilliant that day. I was injured and missed the game but went down to the car park afterwards to catch him before the Arsenal bus left. I was player-manager of the Irish team at that time. It was just to say hello and we had a chat. I think I mentioned that I'd played for Ireland with his brother Ray. I wanted to bring him on tour to South America with us that summer, but his manager at Arsenal, Bertie Mee, wouldn't let him go. Clubs didn't have to in those days. I don't think he even told Liam about the call-up.

I knew immediately we'd be seeing a lot of Liam. When it came to my first competitive match, a European Championship qualifier against the USSR at Dalymount Park, I put him straight into the team.

He told me later he was very nervous before that match. But that was normal. I was nervous from the minute I woke up in the morning before every match I ever played. You should be nervous, but it's different to being scared. When you watched Liam play, you wouldn't think he had a care in the world.

There was a saying in those days, that international football was different to club football. I never really subscribed to it anyway, it was still just a game of football. But to Liam it was no bother. I remember knocking the ball back to him from the kick-off, just to get him into the game straight away. But he played that afternoon like he'd been in the team for 10 years. He was so young, yet so mature. He was brilliant in a famous win for Ireland over a world-class team.

Liam was a beautiful footballer. He was beautiful to watch as well as being effective in what he did. There are a lot of great players who you wouldn't necessarily describe as beautiful. They might be workmanlike, or great tacklers, or able to dominate matches in a physical way. None of the great players are the same. A player is great, in my opinion, based on what he contributes to the team. And Liam certainly contributed his greatness to the team.

Liam was among the most stylish players to ever play the game. He always looked comfortable on the pitch. He had natural balance and his control was brilliant. He had this deceptive change of pace, where he might seem to be strolling along, but could inject a burst of acceleration to go past people. But he could also go past people with trickery. He could beat people easily. In the cup final he won, in 1979, he opened up the whole game for Arsenal with the way he was beating players in midfield.

Apart from his great talent on the ball, he had the awareness and knowledge to deliver the ball at the right time and the vision to see a pass. He could score goals too. He had a great shot in his left foot.

Liam was a joy to watch but he was also a joy to play with. I played with him in the Irish team for five years and he ranks among my favourite teammates. He had the ability and the knowledge and the temperament to always do what was best for the team. He wasn't a show-off. He never did tricks for the sake of it.

We had a perfect balance in the Irish midfield at the time. Mick Martin was a fine all-round midfielder. I played in the middle of the park, trying to dictate the play. And Liam was to the left. When I got the ball, Liam was always in a good position to receive it. You could give it to him with men around him. He'd just do his shuffle or throw his shape, whatever he did, and he'd be out of trouble. I couldn't do the things Liam did, beating players so easily. But we worked well together. That's what you find with good players. You know exactly what they are going to do, and they know what you're doing to do.

We got on well, off the field, from the start. He is good as gold, Liam. And he was always a very direct character. He learned the game on the Dublin streets in the traditional way. And he went away when he was 15 to England, same as most of us. That made him streetwise and independent and able to look after himself. He became one of the big stars of the English game at Arsenal, but he never lost the run of himself, never became big-headed, was always one of the lads. After a match in Dalymount, he'd still give us his party piece, 'Ruby, Don't Take Your Love to Town'.

We always stayed in touch and we are still great friends. When he was thinking of leaving Arsenal, he was coming under severe pressure to sign a new contract, and it was difficult to handle for such a young lad. I advised him, if he really wanted to go, to in no circumstances sign a new deal and I put him in touch with my solicitor, Ronnie Teeman, a very good friend who helped me when I needed it. Ronnie looked after him from there.

He was leaning towards going to Germany, at one stage, rather than Italy. He told me he was worried about the Italian reputation for tight marking and thought he might get more space in Germany. We spoke about it and I told him he'd be alright in Italy because it was the forwards they marked tightly, in my experience of European games against Italian clubs, while you got more space in the middle. As it turned out, he did brilliantly, winning two titles with Juventus, and became a great ambassador for Irish football at all his clubs in Italy.

In later years, it was a pleasure to work with him as a pundit. Talking about football was no bother to Liam. He came on the RTÉ panel when it was already established. Eamon Dunphy had this saying, that we'd 'run it from the floor', meaning we could decide what to talk about ourselves rather than have to follow whatever the producers had decided. It was a policy that worked well, I think, particularly with somebody as good as Bill O'Herlihy steering the ship. When Liam came on, he added to that. He always had a good knowledge of the game and expressed himself well.

I know himself and Eamon hadn't got on in earlier years. Eamon had written some harsh things back when Liam was still playing. But Eamon made him very welcome and Liam did his stuff. And in the end they became big pals.

No more than I'd love to have done so myself, I wish Liam could have played in a major tournament with Ireland. He deserved that stage. It was one of the downsides of Jack Charlton's great era that he didn't have more use for the creativity Liam could bring to a team.

Liam always took great pride in playing for Ireland. But he could have played for anyone. He is a credit to the game and a credit to himself and his family. One of our country's great footballers, and definitely our most beautiful.

John Giles

1

Dalymount Debut

DOUBTS BEGIN TO CREEP into my head in the Dalymount dressing room with my first Ireland senior shirt in my lap. Later in life, you learn to control your emotions better. But I haven't really yet, at 18. I don't have the experience. I'm about to live my dream but start entertaining nightmare scenarios. The Soviets are a top-class team. What if we get hammered? What if I have a stinker?

It isn't that the surroundings are intimidating. The changing room is a bit of a dump. Damp floorboards, chipped panelling on the walls. All a bit tattered compared to the tiled order of Highbury and some of the grounds I play at in England.

But I had left home for London three years earlier, hoping and believing I could follow my brothers and make a career in the game. To return to the home of Irish football as a full international was going to be a serious landmark in my life.

I've read about memory. Smells and sounds aren't supposed to stay with you too long. But I can recall that day's smells and sounds clearly. A cocktail of liniment oil from the players' rubs and Guinness and urine from the bar next door to the home dressing room. It suffocated the small room, where 16 of us elbowed each other for space.

There's the nervous tap dancing of the steel studs that Giles told us all to wear after the autumn showers that had rinsed Dublin. There's the constant clank of turnstiles, and the excitement around a new era for the Irish team. The experienced players reckon it sounds like a full house.

As we had made our way through Phibsborough, crowds had flowed out of the pubs to cheer the bus. Kick-off is 3pm because of the energy crisis that is panicking Britain and Ireland. The news in England is dominated by it. Very few night matches are taking place. Everyone knows the price of a gallon of petrol. The FAI was under pressure to save electricity, so no floodlights.

But today Dublin is buzzing, and most of the feel-good factor is down to Johnny Giles. A hero to me, to Irish football people he is a reassuring symbol of excellence. A determined man who nobody takes lightly and someone who had done it all in English football with Leeds United.

Now he is player-manager, and there is a belief that Giles will get things done. There is optimism in the air. He has been making the set-up much more professional. There had been a summer tour to South America, where the team played well in a narrow defeat by Brazil in the Maracanã and beat a Chile side that had qualified for the World Cup. Arsenal boss Bertie Mee had blocked me going, feeling I needed a rest after my first season with the first team. Though I hadn't found out I'd been selected until I had one of my first conversations with John. That was how things worked then, and the international associations were pretty powerless to make demands.

Giles had been injured when I played for Arsenal against Leeds the previous season, but he boarded our team bus after the game to introduce himself and told me he would keep in touch. I got my chance to play with him a month before the game against the USSR. He brought me on for the second half of a friendly against Manchester United at Old Trafford. We played well together, beating United 2–0, and I'd done fine.

I'd learned only the day before that he trusted me in the first competitive match of his new managerial career. He had pulled me aside and told me I would play alongside him and Mick Martin in midfield. We trained the day before the match and I was bursting with excitement. We finished off the session with a rehearsal of set pieces for and against. 'I know this is boring, but being organised properly can make the difference between winning and losing.' We worked on free kicks and corner kicks. Every player knew their roles for the next day.

But now, with kick-off approaching, fear has reached my stomach. I head for the toilet and bring up what little food I had managed to eat before the match. When I return, all is calm. That was John. He sits us down and briefly goes through what he wants from every player. Simple, sensible stuff. He never overcomplicates anything. He doesn't seem to need a moment to collect his thoughts. He is perfectly at ease with having to perform himself while instructing the rest of us.

When we run onto the pitch the stadium is full. Every vantage point is taken. The terraces are jam-packed and lots of fans have climbed on the roofs of the stands. There is no health and safety in 1974. Some 35,000 are there, our first qualifier for the 1976 European Championships, in a ground that takes around 4,000 now.

As I was growing from boy to man, Dalymount had been a huge part of my life. I watched countless League of Ireland games as a kid. Shelbourne was my team, Ben Hannigan my favourite player, so I was a regular at Tolka Park in Drumcondra. But I would try to go to the biggest game in Dublin every weekend.

Shamrock Rovers at Milltown, Drumcondra and Shelbourne at Tolka Park, and sometimes Bohemians at Dalymount.

It could be a profitable exercise. I'd go with my brother Frank or pals my age and our parents would give us the few shillings to get into the ground. We would ask the adults queuing and nearly always someone would give you a lift over the turnstiles so we could pocket the money.

I went to all the international matches too, some on Sundays, but I preferred midweek under the lights. When Frank played here for Shamrock Rovers in the 1968 FAI cup final I was 12. The atmosphere was tremendous. He was centre half, I hardly took my eyes off him and he played great at the back, didn't give the Waterford centre forward Mick Lynch a sniff. Rovers won 3–0.

And five years earlier Dalymount had changed my life, or at least mapped it out for me. It sounds a big claim, a little crazy even. And hindsight sometimes makes everything fall into place. But it's something I genuinely believe. That afternoon I watched my brother Ray play in a brilliant Ireland victory over Austria. The atmosphere was buoyant. It was an inspiring match, even if you had no skin or blood in the game. Ireland won 3–2, with Noel Cantwell scoring a penalty in the 89th minute. It triggered a huge pitch invasion by overjoyed Irish fans. As an eight-year-old boy this spectacle was thrilling. Alan Kelly, Charlie Hurley, Tony Dunne, Johnny Giles, Cantwell and my brother with them. I decided that afternoon I was going to be a footballer.

I practised, practised and practised even more. On an errand to the shops for my mother, the ball would always come, and I'd play one-twos with the wall of every house I passed. At my local park I smashed balls against the concrete pavilion for hours and hours. I joined St Kevin's Boys and was playing in the Dublin Schoolboys U13 league when I was 10. All I had in my head was football, and I read about the game as much as I could. I was aware that you had to make dreams happen, though, so I never tired of practising. I was going to follow my brothers. And I'm certain it was that afternoon in 1963 that signposted the way back to this stadium to play the USSR, almost 11 years later.

The experts say touch gives you the longest-lasting memories of all. John collects the kick-off from Don Givens and very purposely pushes the ball towards me. His way of saying: 'Come on now, I have every faith in you. I know you can do it.'

I don't know if you could say any fear subsided right then, but I just remember enjoying the game. It's a hard thing to describe, when you feel comfortable in a match. Everything fell into place. I played left of a tight three in the middle, a 4-3-3. Mick Martin was the other side of John. Ahead of us were Steve Heighway, Don and Ray Treacy. In my memory of the game, John is always beside me. And the highlights suggest that's not far off the mark. He's invariably there to receive the ball and give it back. As easy to link up with as those front walls on a jog to the shops.

Except the walls don't talk. And John was always talking. He never stopped. Again all simple stuff. Common sense. He just saw everything clearly and he saw it early.

'Liam, Liam, drop off. Tighter, Joe. Quicker, Mick. Close him down, Ray.'

It's funny. I've watched the highlights of that game back a good few times now. So when I visualise it, I can sometimes hear the commentary too. I can see John hit one of his renowned diagonal passes from left to right into Joe Kinnear's path. On the run, Joe hits an inch-perfect cross met by a brilliant header from Don Givens that flashes past the keeper, Vladimir Pilguy.

'What a beautiful goal. Isn't that a beautiful goal?' shouts legendary RTÉ commentator Jimmy Magee.

There was a sense of control, mainly, from there. And of Soviet panic. Much of that was spread by the dynamism of Ray Treacy, who was relentless in putting 'em under pressure a long time before that was something Ireland fans sang about. Even Olshanski, their big blond captain at the back, appeared rattled. And it wasn't straightforward to panic international defenders in the days when they could always turn and knock it back to their keeper to pick it up.

It was Ray who flicked on for Don's second at the near post, 10 minutes after the first goal. The ground was delirious. I can't recall the great Oleg Blokhin having much impact and the Soviets' frustration spilled over in a goalmouth scuffle that saw Vladimir Kaplichni sent off and my Arsenal teammate Terry Mancini join him for retaliation.

That incident turned out to be a terrible blow for Terry. He was targeted at the corner kick by the Soviet defender, who elbowed him in the face. Terry duly responded with a forearm smash across the nose. The referee had seen what had gone on and both got a red card. It would prematurely end Terry's international career. He had been capped late in his career and a four-match ban put paid to his chances of playing again.

They say 2–0 is a dangerous lead, but needless to say John Giles doesn't believe in that kind of thing. As far as John is concerned, a 2–0 lead is better than a 1–0 lead, and the most sensible approach would be to try to turn it into a 3–0 lead. There was a cup of tea, calm, and then John took complete control. He switched Mick Martin to the back in place of Terry and pulled Steve Heighway into midfield to help us out. He preached work rate and concentration, and he assured us we'd go on and win this game.

There were flurries of a Soviet storm to be weathered early in the second half, but nothing that unduly troubled Paddy Roche in goal. Joe Kinnear did a great defensive job on Blokhin. And then came one of those rewards for a coach who has done his job and payback for us being a little bored the day before – a goal direct from the training ground. A routine we'd gone over and over. John's quick free kick meeting Don's near-post run for his hat-trick.

From there we were comfortable, and Jimmy Magee's commentary reflected the euphoria that surrounded one of the great days in the history of the game in Ireland.

'Irish soccer has been reawakened.'

'Arguably our greatest ever performance at international level.'

'Football to warm the heart.'

As far as debuts go, it lived up to a decade's worth of dreams. Easily the best day of my life up to that point. My mother, father, brothers and sister were all there to to see me play my part in a truly great display by an Irish team. Don Givens rightly made the headlines with his outstanding hat-trick, and the consensus was I had struck up an excellent partnership with Giles, and that I had a bright future. I flew back to London the next day a happy and proud young man. In an international career spanning 15 years and 71 matches, this debut cap remains the one I remember best and cherish most.

2

So Far So Good

A BOOK LANDED ME in the London High Court in 1982. Maybe it served me right for recounting my life story at the age of 24. *So Far So Good* it was called, tempting fate dangerously, and I got involved against my better instincts. It was my agent Dennis Roach's idea. Dennis was considered to be the first major football agent in the late 1970s. A former player in the lower leagues, he met Johan Cruyff on holiday in Portugal after their children started playing together on the beach. Cruyff was so impressed with Dennis's business know-how that he flew him to Spain to negotiate his transfer from Ajax to Barcelona, and an international agency was born overnight. Or at least that's how Dennis told it.

He was a super-confident man who soon represented many of the top players. In 1979, he was involved with the deal that made Trevor Francis the first million-pound player when he left Birmingham City for Nottingham Forest. Players did need someone in their corner. The balance of power was totally with the clubs. With no freedom of contract, a player couldn't just walk away when his deal expired, as the club held on to his registration. Many were taken advantage of and tied to low wages. Especially if you'd come through a club's youth system and hadn't been involved in a transfer where you could negotiate your worth. There was no contractual advice. We were young men, thrilled to be doing what we loved for a living, and not really capable of saying no when new contracts were put in front of us. A lot changed when Kevin Keegan left Liverpool. It opened people's eyes. He joined Hamburg in Germany in 1977 for much more than he had been earning at Anfield.

In 1978, Arsenal were pushing me to sign a new contract. I'd steadily improved over the previous four years and Dennis convinced me I needed his representation. I fell for his sales pitch and signed a two-year agreement to make him my agent. I only wanted someone to handle negotiations and maybe get me a boot deal. But Dennis had other plans. Like many agents I've come to know down through the years, Dennis was keen to control not only the player's business affairs, but also their lives. Agents like to make themselves indispensable. With many of today's players, if they want to book a holiday or a hotel or even have a meal out, it's all done though their agent. Their lives are not their own any more, and the agents are fine with that.

After we won the FA Cup in 1979, Dennis launched a Liam Brady fan club. Send away your postal order for a signed Brady photograph, all that kind of thing. Hugely embarrassing for me. And then he came up with the plan for a ghostwritten book. I have no idea why I went along with it. Naivety, I suppose. You won't find many regrets in the chapters of this book, but this episode remains a big one.

Over two or three months I spoke to the ghostwriter, Tony Roche, a journalist with the *Daily Mirror*, to describe, as the book puts it, 'the 10 momentous years from the hopeful days of playing for St Kevin's in Dublin to lifting the FA Cup at

Wembley with Arsenal'. There are still a few copies around the house, and when I leaf through one now I find it a slightly strange book. It's very serious. Gloomy, even, in parts. I complain a lot. The cover blurb says it 'will probably shatter a few illusions and remove the phoney tinsel from the edges of many a mental picture of life as a professional soccer player'. I can't quite reconcile the tone of it with what I remember as some of the happiest years of my life.

Maybe Tony Roche just caught me at a bad time, while I was in a bit of a quandary about my future. The fans at Arsenal were giving me a bit of stick, because I had hinted I'd be leaving. And the publisher, Stanley Paul, was pushing me to be controversial. Tony knew the game and the questions to ask. And I was honest in response, which probably wasn't wise.

I'm not sure too many people were impressed with the book. It was, rightly, regarded as a bit of a liberty, a guy in his mid-twenties writing an autobiography. Sales were middling and the little money it made certainly wasn't worth the grief. I found the whole process unpleasant – and then it put me the dock.

Exhibit A for the prosecution was a chapter called 'The Press Problem', in which I complain about the practices of some journalists. I had friends among the press. Reg Drury of the *News of the World*, Patrick Collins of the *Mail*, Harry Miller in the *Mirror* and Michael Hart at the *Evening Standard*. Guys you could trust not to spin a quote out of shape. But I was wary of others. It was a time when trust between footballers and the media was being tested. Rivalry was intense among the tabloids for 'exclusives'. I knew there were writers around who would give you a higher mark in their player ratings in exchange for a steer on a story. I never got involved in that.

Footballers were becoming nervy. And soon we'd clam up altogether, except to reveal we'd be taking things one game at a time, at the end of the day. But in those days there was no caller ID, so you'd still answer the phone, as I did to Kevin Moseley of the *Daily Express*.

I didn't like Moseley, was certain he didn't like Arsenal, had noticed he tended to only write negative articles about the club. In the book, I criticise him for a story he wrote about me and the Arsenal manager Terry Neill, and my plans to leave Arsenal. I accuse him of misrepresenting what I said on the phone for a back-page story. In the same chapter, I have a go at the 'certain reporter, who for his professional credibility shall remain nameless' who phoned my teammate Malcolm McDonald's wife, upon hearing a rumour that Malcolm had been killed in a car accident. It hadn't happened, but Malcolm's wife didn't know that, because he was away for the day, and she was beside herself.

Because he was the only reporter named in the chapter, Moseley claimed I had implied he was the man who made that call, and had behaved unprofessionally. And indeed I was implying that, since Malcolm had told me it was him.

Moseley sued for libel on both counts, claiming I'd damaged him as a person and as a journalist. The *Express* joined him on the case, which put me in an even trickier position, given English defamation law at the time, where the burden of proof was squarely on the defendant.

It was late 1982 and I'd just begun my third season in Italy, having left Juventus for Sampdoria. By now Roach was no longer my agent and the Leeds-based solicitor Ronnie Teeman looked after all my affairs. Ronnie had been introduced to me by John Giles, in one of the many pieces of good advice John has given me during my career. Ronnie did his research and arranged an up-and-coming barrister, Richard Rampton, who went on to become one of the most renowned libel silks around. You might have seen him played by Tom Wilkinson in the movie *Denial*, where he was defending a libel suit brought by the writer David Irving, who had been described as a Holocaust denier.

Around a month before our case was due in court, myself and Peter Levine, Ronnie's partner, went to meet Rampton. Sampdoria president Paolo Mantovani had given me time off to try to get myself out of this mess.

Rampton was worryingly frank. 'Look, Liam, you can contest this, but I have to warn you, the case could go either way.'

'How much will it cost if I lose?' I recall asking.

'In the region of a hundred thousand,' he replied. It was a frightening prospect, and Rampton may have noticed the blood drain from my face.

'You can always settle with him . . .'

'And how much will that cost?'

Peter's turn to deliver sobering news. 'In the region of 25 grand and a full apology.'

I remembered how much I disliked Moseley and tried to recover a little composure. 'Let's offer them the sum of money I made from the book.'

'How much is that?' enquired Rampton.

'Around £1,500.'

We all smiled and began preparing for court.

The case opened in October 1982. I'd arrived again from Genoa, not needing this interruption to our fine start to the season. The media was all over it – who doesn't want to read about a footballer in court? Peter and Richard were flanking me, with Ronnie's daughter Miriam assisting them. Ronnie figured it would be a good idea to walk into court every morning with my wife Sarah. Our first child was due in January and he felt it couldn't do any harm for the jury to see she was heavily pregnant.

Prosecution counsel David Eady set out Moseley's case, claiming I'd launched 'a fundamental attack on his professional reputation and portrayed him as someone very heartless and inconsiderate'. The judge was Lord Justice Bernard Caulfield, renowned for his florid summations and who later became well known for directing proceedings in the Jeffrey Archer libel case against the *News of the World*.

But on the first couple of days of this one he appeared to have little interest. He had a stinking cold and a box of tissues perched in front of him at all times. Whenever I glanced his way he was blowing his nose or seemed to be dozing. He said very little, though one morning, as the rain pelted the windows of the courtroom, he noted, to nobody in particular, that there would be 'empty spaces on the terraces this weekend'.

Eady introduced a string of character witnesses, vouching for Moseley's absolute trustworthiness and unimpeachable integrity. They were mainly other journalists and they portrayed him in a shining light. I don't know if it made any impression, but I quickly tired of hearing Moseley's bona fides as a reporter being lauded in various long-winded ways.

These fine tributes were punctured somewhat when, for my side, Malcolm took the stand and confirmed that, yes, Moseley was the journalist who had phoned his wife and, yes, she had been very upset and shocked and, yes, he had told all his Arsenal teammates about it. Eady mentioned integrity less after that.

It was difficult to judge how things were going as the trial neared an end, but I still had to take the stand myself. 'How you cope under cross-examination will be crucial,' Rampton warned. 'Just be yourself and tell it like it is.'

First it was his turn, and he fed me a few tap-ins we'd prepared well. I recalled the short conversation with Moseley that he'd trumped up into an inaccurate story. I rehashed exactly what Malcolm had told us in the dressing room the day after he had supposedly had a fatal accident on the M1.

'Have you been unfair to Mr Moseley?' he asked, in conclusion. 'I don't think so,' I replied. I glanced at Caulfield and he didn't even seem to be registering any of this.

Eady countered by asking why I seemed to hold such animosity towards the press. I told him there were a number of journalists I got on with and others I just didn't trust. He got me to admit to some minor inaccuracies in the book around the sequence of events that led to Moseley phoning Malcolm's wife. I apologised for those.

Then he proceeded to the nub of the case – as silly as that sounds – the story about me and Terry Neill. Did I recall, he asked, that phone call and Moseley asking me 'How are you getting on with the Irishman?', meaning Terry.

'That would have been a strange thing to ask,' I replied, 'since there were so many Irishmen at Arsenal at the time.' I saw Eady shoot Moseley a quizzical look. 'We had Pat Jennings, Pat Rice, Sammy Nelson . . .' I continued, determined to labour this point. And before I could carry on, an assertive voice echoed from the bench. Caulfield had woken up and come to life. 'O'Leary and Stapleton . . .'

The courtroom erupted in laughter, except for Moseley's people. It was a knockout punch. Caulfield, the old fox, knew his football. He went on to sum up in a way that seemed extremely favourable to me and the jury took just an hour and a half to return a not guilty verdict.

It was a huge relief. Rampton cheekily informed the jury that I would sign a copy of the book for each of them. Some Arsenal fans had gathered outside and I signed a few more on the steps of the courthouse. But it was a chapter I was extremely glad to close.

I took it as a wake-up call, too. Agreeing to do that book was a sign I had become a little carried away with myself and the attention football was bringing. I vowed to have nothing to do with another book.

Until now. More than four decades on, retired from football, retired from media, I feel I now have a story to tell. Arsenal as a kid and a young man, seven years in Italy, management, coaching, working with Arsenal's youngsters. And even, after all my cribbing about journalists and their ways, a bit of work in newspapers and television.

There have been a few setbacks and disappointments along the way, the odd fallout, an occasional controversy. But very few regrets. If the pages of *So Far So Good* suggest that, at 24, I didn't fully appreciate all that football had already done for me, I hope that, this time round, I can set that record straight too.

3

Rare Old Times

I WAS BORN TO be a footballer. But in which code? The Bradys were a GAA family. Edward Brady and Patrick Brady, my grand-uncles, won the 1902 All-Ireland final with Dublin. The match was postponed and eventually played in 1904 on the same day as the hurling final, won by Cork. The double bill drew a huge crowd to the opening of the Cork Athletic Grounds, now Páirc Uí Chaoimh.

I know this, because it's a story that never got old when I was growing up as a kid in Glenshesk Road, Whitehall, then on the outskirts of Dublin, now pretty much in the heart of the city. The Bradys played in defence and must have done alright that afternoon because London were beaten 2-8 to 1-2. They played their club football for Parnell's, one of the great old Dublin GAA institutions. My family maintained links with the club across the decades. My father Ned played for Parnell's and won, alongside his younger brother Jimmy, the Dublin Senior Football Championship in 1939. Dad was 28 and Jimmy 26. Jimmy won an All-Ireland Minor medal in 1930. It's an irony that I would encounter trouble in making a choice between our national game and the English game. I blame it all on my dad's uncle Frank.

My grand-uncle Frank, although a fine Gaelic footballer, broke the mould when he opted for soccer instead. I guess it was because there was the option to make a few quid out of your talent, but I would love to know the sequence of events. He was born in 1902 and growing up was steeped in the GAA and Parnell's. He was a teenager while the war between the IRA and the British forces in Ireland was at its worst. Atrocities and tit-for-tat killings were a common occurrence. Frank would have been 18. What was happening in his life? What was going through his mind? I know he played for Belfast Celtic, then found his way to Cork and played for the Fordsons factory team in the League of Ireland. We knew all about his achievements, especially his Ireland caps. He played twice for the Irish Free State in the 1920s, home and away against Italy. Soccer was now in the Brady family, though there was never any sense, in our house, that one sport was more worthy than another. Or more Irish.

I am the seventh child of Ned and Eileen. Paddy and Ray arrived a generation before me, in 1936 and '37. Sylvia and Breda followed not long after. Eamonn and Frank were next, before a seven-year gap to me, a pretty unexpected addition, in 1956. Born in extra time, you might say.

We were not a large family, by the standards of the day. Not every house had a TV, which was the only acceptable birth control, under the watchful eye of the Catholic Church.

Sylvia died when she was just five, from meningitis. Myself, Eamonn and Frank never knew her. My mother sometimes talked about her but my father never did. He wasn't a great talker on personal matters, Ned Brady, like a lot of men. It frustrates me that he never talked much about all the turbulent events in Irish history that he grew up experiencing as daily news. Because the period has always fascinated me.

The Easter Rising of 1916 took place a few streets away from where he grew up. Bloody Sunday, in Croke Park, was a stone's throw. He was a child during the War of Independence against British rule between 1918 and 1921. And the Civil War that followed the signing of the Treaty. What was that like? What was my grandfather doing? Which side the Bradys were on is what I'd like to know, I suppose. Steeped in GAA, you'd suspect we had republican leanings. But I know that my father held Michael Collins in the highest esteem. Those were complicated times. History and politics were rarely discussed at home. So there's so much I regret not asking him.

In later years I'd probe him more about his childhood. And one day, over a pint in our local, he told me about his mother. Ellen Melsip came from Lancashire, England and had been sent to Dublin to one of those institutions run by the nuns. A laundry, we think. To have, as they used to describe it in harsh and dehumanising terms, a child out of wedlock.

In Dublin a while later, Elizabeth met my grandfather James Brady and they married, soon starting a family. My father had two siblings, May and Jimmy. But when he was just three, their happy life fell apart, when Elizabeth succumbed to tuberculosis, a disease that ended many lives in Dublin then and for decades after. James married again, but I get a sense my father's step-mother found it difficult to take on an instant family. Maybe my father didn't talk too much about his childhood because some things were too painful to recollect.

My mother, Eileen Henvey, worked in service, as a maid in a big household. She was from Coolock, now very much part of Dublin City, but which was out in the country then. That gave her an accent totally different to my father's, though they were born around 10 miles apart. She told me I was a quiet child, compared to the rest of them. Walking at 10 months and out at the garden gate at 12 months watching the older kids playing football in our road.

It's funny, I can recall some of the games and goals in 'The Keyhole', a Northside Dublin name for a cul de sac – often it was 20, maybe 30 boys having a match. I can remember the trouble we caused when someone's front window smashed. There were lots of broken windows and footballs confiscated.

I can only recall being a really happy kid. 'The Rare Ould Times' by Pete St John, a fond reminiscence on life in Dublin, is among my favourite songs. 'Ring a ring a rosey, as the light declines.' It never fails to stir a memory of one of those endless games on the road outside. Or of a busy house where somebody was forever running out the front door, often to a match. Or of a dinner table buzzing with sporting arguments and debate, my father in his element on the more comfortable topics of football or Gaelic or boxing or horse racing. Johnny Carey or Duncan Edwards. Kevin Heffernan or Jim Crowley. Rocky Marciano or Cassius Clay. Pat Taaffe and Arkle. Vincent O'Brien and Nijinsky.

I know this carefree existence wasn't the experience all around me. Life was a struggle. Many found work elusive. There was always an awareness we were blessed my father had reliable employment on the docks, like his father before him. My older brothers had grown up in much more difficult times. I was cocooned, no doubt, from the stresses of the time.

It was a life full to the brim with football. Paddy and Ray were excellent players with Home Farm, the renowned schoolboy club just a 10-minute walk from our house. Paddy had represented Ireland U16s against an England team that included the great Duncan Edwards, one of the Busby Babes tragically lost in the Munich air disaster. Ray moved on from Home Farm to play semi-pro with Transport, in the League of Ireland. But his ambition was England. And Ray was the kind of guy who didn't wait for things to happen.

The year after I was born, he left Dublin. Later, he explained to me that the lack of career prospects at home and the claustrophobic grind of a repressive society pushed him to go. Every street both sides of the Liffey was emptying of young men for the same reasons. Ray went to London to become a professional footballer. And that's what happened. He had grown sick of waiting for things to progress in the traditional way – a scout spotting potential and organising a trial. So one day he packed up and got the boat to Holyhead, made his way to London and ended up in New Cross, where one of our neighbour's sons, Georgie Cox, was living. Not long after, he went to watch Millwall, the nearest professional club, play on a Saturday afternoon and thought to himself that the standard of player wasn't all that great and he was as good as any of them at the Den. So he pestered his way into a trial, did enough to earn a contract and made 188 appearances for the club, along with 88 more for Queens Park Rangers (QPR), and won six Ireland caps.

When I was three, Paddy followed Ray to London and later on to QPR too. They were chalk and cheese as characters. Paddy the quiet one, always stuck in a book, Ray a bit of a tearaway. But they looked out for each other and drove each other on.

At home, Frank was starting off on the same journey. Our Sunday mornings were usually spent watching him play for Home Farm and sometimes straight to Croke Park after to see the Dubs. Dublin had a very good team in the early 1960s.

He went on to join Shamrock Rovers and won the family's only FAI Cup medal in 1968. The same year my father took me out of school to watch Frank play for Rovers against Crusaders in the final of the inter-league cup between teams from north and south at Windsor Park. We got the train to Belfast, then had a police escort to the ground, abuse raining in from all these people lining the streets. Because my father was with me, I wasn't really afraid. Though I can remember him bending down to tell me: 'Look straight ahead, get to the ground, watch the match, and we'll get out of here.' Rovers won it anyhow, though by the end I wasn't sure if that was ideal. It was my first experience of the different outlooks that exist on our island. The train journey back involved plenty of discussion about what exactly made the people lining the streets call us 'Fenian bastards' and shout 'fuck the Pope'.

Basically, I was immersed in football. I knew football as a world of drama and excitement that often drove people to do crazy things. By eight, I knew all about the emergence on the Dublin schoolboy scene of St Kevin's Boys, the new club that had formed in the local Ellenfield Park. Kevin's is among the best things ever to happen to Whitehall. A club that just naturally became the focal point for a community, thanks to the enthusiasm and dedication of the many volunteer coaches and officials who looked after us so well. All the kids in our area gravitated there. And some of my happiest memories are of wearing the orange shirt and black shorts.

My first proper manager was club stalwart Des Lawlor. I was 10, playing my first organised matches for the U13s, though I played for the U12s too, whenever I could. Indeed Des often told the story of an afternoon when I played for the 13s, ran to the nearby pitch at the final whistle and got subbed on for the 12s, scored a couple of goals and came off again. I don't remember this one, it sounds a bit of a tall tale, but I know I couldn't get enough of football at that age.

Kevin's was a tiny club then, in the shadow of Home Farm, but is now one of the best schoolboy clubs in the country, with many internationals starting out in Whitehall. Under Des's guidance, our team became one of the best in Dublin and won the U15 National Cup in 1970. But before we knew we were any good, we just loved the place and the game. Des and the other coaches deserve great credit for the happy environment they created. Because my three brothers had all played for Farm, I was often asked to sign for them. But Kevin's with my mates was where I wanted to be.

I was small for my age, but sport came easily to me, soccer and Gaelic. Soccer was the council estate game. My parents had watched all their sons take up the game, and I was last on the conveyor belt. But I never felt under the slightest pressure from them on a football pitch. They only came to watch me in the big matches. There was never a question of letting anyone down if we didn't win or I didn't play well. The games were to be enjoyed.

For most kids in Dublin at the time, our heroes came to life on Saturday nights. My parents would sometimes enjoy a well-deserved Saturday night out having a few in the local pub. My dad would leave money for sweets and fish and chips. So it was home to watch *Ironside* and then *Match of the Day*. That is how I fell in love with football, along with magazines like *Charles Buchan's Football Monthly*, *Goal* and later *SHOOT!* I cut out photos of the players and plastered my bedroom. George Best, Johnny Giles and Colin Bell were stuck to the wall above my bed. Anyone who could do something a bit different. Charlie George at Arsenal came into that bracket too, a few years later.

But a book like this is obliged to reveal one dark secret, so it's time to come clean: I grew up a devout worshipper of Manchester United. My family too. George Best, Bobby Charlton and Denis Law were our holy trinity. Most Dublin boys my age were carrying on the same love affair. Dubliner Liam Whelan lost his life in 1958 in the Munich air disaster. Noel Cantwell was the United captain who lifted the cup in '63. Alongside him were two Dubs, Tony Dunne and Johnny Giles. The O'Reilly family, our neighbours, had one of the few televisions in the area, and they allowed us boys in to watch the match. It is the first cup final I can remember. I could tell you who won all the cups and leagues in those years, and name the teams as well.

United had the pick of Ireland's best young players then, largely down to their scout, Billy Behan. Everybody knew who Billy was, and you could often detect the rumble of excitement that spread around a football pitch when he was spotted before a game. By the time I was 12, Billy had been in contact with my parents, and there was talk of a trip to Manchester for trials. But I think Billy feared I was too small to do myself justice, and wanted to wait until I got stronger.

It's funny how things work, how your destiny spins on someone else's choices. Bill Darby, who would become one of Arsenal's most famous scouts, had just written to the club, pointing out that Manchester United had more or less a free run at all this talent in Dublin. And that if Arsenal had any sense, they would give him the job as their scout. Bill was a nice man, approachable, friendly. He networked well and knew how to get on with the different schoolboy clubs. He was welcome everywhere. Obviously, the letter struck a chord at Arsenal, who sent over their highly regarded Wales scout Malwyn Roberts to see if Bill had an eye for a player. That led to Bill bringing Malwyn to watch my Under-13 side. And it seems both me and Bill passed this test, because Malwyn and Bill's next stop was Glenshesk Road and our house for a chat with my parents. After a fair bit of persuasion that I'd be well looked after in London, a trial was arranged for August 1969. And Bill got a job he'd do extremely well at.

I remember that first trip to London, aged 13, like it was yesterday. A bus to Dublin Airport, flying on my own, no chaperone. Ernie Collett, who played in Arsenal's dominant 1930s teams, picked me up at Heathrow. He was the trusted right-hand man of Gordon Clarke, Arsenal's chief scout.

We drove to Highbury largely in silence as I couldn't understand his Yorkshire accent – I doubt I'd ever spoken to an Englishman before. And I'd hazard a guess Ernie wasn't having much luck making out what I was saying either. We arrived at the famous Highbury Marble Halls, where approximately 30 other 13- and 14-year-old trialists had gathered. We were to be divided into pairs and sent to the relatively plush – in those days – Alexandra Hotel, next to Finsbury Park. Plush to me, for sure, since I had never stayed in a hotel before.

My roommate was the only black kid in the group. Fine with me, but I could see some of the English boys sniggering when we were put together. And it was immediately evident to me, even at 13, that there was a reason we were paired up. I'd heard from my brothers the difficult time Irish people endured in London in the 1950s and '60s. And while Phil Lynott from Thin Lizzy was just about the only black person I'd seen in Ireland, I'd heard a fair bit about racism too. I knew about the 'No Blacks. No Irish. No Dogs' signs outside digs in London. This felt a little bit like that, and it made me uneasy.

Anyway, me and my new pal from Hackney were getting on fine chatting football at the Alexandra, where we were told to have an early night. But next thing he's on the phone in the room to his mates, inviting them round to inspect his new luxury accommodation. I wasn't expecting company, so headed out for a walk to the local park. It was a hot summer evening and I spotted some older lads having a kickabout. Here, I employed the age-old tactic of standing close by looking on until one of them shouted 'Fancy a game, little 'un?' I held my own, and at the end one of them said, 'You're not bad for a kid. We're here most nights if you fancy another game.' I don't think Arsenal would have been pleased with my pre-trial preparation, but there weren't many child welfare concerns then.

Next morning, up at London Colney training ground, competition was stiff, though of course I didn't know it then. Richie Powling and John Matthews were there, who both went on to play first team football at Arsenal. So was Ian Gould, who made it too, but as wicketkeeper for Middlesex and England. And there were others who somehow failed to make the cut at Arsenal, such as Glenn Roeder and Laurie Cunningham. Both ended up at Leyton Orient, which I couldn't understand. Laurie in particular was a brilliant player. I always suspected his failure to be selected had to be down to the culture of the time. At all clubs then – even Arsenal, which later gained a reputation among the more inclusive – there was a reluctance to take on black players. Even then Laurie had electric pace, and whoever overlooked him must have been mad.

It's a cutthroat test. An hour or so to prove yourself, if you're lucky. A game of your life, literally. My new mate from Hackney didn't do enough either, though that may have had something to do with the phone bill at the hotel. Malwyn Roberts told me after that he feared I'd blown it too. I'd started nervously and Malwyn was just as anxious, since he'd apparently told every scout there that he had found a good one. So his reputation was taking a battering until I settled down in the second half and showed what I could do. It just became one of those happy mornings where you fall in step with the game's rhythm. I was dribbling past two and three players and scored a couple of goals.

They didn't give us any verdicts straight away, but you didn't have to be told. Some kids made a lonely walk back to the changing rooms, but I was surrounded by Arsenal staff, firing questions about my background. I knew I'd done what was needed.

Back inside, the chat turned to the next steps. The club was anxious to know how it could tie me down – not straightforward since I wasn't from the UK. Really they wanted something on paper to warn off Manchester United, who they knew were hovering. The chief scout, Gordon Clarke, settled for inviting me over for an extended trial during the next school holiday, and asked me my shoe size. They'd be sending me 'a nice pair of Adidas boots', he promised. The kind of conversation that might take place nowadays, except the kids' parents might get offered a house, a car or a job to entice the kid to commit to the club.

Coventry City were now interested too, and willing to go a little further. Bunny Fulham, a famous League of Ireland player with Drumcondra, was their scout, and Noel Cantwell, the former Ireland and Man United star, their manager. Bunny called round to Glenshesk Road and offered my mother a washing machine if I would sign for him. Bunny and my brother Ray were mates, but I didn't fancy being sent to Coventry.

When I returned to London next time, my brother Eamonn came along as my minder and advisor. He was only 23 so wasn't exactly a super-agent. Indeed he had no idea how the business of football worked. Gordon got me to sign 'amateur forms', which were essentially meaningless legally, but under the curious code of honour football clubs observed it was enough to put United off making any further approaches. As part of the agreement Eamonn somehow managed to extract a job for our dad on £40 a month as another Arsenal scout in Dublin. He wouldn't really have to scout but just send over some fictional expenses to receive a nice little cheque in the post. Not quite within the Football League rules, but my dad wasn't complaining.

The decision to commit to Arsenal had nothing to do with money. Basically, while United had been indecisive, Arsenal acted, along every step of the way, as if they were convinced I had what it took to play for them. And most important, they convinced my mam and dad I'd be looked after. Told them about the family who'd take care of me and explained how I'd be given every chance to become the best footballer I could be.

Next time, my mother and father came with me and got the full treatment from the club, including dinner with Gordon in the fancy restaurant at Highbury. Scene of that old story my mother loved to tell. Gordon leads us in, hands out some menus and my mam looks over at me and says: 'Don't bother with that menu for him – all he eats is chips.' From there, by the indisputable logic of nicknames, I was introduced to everyone at the club as 'Chippy' and continue to be called it to this day by many of my former teammates, despite little encouragement from my end. Even now, when some Arsenal supporters address me as Chippy, I tell them 'only my teammates can call me that'.

There were still 18 months or so of a normal life to live before I'd leave for North London to sign as an apprentice in 1971. Gaelic football was another big part of that life. I loved the game and played for Whitehall Gaels when the matches didn't clash with St Kevin's games. I also played left-half forward for the school at a time when St Aidan's CBS had a super team. Tommy Drumm and Andy Roche, who went on to play with

Dublin, were in the side. We beat all the best teams in Dublin. I recall playing in a big game against Drimnagh Castle CBS, who had Kevin Moran and Gerry Ryan, who I'd go on to play with for Ireland.

It's another cherished day, the afternoon in 1970 when we won the school its first Leinster senior title, beating Naas CBS. An old *Sunday Independent* clipping suggests I got five points, though Brendan Dalton was the main man, bagging three goals from full forward. We retained that title the following year, when Gaelic football got my picture in the papers and my name in the headlines. Sadly, it wasn't for my contribution on the field, but rather for not making it onto the field one day.

It wasn't a showpiece occasion, rather a friendly – or challenge match, in the vernacular of the GAA – against St Jarlath's of Tuam. Problem was, I'd found out the week before I'd been selected to captain Ireland in an U15 international against Wales in Cardiff on the same day. In my innocence, I figured the principal of the school, Brother Loughran, would acknowledge this as a fairly straightforward choice when I knocked on his office door to declare my unavailability for the Tuam test. I was going to Wales to captain my country. Surely the school would be proud. Instead he told me, in the clearest terms, that I wouldn't be welcome back at the school if I missed the GAA match. I was crestfallen. Surely he wasn't serious.

At the time, the GAA rulebook banned its members from playing – or even watching – other sports, specifically what were regarded as the English sports of soccer, cricket, rugby and hockey, lest our Gaelic bona fides be polluted by contamination from the Crown's games. Though by 1971, blind eyes were often turned to the many transgressors and the rule was actually revoked that year.

But Brother Loughran wasn't budging, even when my father visited the school to plead my case on the Monday after the game in Wales. He just held up his hand, told my father he'd hear no more about it and that I wasn't welcome back. I was raging about the whole thing since I'd been very happy at the school. My parents were upset and concerned I wouldn't be able to sit my Inter Cert exams before leaving for London. My father contacted the newspapers and a journalist called to the house to get the story on the record.

And so, to my huge embarrassment, I endured my first media saga before I'd turned 15. Maybe good preparation for the line of work I was heading into. When questioned by the newspapers Brother Loughran was altogether more conciliatory, suggesting I'd never been expelled and it was all a misunderstanding. That wasn't the case and I never did go back to my class in St Aidan's. I studied for my exams in Plunkett Technical School down the road, though St Aidan's were obliged to allow me to return to sit them in their buildings. And I did well in those exams despite the unwelcome drama.

I would soon be leaving home to go to England, and should have left with the school's best wishes. But they weren't forthcoming. It's long forgotten now. Those were the times. Over the years, the school and I have reached out to patch things up. I've been back a couple of times and been made very welcome. Ironically, they have a fine soccer team these days. I wonder what Loughran would make of that development.

It wasn't easy to leave Glenshesk Road that summer, and it would take a couple of attempts to put down the roots of a new life. My happy childhood was probably a hindrance at first, as I longed for home in those early months in London. I missed my parents and my friends and wondered if I could cope.

But I could always count on the support of my brothers living in and around London. Ray, Paddy and Eamonn knew the life and how hard it was to make it as a footballer. How dedicated you had to be. Their advice along the way was vital. I feel very lucky they were always there for me at what could have been a very lonely period in a kid's life.

Ray's career showed what could be achieved through determination and self-belief. His appearances for Ireland meant the world to him, and that day watching him in Dalymount triggered something in me that never really switched off. In later years, his pub that his wonderful wife, Faith, looked after so well, the Railway and Bicycle in Sevenoaks, Kent, would often become a home from home.

The two older lads had left school at 13, but when Paddy finished playing, he availed of every scrap of education the Professional Footballers' Association offered. And he went on to teach Economics at London University. I may be going out on a limb by suggesting he could be the only Millwall player to take that route.

Because the two of them were more or less finished with football before I started, they always told me that my career gave them another go at it. Another spin through the highs and lows. They willed me onto every next step. Came to the matches. Were there to celebrate or commiserate.

Frank's wisdom was always dispensed quietly, a word in your ear. And he always carried a great spirit of adventure; he emigrated and played pro in Australia for a while. When I went Down Under with Arsenal in '77, I visited his former clubs in Sydney and they couldn't speak highly enough of him.

Eamonn's help was the most important of all, in those days. He was single, living in London, didn't have a family life then. So he looked after me at weekends, brought me to visit Ray and Paddy. He often told us he could have made it as a pro too, if he hadn't joined the Irish Merchant Navy at 16. He played in the same schoolboy team as Eamon Dunphy at Stella Maris and reckoned if Eamon could play for Ireland then so could he.

Breda, the only girl after Sylvia, has been a brilliant sister to all of us. Following the passing of our mum and dad, her home, with her husband Michael, became the place where we all congregated, where we have had so many wonderful family get-togethers and parties. We lost Frank in 2009, Ray in 2016 and Paddy during the first summer of the Covid-19 pandemic. I owe so much to their love and encouragement.

4

Starting Out

As a 12-year-old in September 1968, I was among the throng at Dublin Airport, filling up an autograph book, when my beloved Manchester United arrived to defend their European Cup against Waterford. I was at the match in Lansdowne, captivated by Denis Law's hat-trick.

But then my first love was extinguished by a trip to play at Old Trafford.

It was in my second season with the Arsenal youth team, and I'd found my feet. The FA Youth Cup was everything to us, and the quarter-final draw delivered United out of the hat. Part of our excitement about the competition was getting to play in clubs' main stadiums, so I was thrilled by the prospect of finally getting to run out of a tunnel I'd visualised so often.

You don't cut the emotional ties of childhood overnight, and I still kept a close eye on United's results, though the first team was struggling near the bottom of the league under Tommy Docherty. The Brady clan was buzzing for this match, and gathered in numbers. My mother and father travelled from Dublin and stayed with my uncle Tony, who lived in Manchester. My brothers Ray and Eamonn drove up from London.

The match was tight – a nil–nil draw, meaning a replay at Highbury – and I played well. Walking off, pretty pleased with life, I spotted the family in the directors' box, which was above the players' tunnel in those days. They were waving and clapping, so I waved back. Cue a rude awakening from this happy moment. 'What the fuck do you think you're doing, you wee fucker?'

It was the charming Glaswegian greeting of Docherty, who was standing in the tunnel, clearly displeased that his young lads hadn't progressed. United had a strong tradition in the Youth Cup. He wasn't finished with me. 'Who do you think you are? What are you celebrating for? You haven't won anything yet.'

I was only 16 and usually respectful in my dealings with senior figures, but I did have a capacity for cheek when provoked. 'I was just waving to my family. Anyway, haven't you bigger things to worry about trying to keep your team in the First Division?'

You could say that escalated tensions, and he went purple with rage. Irish this, bastard that, effing the other. I ignored him and walked into the dressing room for a shower. A while later I emerged, looking forward to a reunion with my family, but part two was waiting for me. United legend Paddy Crerand, Docherty's assistant. A tag-team job. 'Don't you dare speak to the manager of Manchester United like that again.'

Given he was a European Cup hero and had once signed my autograph book, I was less confrontational and more conciliatory with Paddy. 'All I was doing was just waving to my family and he had a go at me. What was I to do?'

He wasn't having it. 'You show respect when you come to a place like this. You have done nothing in the game.' Then he called me a 'wee fucker' too.

Tommy went on to be a quite successful manager of United and a huge personality in the game. Though he did take them down the next season, so maybe he should have kept a closer eye on his own team. I know Paddy was just backing his boss. I got to know him later in life when we played in a few veterans' games together. Though I never brought up that night at Old Trafford. He'd probably remember the incident, but not that I was the wee fucker involved.

What do they say about your first break-up? United never meant quite as much to me after that. Tommy the Doc had cured me of my love and fascination. There wasn't a huge rivalry between the clubs in those days, but that Old Trafford tunnel staged plenty more lively exchanges when Alex Ferguson and Arsène Wenger were in charge.

A year before that match at Old Trafford, I was home in Dublin, adamant I'd never go back to London. Just a few months into life at Arsenal, I was ready to quit the club and football for good. I was very homesick, and had had enough of an environment that felt like a boot camp.

Arsenal's double-winning manager Bertie Mee was ex-army. He'd been a physio in the medical corps and carried a military outlook into his management style. A stickler for discipline and punctuality and appearance, his approach set the tone for the whole club. My sergeant major was youth team coach Ian Crawford, a Scot.

Crawford had around 20 young apprentice professionals to deal with, and his priority was ensuring we all fell into line. Fifty years on, I can recite the mantras he drummed into us every day.

'Good better best. I shall never rest until my good is better and my better best.'

'It's better to be 10 minutes early than one minute late' was another popular one.

34

Conformity was very important to Crawford, and nothing concerned him more than the length of our hair. The style of the time meant most of us wanted to wear it long like George Best, or Charlie George from the Arsenal first team. But to Ian this was a demonstration of untidiness and self-indulgence. 'You can grow your hair when you're a fucking pro – in the unlikely event you ever fucking make it,' he would shout at us.

We used to go to a barber shop close to Highbury owned by Alf Rice, brother of Arsenal legend Pat. Alf had this method of turning up our hair at the back to make it look short enough to get Crawford off our backs.

This first taste of football life was a culture shock for a kid who expected more of it to revolve around football. I hated the rules. I imagined this was like life in the army. We seemed to spend more time scrubbing floors and cleaning baths in the home and away dressing rooms.

We had a Dublin kitman, Tony Donnelly, who was in charge of dressing room duties. You might have thought he'd make life easier for us Irish lads, but it was quite the opposite. He seemed to come down harder on us. Most days, we were on duty at Highbury by 8am, helping Tony load kit into a van to be brought to the London Colney training ground in St Alban's. We'd follow on the bus, about a 40-minute trip, where we'd lay out all the gear for the first team, reserves and youths. Any mistakes and Tony always seemed to have another chore for us to do. We'd train from 10 to 12:30, and twice a week there would be an afternoon session too. We finished around 5, once we had done the baths, showers and toilets. Tony would come in and inspect the work with his customary catchphrase: 'Call that clean?' When we did train at Highbury, it was usually for a physical day – running around the pitch, or up and down the terrace to build up our stamina. When that was finished, with our legs like jelly, we had to scrub the dressing rooms, the showers and the big first team bath. We dreaded the Friday before a home game, when Tony's attention to detail went to another level.

We cleaned the first team boots too. I looked after John Radford and Alan Ball, who were generous with their Christmas tips. But by that first Christmas, I'd become disillusioned. Some afternoons, we had to attend classes at a local college and I'd missed one, copping a month of extra dressing room-cleaning duties from Crawford. I can recall a late evening alone in the Highbury dressing rooms, polishing the silver pegs and just feeling so far from home. This was not what I signed up for.

That Christmas break in 1971 was meant to last a week but I couldn't face going back. I wrote to Gordon Clark, the Arsenal chief scout, to tell him. I missed my family and friends too much and wasn't happy with life in London. Gordon got me on the neighbours' phone. There are important forks in every road, and I sometimes rewind that conversation with Gordon and wonder how my life would have unfolded had he not reacted so calmly and sensibly.

'This happens quite a lot to boys living away from home. Take your time and see how you feel in a couple of weeks.'

It was the perfect response to a 15-year-old who was finding life difficult. It didn't take me long to miss playing football every day and to realise what a privilege it was to learn and develop in such a professional environment. When I told Gordon a few weeks later that I was ready to come back, he could probably hear the penny dropping. He sent me on my way with one piece of advice for getting Crawford, literally, out of my hair. Get picked for the reserves, where I'd enjoy playing seasoned pros in proper stadiums.

'But you can only do that by playing really well in the youth team.'

In many ways, I was blessed and had little to complain about compared to some of the other lads from all around England, Scotland, Wales and Ireland. My digs were with the Rowland family in Finsbury Park, one of the less salubrious areas in North London then, but a house that would go for well over a million now. John Rowland and his wife were Arsenal season ticket holders, and were special people. John was like a surrogate father to me for a couple of years. Not long after I arrived, he lent me his patent leather shoes to go to Claridge's for a dinner to celebrate the club's double winning season. My tuxedo was from Moss Bros and I wore my landlord's shoes. 'Start from the outside with your cutlery, Liam, when the first course is served.' I started to eat more healthily. I couldn't take Mrs Rowland for granted like I did my mother. Some of the other lads weren't so fortunate and lodged with families who were only interested in making a few quid off the club. Their lot didn't compare to mine.

I had the support of my three brothers too, who were living in England. I often went down to Kent to stay in Ray's pub in Sevenoaks. Even though Eamonn lived in South London he would come to all my youth team matches. Sometimes on Saturday afternoons when Arsenal weren't playing at home he'd bring me to Cold Blow Lane to watch Millwall, who had an opinionated ball player called Eamon Dunphy pulling the strings in midfield.

Back at the club, Crawford would often wonder why we couldn't all be more like Pat Rice. The Rices also ran a green-grocer's next door to Alf's barber shop, and Pat, a first team regular, often worked there in the afternoon. It epitomised his work ethic. Crawford never tired of telling us how Pat was an average player at our age, but had sweated out every drop of talent through extra training in order to forge such a great career.

I can't claim to have really listened. When I look back from this distance, there's a little bit of regret that I didn't push myself harder. With more dedication, I could have been a lot better with my right foot and a lot stronger physically. It was complacency, to some extent. I knew I had more ability than my teammates in the youths. Despite this self-belief, though, I was still worried about making the cut for a pro contract. There was no safety net of big money like with today's kids. Get the boot on a Friday, I'd have been scratching around for a job in Dublin by Monday.

By now I began to enjoy life in London. I made a few good pals like Richie Powling, John Matthews and Wilf Rostron. I'd take a few drinks and go to a disco at the weekend. I developed an unhelpful addiction to snooker, which began to dominate my free afternoons. Alex Higgins was about to win his first world title, and the snooker craze was building. A snooker hall popped up above nearly every Burton's department store.

My regular was in Southgate. First team stars like George Armstrong and Peter Simpson were often on the next table. Except they soon went home to their wives and families, while I stayed playing until I ran out of money for the light above the table. I was often there for five or six hours. Fun times for sure, but time that would certainly have been better spent working on my right foot and upper body strength like Pat Rice.

All the same, I did start to play really well in the youth team, as Gordon advised. We played in the South East Counties League, and when we didn't have a league game we would play against the likes of Oxford or Cambridge University, or maybe the RAF or the Army. Those games were my first taste of football against men, and I found myself able to adjust. When it got a bit too physical in the midfield, I could move the ball on quickly, rather than invite a crunching tackle. The club was evidently satisfied with my progress, because around the time I turned 16 in February 1972, I got the call for the reserves.

The manager was Dave Smith, a lovely guy, who favoured the arm round the shoulder in most scenarios, rather than the boot in the backside. It was a huge thrill playing in a team with some Arsenal heroes who had won the double less than a year before. Most were helpful and encouraging and I learned a lot from them. Though their mood, ahead of these matches, usually depended on why they were playing. If you weren't a young hopeful like me, only two things brought you to the reserve league, the Football Combination – you were returning from injury or had fallen out of favour with the first team boss, Bertie Mee.

Charlie George fell into the latter category when I got to play with him in a reserve match at Highbury. A great thrill for me and no doubt the few hundred diehards inside the ground were delighted with his unexpected appearance too. I loved him as a player, his talent and flamboyance. Comfortable on both feet, great shot and vision. But it was pretty obvious, from an early stage in the match, that Charlie was in no humour to parade those gifts on this stage or on this day. After about half an hour, the ball came his way and he controlled it, flicked it in the air and volleyed it high into the seats in the Upper West Stand. 'What the fuck am I doing here,' he roared, in case it wasn't clear this was a man in existential crisis.

Having been taking the match extremely seriously, I was shocked. But Dave Smith had seen it all before and just had a quiet word at half-time, got Charlie to calm down and play properly. He rifled in the winner in the second half. Sadly, that rebellious streak in Charlie began to surface more often in those final years of his Arsenal career and he fell out with Bertie regularly, as well as suffering with injuries. I was gutted when he eventually left the club for Derby, where he played brilliantly when he got over his injuries.

That great double side was breaking up quickly. I remember a brief conversation with George Graham, just a few months before he left for Manchester United. George had been a vital part of the '71 team. Having come to the club as a striker, he evolved into a goalscoring midfielder, fine passer and brilliant header of the ball. Though his place now in the first team was not guaranteed since the arrival of World Cup winner Alan Ball.

'How you getting on, Chippy?' he said, having climbed onto the treatment table next to me. That's all anyone called me by this stage. 'I'm fine, I'm getting some games in the reserves and I think I'm doing OK.'

'Good lad,' he replied. 'I've heard this Liam Brady kid is pretty good.' No doubt I'd gone bright red. 'He's fucking brilliant,' I managed to utter and quickly made my way out of the treatment room. George was never the wiser.

That spring Gordon Clarke contacted me with an unusual request. Could I come to Highbury on a Sunday morning for a trial match to select next season's intake of apprentices? Frank Stapleton came from Artane, barely two miles from my home in Northside Dublin, but our paths had never crossed. He played very well in that trial, scored the kind of terrific header that would become his trademark. When Gordon introduced us afterwards, I told Frank I was very happy and the club had been good to me. He had plenty of options – United were also interested – but he chose Arsenal. A year later, a gangly lad called David O'Leary made the same decision. There was a bit of a pipeline being constructed between North Dublin and North London. Within two years Arsenal recruited three Northside Dublin kids who would play over 1,200 games for the club, David holding the record at 722, a mark I can't see ever being overhauled. That letter from Bill Darby to Gordon Clark was a landmark document in Arsenal's history.

As a young footballer, you're always chasing a specific target. The big one at this age is a pro contract. That brought a certain amount of pressure, whenever you kicked a ball, but at least it was something to focus on while you were wiping grime out of a bath, or squeezing out the next 20 push-ups.

All the indications were the club was happy with my progress, but there were enough friends regularly departing the place in tears to keep the rest of us on our toes. So it is very easy for me to recall that cold morning inside Bertie Mee's office – 13 February 1973, my 17th birthday, was warmed up by relief.

It was a conversation insofar as Bertie talked and I listened. I would have three more years to learn my trade. I'd start on £25 a week. And there was fine print. It would mean the end of my dad's scouting deal and that £40 a month he was getting, a considerable amount in those days. The club figured that I could look after my parents now on my huge wage packet! Looking back, there was no negotiation, no one to speak on my behalf. Bertie had all the cards stacked in his favour. But I would have another platform to improve. Life as a pro meant regular appearances in the reserves and the licence to have your hair cut however you wanted. And overnight, the big target changed – get in the first team.

A Friday morning, the following October, I'm sitting in the youth team dressing room. I'm a pro now so I'm not mucking out any more. One of the younger lads charges in. He'd been sweeping out the first team dressing room when he glanced at the team sheet on the wall. 'Chippy, your name is on the sheet.' I rush down the corridor to take a look at this apparition for myself. This lad isn't one of the usual jokers, but you never know.

He's right. My name is there. Number 12: Brady. The one substitute allowed for tomorrow's First Division game with Birmingham City at Highbury. I scan the sheet for the other names. Bob Wilson, Pat Rice, Peter Simpson, Bob McNab, Peter Storey, Eddie Kelly, Ray Kennedy, George Armstrong, John Radford.

The weekend is a blur. In my mind I go through how I might make my debut. If I'm lucky I'll get a short run in the last five if we're winning. Or maybe we'll be losing and Bertie will need to change something. But after 10 minutes our new big-money signing from Leicester, Frank McLintock's replacement, Jeff Blockley, goes down injured and I am on. There's no time to worry. The game is faster but not too fast. I'm on the ball a fair bit, beat a player or two. Passes go where they're supposed to. The crowd is encouraging, always willing to detect promise and help a young player. I'm on the left, knocking it to Armstrong and Radford. A few months before I was babysitting their kids. The move finds Ray Kennedy in the middle. He slams it in. I'm celebrating in the corner of Highbury with the double heroes.

In the second half I'm tired, but it's still going OK. We haven't conceded. The ball finds me at the edge of the box. I try a lob. Birmingham's new keeper Gary Sprake touches it over. The crowd applauds generously.

We win and the dressing room is loud and happy. I'm in the first team bath. 'Well done, Chippy,' my heroes are saying.

Coach Bobby Campbell tells the press I have a left foot like a wand. I'm on the phone to my parents. They're telling me what the radio has been saying in Dublin. Am I a different person to the kid who woke up Friday morning, still dreaming of this?

When the madness subsides and I can take it all in, there is sadness that someone important was missing. I wish John Rowland had been there, my surrogate dad. He looked after me so well, made London my home and his home my own. He even got me into test cricket, which I still enjoy today. He had died just months before, having suffered a heart attack leaving a Chelsea v Arsenal cup-tie at Stamford Bridge. I know what a thrill he'd have got seeing me play for the first team. I moved out of my digs as Mrs Rowland went to live with her son.

Football has its own mysterious ways of keeping you on an even keel, I've always found. It'll give and take. When you're a bit low, it might throw you a lucky break, if you deserve it. When you're in the clouds, it'll often give you a little tug back to earth. Bobby Campbell was pushing Bertie Mee to give the youngsters a chance and I was in the starting team to play Tottenham in the derby at White Hart Lane the next Saturday. This time it was all too much. I barely got a kick, Alan Gilzean and Martin Chivers scored for them and we lost 2–0. The following week I was back in the reserves.

But I'd had a taste and was hungry now for more. I worked harder and kept learning, got a few more runs, sometimes as a starter, sometimes as sub, and I was getting stronger. April came and a serious match that I associate, even more than my debut, with the beginning of my life as a first team footballer.

The night before, I'd reported to Highbury for the Youth Cup semi-final with Tottenham. A big match I'd really looked forward to. We were 1–0 down from the first leg at White

Hart Lane. Inside the dressing room, Ian Crawford pulled me aside. 'I've been told I can't play you because you're in the first team squad for Liverpool tomorrow night.'

It may only have been my second time in Bertie Mee's office. He was at the ground to watch the game. A tentative knock, unsure how to approach this very regimental man.

'Can I please have a word with you, Mr Mee?'

The reply was stern. 'What do you want?'

'Well, I'm here to play for the youth team and they're telling me I can't.'

'Of course you can't – you're in the first team squad to go to Anfield tomorrow night.'

'Yeah, I know, that's great, but I'd rather play against Spurs than be a sub up at Liverpool.'

'I think you should just get out of my office. I have never heard such nonsense – you stupid boy.' It felt like *Dad's Army*. I was Pike and Bertie was Captain Mainwaring.

I was even more annoyed after we drew nil–nil and lost on aggregate to miss out on a chance of playing in the FA Youth Cup Final. I travelled to Anfield the following night fully expecting to be 12th man. Bill Shankly was standing at the door to the dressing rooms. Staring at us, staring at me. Sizing us up. You're at Anfield, son. We were middle of the table and the expectancy was that we were getting rolled over. Bertie read out the team and to my great surprise, I was starting. Then, after a quick team talk, he walked out of the dressing room and all the other players started laughing and saying, 'Good luck, Chippy.'

'What's so funny?'

'Well, you're outside left and Tommy Smith is right back. All the best!'

I believe Anfield is out on its own when it comes to atmosphere in a football ground. When I ran out of the tunnel, the noise was incredible, a hundred times louder than anything I'd experienced. Liverpool were neck and neck with Leeds for the title with three games left. On the other hand I was among lads who had done the double. Alan Ball was alongside me in the middle of the park and he revelled in this kind of game. I felt strong and confident, not scared.

I got the ball in the opening minutes, jinked past Smith and put a decent cross in that Ray Kennedy nearly scored from. Well pleased with myself, I was jogging back for the goalkick when I was treated to an up-close view of the most fearsome face in football. It resembled the Charles Bronson vigilante from *Death Wish*. A face pitted with pockmarks and vengeance. A moustache like a yard brush. As Shankly famously put it, Tommy Smith wasn't born, but quarried. His tackles were infamous. He'd once handed Jimmy Greaves a card when he trotted out at Anfield. It was the menu from Liverpool Infirmary.

Now he stuck his head right in my face and calmly, but firmly, informed me: 'You do that again, you little Irish twat, and I'll fucking break your leg.' I could tell this wasn't an idle threat or an empty promise. Players could get away with all sorts of tackles in those days and I wasn't keen to find out what Smith was capable of. I didn't give him an opportunity to nail me. Any time the ball arrived and he was nearby, I quickly laid it off. But I played well and Ray Kennedy scored in a 1–0 win. It was a night that cost Liverpool the title and did John Giles and Leeds a big favour. And it was a night when I didn't feel like the kid showing flashes of promise, the boy you make allowances for. I felt like I could handle being part of this team.

5

Arsenal in Transition

I RETURNED AFTER A summer in Dublin to a seat and a peg in Arsenal's first team dressing room. On one side of me sat the marvellous double-winning winger Geordie Armstrong. On the other was Alan Ball, England's youngest World Cup winner, who had signed in '71, after the double was won.

It was a thrill. I was 18 and this was a coming of age moment. But I had already seen enough disappointment around me in football to know that nothing was guaranteed. I had two missions: stay in this room and secure a place in the first team; and win an international cap. I set goals like that at the start of every season I spent in football.

Although I couldn't have been happier, it didn't take me long to work out that the Arsenal dressing room wasn't a terribly happy place. Much like the world around us. Outside our cocooned lives, Britain was in a mess. Everyone was angry. The punks were taking over from the glam rockers.

The Tory Prime Minister Ted Heath was clinging to power and there were strikes everywhere. We had the three-day week, with businesses shutting to conserve power. There were two general elections within a few months. A state of emergency was declared in Northern Ireland and the IRA was mounting a deadly campaign in England. There was a bomb at the Houses of Parliament and the pub bombings in Guildford and Birmingham were devastating. For an Irish teenager in London, it was an anxious time. My accent was heard differently. I kept my head down away from familiar company.

Football had been rocked by seismic change too. Don Revie resigned from Leeds United to manage England after 13 years of outstanding success. Leeds would never be the same. The legendary Bill Shankly called time at his beloved Liverpool. While Brian Clough, who had won the title at Derby in 1972, resigned from Brighton and Hove Albion in the third division to take over at Elland Road.

And that great Arsenal team – Fairs Cup winners in '70, double winners in '71, cup finalists in '72, league runners-up in '73 – was disintegrating. The captain, Frank McLintock, had gone at the end of the '73 season, after a falling out with Bertie Mee. George Graham had left before him. Now our outstanding goalkeeper Bob Wilson retired to concentrate on his TV work. Mee also shocked everyone by selling Ray Kennedy, who was only 22, to Liverpool. Shankly's successor, Bob Paisley, converted Ray to midfield and he had a brilliant career for them.

Replacing those two were Manchester United men. Jimmy Rimmer had arrived the season before as backup for Wilson. While one of my 1968 posterboys, Brian Kidd, was part of the Old Trafford exodus following United's relegation. Arsenal was, as they say in football, in transition, although it's debatable if change needed to happen so quickly.

We did have Bally. In some ways he was the perfect role model for a teenage midfielder with a lot to learn about his trade. In other ways, maybe not. Even though he was injured, Alan adopted me, you could say, that summer, and involved me in his other passions of partying and betting on horses. A path I would have been better off avoiding, for the sake of my life savings.

It was all very enjoyable, nightclubs in the West End of London and race tracks like Epsom, Ascot and Windsor on a Monday night. One of Bally's favourites was the Friday evening meeting at Newmarket. The only problem was that it usually fell during pre-season training, so tended to be followed next morning by our regular pre-season cross-country run across the fields and hills of Hertfordshire. I was lucky to make the middle of the pack on a good day and I never saw Alan finish one, because he finished them at least 10 minutes before me.

He was a man of extraordinary stamina and appetite for training. I'd rank him among the best I've played with. Always thinking. Like a good snooker player, he was invariably a pass or two ahead upstairs. And he was one of the best one-touch players to play the game. For someone like me, who liked to carry the ball, watching what Bally could create with a single pass or flick was an education.

How many great players have arrived at a great club at just the wrong time? You're never entirely in control of your own destiny in football, whatever we like to think. He played 175 league games for Arsenal, scored 45 goals, some record from midfield. He would be regarded as a club legend if he'd played in a more successful period.

Like many in that dressing room, Bally wasn't slow to make clear his frustrations. And some of the others who had been there for the double, especially the homegrown lads, didn't appreciate that Alan was earning a lot more than them, something he wouldn't have been shy about disclosing. There was a lot of friction, players blaming each other. Bally and Charlie George never really got on and that didn't help the vibes.

We went 10 games without a win early in that campaign and sank to the bottom of Division 1. I was in the team, but got a pass from the flak, from the fans and my teammates. I was too young to shoulder much responsibility and stayed well away from any disputes. I was playing OK too, I felt, considering the team's struggles.

Everything was still a novelty. There was a 4–0 win over Manchester City, who had Bell, Summerbee and Lee, icons who'd also featured on my bedroom wall. The call came to train with the Ireland squad at the Crystal Palace athletics stadium and I worked with John Giles for the first time, in among some of the players I'd watched when I'd been lifted over the turnstiles at Dalymount Park. It was a welcoming group and it was immediately obvious John commanded total respect. He mentioned, during that two-day camp, that he'd wanted me on the South America tour that summer, but Bertie had said no.

I was raging at missing out on the Maracanã and though I was still terrified of the boss, when I returned to the club I knocked on his office door and explained my unhappiness. This time, he didn't dismiss me like a silly kid. 'I'm sorry, Liam, I thought it was in your best interests. It was wrong not to tell you.' Mee was a fair and decent man, behind the sergeant major approach.

As part of Ireland's preparation for the European qualifiers, John also organised a match at Old Trafford against Manchester United. Another encounter with Tommy Docherty went off peacefully and we won 2–0, with Mick Martin, a United player, scoring both our goals. I played the second half in midfield alongside Mick and John and did well enough to earn that memorable debut against the USSR.

With the league title off the table almost from the start, those transition seasons revolved, in many ways, around the FA Cup. Wembley was a cherished prize. We played eight FA Cup ties in 1974–75, but still went out in the quarter-finals. We needed replays to get past York City and Coventry, while it took three matches plus extra time to beat Leicester, who had knocked us out of the League Cup. But two Alan Taylor goals for West Ham at a waterlogged Highbury ended the run. Taylor scored twice in the semi and final too, as the Hammers lifted the trophy. We finished the season in 16th place, far from the standards the club had set.

It has always been important at Arsenal to have players in the team who have been educated at the club. To grow our own. And plenty more were about to join me. Mee may have had his arm twisted to some extent by Bobby Campbell, who had come in as first team coach and wanted to promote the youngsters. But the following season, the job began of rein-venting Arsenal, you could say, even if Bertie perhaps sensed he wouldn't be around to enjoy the rewards of that process.

Frank Stapleton began to get games up front. Trevor Ross and Richie Powling, who'd been at my first trial in 1969, became regulars. John Matthews, Brian Hornsby and Wilf Rostron were making progress. Wilf and I shared digs and became great mates and were always out socialising together. David O'Leary turned professional that summer of '75 and made the first 30 appearances of his record 722 for the club. He wowed everyone instantly with his searing pace and ability to match the runs of the fastest forwards.

Space had to be made for this infusion of youth. The rela-tionship between Bertie Mee and Charlie George had always been uneasy. Charlie the long-haired rebel who Bertie could never quite drill the way he'd have liked. Charlie was sold that summer to Derby, to my great disappointment. Bob McNab, another double hero, went to Wolves, having lost his place to Sammy Nelson at left back.

The upheaval in the dressing room and the inexperience in the side meant results were poor. We suffered early cup exits, and relegation was a real prospect at different times. And it wasn't lost on Arsenal supporters that Frank McLintock was virtually ever-present for QPR, who were pushing Liverpool all the way at the top. They eventually finished second in the club's best-ever season. Shouldn't Frank still have been at Highbury tutoring the 18-year-old O'Leary at the back?

Around six weeks before the end of the campaign came an announcement that took us and the whole of football by surprise. In an emotional press conference, Bertie Mee confirmed he would be resigning at the end of the season. He had been pushed, it was clear, but it was a reasonably dignified exit, in the Arsenal style, for a man who had given the club so much. Bertie insisted he would have done nothing differently, if he had his time over, except for one regret – letting McLintock leave. We finished 17th, which was an escape, considering the dressing room was virtually in civil war.

The established players, marshalled by Bally, wanted Bobby Campbell to be the new manager. The word was that Alan might become his player-coach. While the younger contingent mainly hoped for someone new. The renowned Yugoslavian coach Miljan Miljanić, then at Real Madrid, was heavily linked with the job. Frank and Wilf were of the same mind as me that a fresh voice would be for the best. Bobby had been pretty harsh on some of us. His mood fluctuated hugely with the results and when we lost he could be very tough, particularly on the younger players.

It even went to a dressing room vote, which was a bizarre attempt at making player power a democracy. Bally, my mentor, was disgusted I hadn't taken his side. Nevertheless, Campbell won the vote and I recall Alan visiting the directors to tell them Bobby had the full backing of the players. Of course the board had no intention of listening to a group that had almost got one of England's most famous clubs relegated. So instead Terry Neill got the job, in a surprise switch from Tottenham.

Another Irish voice in the dressing room. Terry, from Belfast, was still only 34. He had started out as a kid at Arsenal and had been a good player for the club, leaving to become player-manager at Hull City. He also managed to coach Northern Ireland at the same time, and had only stopped playing a couple of years earlier to focus on management.

Though young, in one sense he was a good fit. He knew the club, had had reasonable success at Hull, and had already followed a legendary double-winning manager at Spurs, where he had taken over from Bill Nicholson. He'd done OK, steadying a ship that had been lurching towards relegation like ours.

Terry ticked a lot of other boxes too. Well-spoken, smart, good with the media. He fitted the bill as a safe pair of hands at a club with standards to uphold. Bobby Campbell, disappointed with being overlooked, left to become Fulham manager, while Terry brought his coach with him from Spurs, Wilf Dixon.

'This club needs a good shake-up,' Terry said, during his first meeting with us. 'Anyone who doesn't agree, there's the door.' And yet nothing much changed at all, for a while. If anything, the internal politics and infighting got worse. For a start, Terry didn't find it easy managing some of his former Arsenal teammates. The likes of Peter Storey, John Radford, Peter Simpson and Geordie Armstrong had all been around during Terry's playing days. They weren't trouble-makers, but Terry was only a few years older than them. It was easy to detect friction. Nothing major, just little tests of the manager's authority. It was even more obvious that Alan Ball didn't take to Terry, and that Bally wasn't Terry's cup of tea either.

But Terry did make a big early statement, the signal of intent a new manager needs to let everyone know 'this is my team now'. Malcolm MacDonald came from Newcastle, where he was idolised, and had been the First Division's leading goalscorer the previous season. The fee was, famously, £333,333.34p, a record for Arsenal. After protracted negotiations, the chairman Denis Hill-Wood had picked up the phone to Newcastle and made a final offer of a third of a million pounds, 'and not a penny more'.

I soon got on well with Malcolm, but he was another brash character, with no shyness about letting his opinions be known, so it added another spiky element to an already disgruntled dressing room. He and Bally quickly teamed up as the two biggest personalities in the team. And it was exciting playing with them. Malcolm's pace and goalscoring made a big difference to us. Never lacking confidence, he promised 30 goals and fell only one short of delivering.

However, nobody was impressed with Wilf Dixon's coaching, and it didn't take long for some of the older players to begin to openly challenge him, Bally especially, who'd had Wilf before at Everton. Training wasn't enjoyable. It wasn't stimulating and a lot of the players just switched off, didn't respond to Wilf at all. He was a nice guy and it was rough on him, but he never really got to grips with it.

So no wonder results were mixed. There was plenty new about that season. Goal difference was brought in to separate teams. Referees were given red and yellow cards for the first time, which some of them seemed to enjoy greatly. On the first weekend they were introduced, George Best was shown a red for swearing.

For us, the comings and goings never stopped. Brian Kidd left. Terry Mancini was released, depriving the dressing room of much-needed good humour. Eddie Kelly, who Bertie had made captain the previous season, joined Frank McLintock at QPR. John Radford had lost his place to Frank Stapleton and moved to West Ham. Another youngster, Steve Gatting, made his debut. And another Dubliner, John Devine, signed as a professional.

Malcolm and Frank were now our strike partnership. Malcolm was quite a selfish player, with a close eye on his goal tally, so most of the running and chasing and harrying defenders was done by Frank, who was unselfish and played for the team. But they did make a very dangerous pairing. And Frank's hard work and form was rewarded with a place in the Ireland squad that autumn. We played together in green for the first time in a 3–3 draw in Turkey, with Frank scoring.

For Arsenal, the pivotal game of that season was arguably our 2–1 defeat by QPR in December in the quarter-final of the League Cup. McLintock and Kelly in their team. Alan Ball missed a penalty in what was more or less his last act for the club. In the inquest that followed, Terry demanded to know why we were so inconsistent. And another row about the coaching followed, with Bally at the forefront. More harsh words were said and Terry was fed up with it. There was just too much friction between them. He moved Alan on to Southampton within a few days. I was sad to see him go, still rated him as one of the best around, and I agreed with him about the coaching, as most of the players did. Though looking back, I could see too that Terry needed to assert his authority.

To replace Ball in midfield, he got Alan Hudson because, according to Alan at least, Stoke needed the money to replace the roof on the Victoria Ground stand, which had blown off in a storm. His arrival was a huge surprise to us, because Huddy had a well-earned reputation as one of the biggest drinkers in the First Division. Terry certainly wasn't making things easy on himself. Huddy was a brilliant midfielder, a stylish, elegant player who had grown up among Chelsea's flamboyant team of the early 1970s. I loved playing with him. He probably needed help with his drinking, but in our time that kind of support for players just wasn't around. So Huddy was impossible to keep on the straight and narrow. Nor was he easy to coach. He once volleyed the ball at Terry on the bench during a game because he didn't agree with whatever instructions were being shouted. Terry had bitten off more than he could chew.

We finished a strange season in eighth place, an improvement on paper, despite losing seven games in a row at one stage. I played well, was becoming comfortable with the standard. But overall there was no sense of positivity. I started to wonder, for the first time, if my future was at Arsenal.

My best pal, Wilf Rostron, was sold to Sunderland. He went on to have a great career, especially under Graham Taylor at Watford. Though he missed out on captaining them in the 1984 Cup Final because he was sent off in their final league game and suspended. That must have been heartbreaking for him. We'd lost touch by then after I left for Italy. Such is the life of a footballer.

My other great friend, Richie Powling, also played his last game for the Arsenal first team that year, though he stayed around for another three seasons. What happened to Richie, a talented lad with great game intelligence, was cruel and made me count my blessings regularly. It started out as a knee cartilage problem, which could easily have been rectified with modern sports science, but he deteriorated to the point where it was a career ender. I deserved nothing that came my way in my career more than Richie did.

Change kept coming even as that season petered out. Peter Storey left, Willie Young came in. Life at Arsenal was a spinning carousel, so no wonder it was hard to think we were going in the right direction. You often hear that a manager has lost the dressing room and that's essentially what had happened. Things came to a head on a summer tour to Singapore and Australia. Most of the lads were furious because the trip cut into our holiday by two weeks, but Terry promised we'd be compensated for travelling with generous spending money.

We played a tournament with Celtic, Red Star Belgrade and the Singapore national team, and we didn't play very well. There was still no sign of our cash and the older lads were mutinous. Most had fallen out with Terry by now and he lost control. We were treating the tour more as a holiday than preparation for the next season. Players were openly drinking after the matches, with the younger lads taking their cue from the others. On the flight from Singapore to Sydney, it was obvious Huddy and Malcolm were the worse for wear. Things got raucous, to the amazement of the rest of us. On arrival, they were dispatched very quickly back home from Sydney on a flight to London. Of course the press were waiting for them and it turned into a circus that dominated headlines. In truth, that episode summed up the unhappiness at the club at that time.

Somehow, at the lowest point of his time at Arsenal, Terry turned things round. First, there was a helping hand from Tottenham, who made the calamitous decision to allow Pat Jennings to leave the club. Pat was 32 and had been a great goalkeeper for them, but their manager Keith Burkinshaw felt he was coming to the end. They wanted to sell him to Ipswich, but Pat didn't want to uproot his family and he was so disgusted with how he was being treated that he put the rivalry to one side and came a few minutes over the road to Arsenal. For just £40,000. One of Arsenal's greatest ever pieces of business, considering Pat kept going for eight more years and played 327 times. It's a mark of his greatness as a player and a man that he's the only player so highly regarded on both sides of the North London divide.

It was hard to beat that signing for impact on the club, but Terry then made an even more important one. He brought home Don Howe. Don had been Bertie Mee's coach in the double season, leaving to become manager of West Brom. Now he returned as head coach, with Wilf Dixon going to concentrate on scouting. It was miraculous how quickly Don got hold of our dressing room. In football, or any walk of life, there are few things more powerful than someone who knows what they want and can communicate it clearly. Don gave the team a sense of purpose, a reason to knuckle down.

Everything stepped up a gear. Don wasn't a man for small talk, for being pals with the players. There were plenty of harsh words. He spoke his mind but it was fair. It felt like everyone was equal. He'd bollock Malcolm or us youngsters exactly the same way. If he could think of any reason to bollock Pat Jennings, he'd have done that too. Malcolm and Huddy fell into line. The moaning stopped. Nobody was late any more. Excuses weren't tolerated.

He organised us as a team and he improved every player individually. He told me I was only doing half my job in midfield. That I wasn't tracking back enough and wasn't fulfilling my defensive responsibilities. Don had this unfair reputation as a long ball coach, because the double team had Radford and Kennedy up front, brilliant target men. But the best coaches adapt to the players they have. He got our team playing much more fluently than we had been. Making use of Dave O'Leary's ability to bring the ball out at the back. Using Sammy Nelson's strengths as an attacking full back. Working things through Hudson and me. Integrating the skill of Graham Rix.

It took time to make us a proper team, too long for a title challenge. There were a few more changes to make. Geordie Armstrong said an emotional farewell. Alan Sunderland and Steve Walford arrived from Wolves and Tottenham. Terry Neill had made a lot of difficult decisions. As a young manager, he probably made some mistakes. But he has to take great credit for getting the team he wanted together, and for not being too proud to realise he needed Don by his side.

We finished fifth, lost narrowly over two legs to a great Liverpool team in the League Cup semi-final. And we reached Wembley for the FA Cup final against Ipswich Town. Realistically, we had a kind run – Walsall, Wrexham and Leyton Orient in the last three rounds – but that was forgotten. The FA Cup final was like the Super Bowl then. The showpiece event of the season. This was everything I'd worked for since I was a kid.

Was our focus fully on the job? We probably got carried away with ourselves. There were endless interviews and so many requests for tickets. The pitfalls experienced players avoid. We recorded a cup final song, 'Roll Out the Red Carpet'. *'Liam to SuperMac / we're gonna knock in four or five'*. We didn't make *Top of the Pops*. And neither me nor SuperMac were fit enough to knock in any.

It went wrong for me two weeks before the final, when I rolled my ankle at Anfield. On the stretcher I could hear the Kop singing 'You're not going to Wembley'. Malcolm had torn knee cartilage but the club was postponing surgery until the cup run was over. We shouldn't have played. I had an injection before the game and another at half-time. The ankle was heavily strapped. But I couldn't play freely and was subbed for Graham Rix around the hour. Ipswich and the great Bobby Robson deserved their win. They had a strong forward line led by Paul Mariner, and Roger Osborne got their goal. It was a horrible feeling. I gave my loser's medal to the kitman Tony Donnelly, who was by now my friend.

It was Alan Hudson's last game for the club. Despite having enormous respect for Don, he still couldn't get on with Terry. He left for Seattle Sounders in the North American Soccer League. Huddy was a unique character, who probably only gave us glimpses of his massive talent, but I'm glad I got to play with him and know him. This time Terry made no move in the transfer market to replace him. He put his faith in the young players he had.

6

North London is Green

WE WERE LIKE BROTHERS, the Irish lads at Arsenal. The way families often work, that didn't mean we were in each other's pockets the whole time. I hung out more away from the club with some of the English lads like Richie Powling and Wilf Rostron, because we had similar tastes in music. But the Irish lads always had each other's backs. We looked out for each other.

It drew a huge Irish community to Arsenal, the fact there were so many of us in the team. We were proud of that. Myself, Dave O'Leary and Frank Stapleton were three Northside Dubs who took the same road, around the same time. John Devine followed a few years after us. Then you had three from the north – the two Belfast boys, Sammy Nelson and Pat Rice. And big Pat Jennings from Newry, maybe more uncle than brother, always the calm voice of reason.

Jimmy Harvey from Lurgan often gets left out of that list. He arrived same time as John and played a couple of times in the '79 season. Though he didn't make the breakthrough at Arsenal, he went on to have a fine career in the lower divisions.

It will never be seen again, I suppose, so many players from our island in a small squad in the English top flight. We made no distinction between north and south. And the English lads certainly didn't.

Sammy Nelson, a great friend who I still regularly play golf with, is a northern Protestant. I only knew this because the first time we met I introduced myself and Sammy, in his rogueish way, replied: 'Liam? From Dublin? You'll be a Fenian bastard then.' It broke any ice immediately. We never gave a second thought to our different backgrounds again.

There was just a genuine Irish vibe about that team. The accents, the music played. You had to be sensible, of course. The Dubliners could be played on the team bus, but not the Wolfe Tones. If Luke Kelly and the Dubliners or Paddy Reilly were in town, Pat Jennings would often go to see them and bring me for a drink with them afterwards. Luke was a big pal of Pat's and loved being around the team.

Nobody manufactured it. It just happened naturally. And Don and Terry tapped into that Irishness that developed, with Scot Willie Young also contributing to the Celtic spirit. There were some epic Ireland v England five-a-sides in training. Most of us had grown up at the club too – throw David Price and Graham Rix into that mix as well. So there was a real togetherness about the team in those seasons.

Outside the club, things weren't as straightforward. Irish players had to handle a fair bit of abuse from opposition fans, and sometimes from opponents. It was Paddy this, Paddy that. 'Fuck off back to the bog' and so on. You would constantly have to laugh off jokes about Irish people being stupid. Before the 1978 cup final, there was a photoshoot for some newspaper or magazine and the photographer brought shovels along with him to hand to the Irishmen. I think it was Frank who told him where he could start digging.

There was also a significant anti-Irish sentiment due to the Provisional IRA bombings in England. That occasionally meant abuse out at night or on the streets, when somebody heard your accent. Frank reminds me of all the times we were stopped and searched at Heathrow when we flew in after a trip home. Two or three detectives would be waiting on the Aer Lingus flight. And we probably looked likely lads. Young, long hair, denim jeans. When we told them we were footballers, they would still check it out before letting us on our way.

But I had a much more serious encounter with that anti-Irish feeling during that 1978–79 season, an experience that shook me up. It was January on the London Underground. Some guys from Birmingham started to make lewd remarks to the girl I was with. I don't think they recognised me as an Arsenal player because there was no mention of football. I told them to leave it out and they copped my accent. Immediately, they set upon me, shouting about the bombings in Birmingham, blasts that killed 21 people in two pubs in 1974. I have never seen a packed carriage empty so quickly. It got pretty brutal. They gave me a good kicking and tried to smash my head off the windows of the carriage.

My friend did her best to pull them off me and when the Tube reached its next stop they jumped off, leaving me battered and bruised. I was dazed when eventually one guy who had recognised me came over and asked if I needed help. He seemed genuine and I told him what had happened. Next morning the story was all over the back pages. He was a freelance journalist who cashed in on a scoop.

These were isolated episodes. Overall, we were treated fantastically in England, a place that has been my home for a long time. I mainly found English people didn't have a clue about what had happened on our island and had no real interest in finding out. My wife Sarah was educated in England until she was 15 and told me she'd only ever read a paragraph or two about Ireland in any of her history books. English people had no idea about the famine or why there was a sectarian situation in Ulster. They just weren't educated about it.

Thankfully, the way fixtures fell, with postponements due to it being one of England's coldest winters, that beating didn't cause me to miss a match. It happened during our famous FA Cup saga with Sheffield Wednesday, a five-match series that our season hinged on.

It had not been a great first half to the campaign, despite the momentum built at the end of the previous one. There was no sense, inside or outside the club, that we were set to kick on and become serious title contenders. The board made little investment in the team. For around £70,000, Paul Barron came in from Plymouth to cover for Pat in goal. But there wasn't enough depth or experience and when injuries struck early we struggled.

The ankle had healed fine, I was playing well and scoring more goals than ever, but results were inconsistent. By the time we lost to champions Nottingham Forest in September we had dropped to 13th. This season was going to revolve again around the cups.

But one route to Wembley was shut off when we had an embarrassing disaster away at Rotherham in our first outing in the League Cup, losing 3–1. It was a match that more or less brought an end to Malcolm MacDonald's Arsenal career. Fred Street, our physio, must have been on at least four times during the game, trying to unlock one of Malcolm's troublesome knees. He was having fluid drained off every few days and it was really hampering his movement by now. After the game, I had a blazing row with Terry Neill in the dressing room.

'Malcolm shouldn't be playing,' I said. 'How can you expect us to win matches starting with 10 men? It's not fair on Malcolm or us to send him out in that condition.' This was in front of Malcolm, who I got on fine with. He knew the score too and was becoming extremely frustrated.

Terry, understandably, stood his ground. 'It's not up you to question the manager. I am in charge here.'

Malcolm did have an operation not long after that match, but in the days before keyhole surgery, they were traumatic and risky procedures. His Arsenal career was effectively over, which was devastating for him and a huge blow to the club's supply of goals. As it happened, Don and Terry pushed Alan Sunderland up front with Frank and they worked better as a partnership, quickly striking up a good understanding. Both began to score regularly.

We were also out of the UEFA Cup by the turn of the year, losing to Red Star Belgrade 2–1 on aggregate, a tie I missed, having been sent off in the previous round against Hajduk Split. I had retaliated after receiving some 'close attention'. It was around that time that certain teams started to put a man-marker on me, especially in Europe. I was still learning that side of the game. On some days, it was possible to get the better of my direct opponent, but I could be rattled by the tactic too, and get frustrated.

Our season arguably turned on 23 December with a Christmas present for our fans. A 5–0 derby win over Tottenham at White Hart Lane that still counts as a highlight in Arsenal's history. It all came together that afternoon, including the BBC's decision to put us on *Match of the Day*. In those days, you rarely appeared on TV, as few games were shown, so it was nice to make the most of the stage. We played brilliantly. Alan Sunderland got a hat-trick. Frank Stapleton scored with a diving header after a slick move. And I hit one of the most spectacular goals of my career. It was a moment that stirred memories of all those hours kicking the ball against the pavilion wall in my local park. I loved to spin and swerve the ball with the outside of my left foot, just to see the effect it had. At White Hart Lane that day, the effect was beautiful. And John Motson's famous commentary means it often gets pulled out of the archives. 'Look at that! Look at that!' It was a delight to work with Motty later in life and get to know him.

So we were in better shape by the turn of that year and ready for another go at the FA Cup. It was the 'Winter of Discontent' in Britain. Public workers were on strike over pay, and rubbish piled high on the London streets. The Labour Prime Minister James Callaghan was hanging on. Then the temperatures dropped, making it one of the harshest Januarys since records began.

Our marathon with Sheffield Wednesday began on 6 January at Hillsborough. Though that game should never have been played. The pitch was frozen and Terry was furious it passed an inspection. The second half was delayed when their supporters began to pelt Pat Jennings with snowballs. An announcement over the PA didn't stop them so eventually their manager, Jack Charlton, went behind the goal and persuaded them to call off the bombardment.

Wednesday were in the third division, but a few of us had faced Jack before when he managed Middlesbrough, so we knew what to expect. And they were as tough and tall and direct and spirited as predicted. We were content to get home with a 1–1 draw.

Back at Highbury, three days later, it was about to become a Winter of Despair when we trailed 1–0 with two minutes left, their keeper Chris Turner having defied anything we threw at him, before I managed to squeeze in the equaliser. And then, with Jack opting for a neutral venue rather than toss for home advantage, the series continued at Leicester's Filbert Street. It was 2–2 next time, our former teammate Brian Hornsby equalising twice. He did it again with an extra-time penalty in game four, a 3–3 thriller. Before we finally finished it off in the fifth game, again in Leicester, 2–0 – Steve Gatting and Frank. I missed that one due to injury. Afterwards, Terry paid generous tribute to the spirit of Jack's underdogs. 'They did the city of Sheffield and their manager proud.' It was an extraordinary achievement by a third division side, to match a top-flight club over five games in 17 days. You couldn't imagine it happening these days, even if replay sagas were allowed, with the gulf in standards between the divisions.

We had played enough games to reach Wembley, ordinarily, but instead we had Notts County in the fourth round five days later. I doubt we'd ever have recovered if that 540 minutes of toil against Wednesday had been wasted. Thankfully, we won 2–0, with Brian Talbot getting his first goal for us. Arsenal had got the chequebook out of cold storage that January for Brian – he had played against us for Ipswich in the '78 final. He slotted in beside me in midfield and was exactly what we needed. Brian could run all day, tackle well and get into the box to score. He made us less vulnerable to counter-attacks and allowed me more scope to roam. I began to interchange a lot with Graham Rix on the left, little moves Don had taught us.

You often hear the description a 'good cup team'. The Arsenal side of George Graham's later years was another example. What exactly makes a good cup team? Often, it's just a very good side that doesn't quite have the strength in depth to become a league-winning team, but has enough about it to show up on the big days. That was us, to some extent. But what helped make us a good cup team was Don Howe. We had our way of playing, but Don was also a master at plotting around the strengths and weaknesses of the opposition and adjusting accordingly. He was thorough and prepared. We would work on things midweek and sure enough, on a Saturday, we would find out that Don had been right. It made us formidable opponents for anyone in one-off occasions.

The fifth round took us to Brian Clough's league champions, Nottingham Forest. Forest were again vying with Liverpool to be the top team in the country. In the build-up, Clough riled us by labelling us soft. He was never shy about throwing a grenade in the days before a big game.

Not everything Don prepared worked at the City Ground. Forest had lots of good players and battered us for spells. But Pat Jennings was magnificent that day. And with around a quarter of an hour to go, we won a free kick. By now, Frank Stapleton and I had developed a good understanding. We were on each other's wavelengths. It wasn't all down to Don's work on set pieces. We'd practise together after training and we'd played together often with the youths and reserves. The moves were simple enough. Frank would feint to go near post, then pull to the back. Or he'd amble towards the far post, then dart to the near. But we could read each other. If he looked uninterested, I knew he was alive. If I seemed to be dawdling over the ball, he knew the delivery was coming quickly. It was enough to sometimes buy him that half a yard of space. My job was to put the ball where he was going to be.

It wasn't just a natural spring and bravery that made Frank one of the best headers of a ball I've ever seen. He was also one of the most dedicated players I've played with. He was one youth player who did listen to the advice of Ian Crawford and followed the example set by Pat Rice. Frank worked diligently on his game from the minute he arrived from Dublin as a kid. He wasn't a giant, but he worked on his strength and could hang in the air, fending off defenders. On this afternoon, the old routine worked. Frank shaped to go near post, then ducked behind Larry Lloyd. I put it on his head and he powered it past Peter Shilton.

With Malcolm out, Frank was very much the main focus of our attack. The responsibility for goals fell on him and Sundy. They were rarely injured but we had little backup for them. Australian John Kosmina played a couple of times, but he was raw. Alan scored both goals in the quarter-final replay win over Southampton. He and Frank shared the goals when we beat Alan's old club Wolves in the semi-final at Villa Park. I missed that game through injury and the inexperienced Steve Gatting had a tremendous game in my place alongside Talbot. I had learnt my lesson. No more pain-killing injections. If you needed one, you weren't fit to play.

Before our quarter-final tie with Southampton came news that still fills me with great pride. I had been named on the six-man shortlist for the Professional Footballers' Association Player of the Year Award, having been in the running for the Young Player award in the two seasons before. But the ceremony was on Sunday night, with the Southampton game on the Monday. There was no hope Terry would let me go. He phoned the PFA chairman Gordon Taylor to tell him and Gordon replied that I had to be there, because I had won.

So it wasn't a surprise on the night but it was a huge honour. To be selected by your fellow players is the highest accolade you can get. It had been my best season for Arsenal. It helped that our first game of the campaign, against Leeds United, had also been shown on TV, on ITV's *The Big Match*. I scored twice and it seemed to catapult me into the conversation as one of the best players in England. That goal against Spurs played its part too, no doubt.

When Terry told me, I got hold of my best mate Kyran Deegan to come over from Dublin to go to the awards ceremony. I wanted him to share this occasion. But when we arrived at the Hilton Hotel banquet hall in Mayfair, there were no seats left at the Arsenal table. The rest of the team had gone to Southampton but Malcolm, who was injured, had hoovered up all the tickets for his pals. They included several journalists from the English press as well as Jack Charlton, for some reason. There was no seat for me and Kyran at the table and I was fuming. They offered to shove over and make space, but I didn't want to sit at a table full of journalists anyway, so we found a couple of seats down the back of the room. A car arrived early to take me to Southampton, so it wasn't exactly a night of wild celebration.

It was an eye-opener to see Malcolm and Jack holding court with their media buddies. Malcolm was one of those players who always had a story for the press and was getting well paid for exclusives, which often annoyed the rest of the lads. It didn't help when, before the '78 cup final, he announced that he didn't want to be part of the players' pool, the collection for whatever we'd make from media work and sponsorship and even the cup final song. He gave some excuse about tax reasons, but the lads felt he just didn't want to share his own deals.

I have mixed feelings on Malcolm. I like him and he gave the team a massive lift with his arrival. He could sometimes win a game on his own with his pace and powerful shooting. But the single-minded nature that made him a great goalscorer made him a selfish player too and I think the team gelled better with Frank and Alan up there, neither of whom put personal glory first. I was still gutted about Malcolm's injury problems, which were heartbreaking for him.

This time I was fully fit heading to Wembley. Before the final I got a call from John Giles. He said he'd been going to phone me the year before and was sorry he hadn't. He just wanted to remind me to shut out the hype, to ignore the media and try not to get caught up in the madness around tickets. There was huge build-up to a final with Manchester United, who were always among the most glamorous clubs around. It was a real north v south affair. But this time we seemed better able to handle it. We still recorded a cup final song, but I don't think we paid as much attention to the sideshows.

It's talked about as being among the cup final classics. 'The five-minute final.' But for long spells, nothing much happened. Lou Macari was shadowing me. After a cautious start, we got in front after 12 minutes. Frank passed to David Price, who pulled the ball back for Brian Talbot to nip in and take the opener off Alan Sunderland's toes. Gordon McQueen almost pulled off a Hand of God for them, when he out-jumped Pat and punched in. But the referee spotted it.

Then, just before half-time, Frank produced another version of our old trick, though this time from open play. As I dribbled down United's left, he ducked towards the near post, then drifted behind their full back, Jimmy Nicholl. It's one of the goals I'm proudest of, because people constantly pointed out I had no right foot. Lefties always get more grief for being one-footed, I've noticed. In the footage, I look up for Frank, and then you can see me really focus on the connection. For once the cross was sweet and precise and Frank nodded in.

Was it job done? I don't think there was any complacency. United never gave up, but we were professional and smart and it felt like the cup was ours. Then with just over four minutes left, McQueen turned in a scramble, with his foot this time. We were on our heels a little, I see now, in the video. Tiredness maybe, it being a warm afternoon. United were injected with life. Straight from the kickoff they attacked. Sammy McIlroy wriggled into the box and somehow squirmed his shot past Pat.

The Wembley penalty area was a scene of devastation, half the team slumped in it. We were in a state of shock. Even unflappable Pat was stretched on the pitch. On ITV, Brian Moore summed it up. 'Arsenal were preparing their victory speeches and now they are dumbstruck.'

We actually lost the ball again from the kick-off, but Sammy Nelson won it back. His forward pass found Frank, who knocked it back to me. I can recall what was in my head. 'We are dead here. Just carry it forward into their half, at least, and get us to extra-time.' Maybe United relaxed for a spilt second, but space opened up. I sensed Graham Rix was making up ground outside me. I nudged it into his path and his cross carried just enough air to tempt Gary Bailey in goal, but still elude him. It nearly caught out Brian Moore too.

'The despair on the face of Don Howe and Terry Neill . . . but wait a moment . . . it's there by Sunderland. And they're back in the lead again.'

There was still time for a Jimmy Greenhoff chance that would have made it 3–3, but Pat made a comfortable save. After the frenetic closing minutes, the final whistle released our last ounces of energy. The celebrations were first relief, then satisfaction. A lot of us just sank to our knees. It really hit, walking up the Wembley steps, that a lifetime's ambition had been realised. A dream was fulfilled that afternoon. We had brought silverware back to the club after an eight-year gap. Seven of us had come through the youth system. Five of us had been told to get our hair cut by Ian Crawford. Maybe Ian was on to something.

The celebrations lasted three days. There was a bash at one of London's best hotels that evening near Marble Arch. Next day, an open-top bus paraded us through packed London streets to a reception at Islington Town Hall. The tricolour was draped across the front of the bus. That was something extraordinary, when you think about it, at one of the most English of all football clubs.

After the reception, Graham Rix and I went to my brother Ray's pub in Sevenoaks to continue the party. A proper Irish celebration had been in full swing since the evening before. My sister Breda was out in Dubai, but my parents were there with all my brothers.

We still had to play our final league game against Chelsea at Stamford Bridge. It was Malcolm's last match, as he had been told that his knee problem wasn't going to get better. True to form he scored, in a 1–1 draw. The following season he was manager of Fulham.

It is special to me, my only trophy at Arsenal. The FA Cup no longer holds the importance and prestige it once did, but that day at Wembley in 1979 was as big as it got in English football, and three lads from Northside Dublin were at the heart of it.

There was such a bond between us. The camaraderie was still there when we got the squad together for a 40th anniversary lunch at the Emirates Stadium in 2019, which the club was very good to host. Terry was there. Fred Street too. Sadly, Don Howe had passed away and Tony Donnelly, our kitman, had gone too. We then lost Terry in 2022. He will be missed when we hopefully make it back together for the 50th.

7

Arrivederci

MY LAST SEASON AT Arsenal was my longest. Almost brilliant, it ended in crushing disappointment in a tearful bath in Middlesbrough. We fought on three fronts and wound up with nothing. We played a record 70 matches, more in a season than any English club before or since. Nine of us played at least 59 times, while one started all 70. I wonder how many can name that durable warrior before reading on to find out.

We went toe to toe with the great Liverpool team that season and were unbeaten against them in six matches. We overcame a star-studded Juventus side in the semi-final of the European Cup Winners' Cup. Those feats proved to me, at least, that we could have achieved great things, could have won titles, with just a little more backing. But ultimately, lack of investment found us out. We came up short.

Not long after beating Manchester United at Wembley, I announced I would be leaving Arsenal to move abroad when my contract expired in the summer of 1980. It wasn't a snap decision. I admired how Kevin Keegan became European Footballer of the Year after leaving Liverpool for Hamburg.

I had been thinking for some time that I wanted to test myself against the best.

Players were moving everywhere for huge sums of money. Trevor Francis had just become the first million-pound player when going from Birmingham to Nottingham Forest. Tony Woodcock's situation, though, was a bit more like mine. He'd come through the youth system at Forest and had won the title and European Cup under Brian Clough. But he was still getting paid much less than their big-name signings like Peter Shilton and Archie Gemmill, and now Trevor. When Forest wouldn't pay him what they were on, he refused to sign a new deal and left for Cologne in Germany.

My agent, Dennis Roach, had been involved with the Trevor Francis deal, but I was having serious doubts about Dennis and the way he was roping me into book deals and fan clubs and other stuff I had no interest in. So John Giles had recommended his lawyer – the man he trusted with everything – Ronnie Teeman.

Ronnie had expertise in European law and knew that the balance of power was shifting from the clubs towards the players. Employees could move between EEC countries when their contracts were up as long as compensation was paid. UEFA introduced a formula for calculating that amount based on the player's age and salary. It was a precursor, really, to the Bosman ruling that changed everything for footballers in 1995. What a European club would have to pay for a player out of contract would be a fraction of the transfer fee an English club would have to cough up. Arsenal were talking about £1.5 million for me, but Ronnie figured a foreign club would have to pay no more than £600,000.

Word was, too, that Italy was about to open its doors again to foreigners, having banned imports following a disastrous showing at the 1966 World Cup. Ronnie advised me to make my position clear, that I wanted to move but didn't want to play for any other English club.

That said, my mind could have been changed. I truly saw that Arsenal team as having the potential to win league championships. We had talent and togetherness. But cup glory aside, we'd finished seventh in 1979, 20 points behind Liverpool when it was two for a win. We needed improvement. Especially as everyone was spending. Man City had splashed £1.4 million on Steve Daley from Wolves.

But during pre-season training, the Arsenal chairman, Denis Hill-Wood, wrote a piece in the Arsenal annual review that made it clear there would be no lavish outlays:

> Many of our supporters may be wondering why we have not decided to compete in a big way in the transfer market in the close season. The answer is that we feel that transfer fees have got out of hand. The £450,000 we paid for Brian Talbot to Ipswich we considered to be a realistic price. But I am very perturbed by the escalation in prices. I doubt very much that the time would come when we could risk £1,000,000 for a player. Naturally that makes the task of the Manager Terry Neill very difficult as he tries to strengthen the side with the sort of high quality signing that is required.

After the cup final, Hill-Wood had told the press he wanted to keep me at the club until my playing days were over. And here he was, explaining in a nutshell why that was unlikely to happen. On one level, it was understandable. It was the Arsenal way, to balance the books, to remain conservative and prudent. A similar outlook was in place when I returned to the club many years later.

The Hill-Wood family had been involved for decades. They were considered upper class, Eton and Oxford educated, from banking stock. Denis's father Samuel had been chairman for 20 years and Denis's son Peter would maintain the tradition. Denis was well liked by the players. He kept his distance, was never publicly critical, or privately either. But he ran a tight ship financially. And I knew that's how things would remain.

I don't think we needed to break the bank. Just a couple of shrewd additions would have been an enormous help. Gordon Clarke's work as chief scout had paid off big time with a core of good homegrown players, but Terry should have tried to persuade the board that we needed more. Laurie Cunningham from West Brom, maybe. And Mark Lawrenson from Brighton. Laurie went to Real Madrid that summer. Mark stayed two more seasons at Brighton before moving to Liverpool.

Instead, John Hollins was our only arrival. He was 33 and cost just £75,000 from QPR. John proved a very good signing and stayed four years, but it didn't send any kind of message to our rivals that we meant business. It convinced me I'd made the right decision to leave.

Did I make a mistake, though, by going public? Keegan had done the same, letting the club know his intentions a year in advance of his departure. Speaking to him recently about his last season, he felt his relationship with the fans changed instantly. If he had a poor game, his heart wasn't in it. If he played well, he was putting himself in the shop window for a big move. They could have few complaints, in the end. He gave everything, as usual, and left after winning the league again and the European Cup.

When I speak to Arsenal fans now, they remind me of the 'Don't go, Brady, don't go' chants. They tell me support never wavered. But that's not how it felt at the time. Like Keegan, I began to get nasty letters telling me I was greedy and had no loyalty. In the early part of the season, I noticed the groans from the terraces when I made a mistake. I understand it now, they were hurt. Fans will never understand how you might see a future away from their club. But I found it hard, their coolness towards me.

The club was still trying to persuade me to stay, and Ken Friar – then club secretary, later managing director – had taken over contract negotiations with me and Ronnie. Ken is, in my view, Arsenal's greatest employee. He served the club for more than 70 years, starting in the ticket office when he was 12. The Ken Friar Bridge, joining Emirates Stadium to the Arsenal underground station, is a fitting tribute to a man who is Arsenal to the core.

After training one afternoon, he called me to his office for a chat. He mentioned the general election and the fact that the Conservatives were back in power, which would mean that if I signed a new contract and stayed in England I would be far better off with the new tax rate. The new Prime Minister, Margaret Thatcher, cut the highest rate from 83% to 60%, causing footballers to take a rare interest in politics. I was no fan of Thatcher but I suppose I didn't protest too loudly about this policy.

However, I told Ken that I really wanted to try my luck playing abroad.

'But Liam, you'll be going to a foreign country, with all the problems that will entail.'

'Mr Friar, I've done it once, I can do it again.'

It was tongue in cheek but I think Ken knew then I wasn't bluffing.

Early in the 1979–80 season, I was contacted by Gigi Peronace. I knew the name. As a Manchester United fan, I recalled his role in bringing Denis Law back to England from Torino in 1962. Gigi had been the middleman in many deals between British and Italian clubs. The maximum wage for footballers then was £20 per week, and the wealthy Serie A clubs saw the opportunity. It helped that John Charles, the brilliant Welsh forward, had taken the Italian league by storm. Gigi was also involved with that deal. He then helped move Law to Torino, Jimmy Greaves to AC Milan from Chelsea, Joe Baker from Hibs in Scotland, also to Torino, and Gerry Hitchens from Aston Villa to Inter Milan. The money these players earned was phenomenal compared to England, but life was totally different. Law and Baker couldn't handle the strict training camps, often lasting four days before a game. Greaves hated the regime at Milan. So although these players had done well on the pitch, they soon wanted to come home. At the same time, English clubs caved to the pressure from supporters and lifted the maximum wage. So Gigi stepped in again as organiser of transfers back to England. He became a very well-known figure in football. Not quite an agent, but a guy who made things happen.

Early in the 1979–80 season, Gigi contacted me and invited me and my girlfriend Sarah to his family home in Twickenham. We enjoyed his hospitality with his wonderful wife Teresa and their four children. He was 99.9% sure Italy was about to open its borders again and assured me that the biggest clubs would be interested in signing me. My preference at that stage was Germany's Bundesliga, like Keegan and Woodcock, but Gigi's charm and enthusiasm for Italian football and its great clubs was thought-provoking. I promised to keep him informed of my intentions.

By the second half of the season it had been confirmed that one foreign player would be allowed at each Italian club from the following summer. Gigi became very active and was in regular contact with Ronnie. Roma were very interested but the press got wind of it and that ended the link.

Meanwhile, Roach was also working on a deal and told me Bayern Munich was as good as done. I met their general manager, Uli Hoeneß, at Wembley after Ireland played England. He told me they were very keen. Sarah and I even started German lessons on Linguaphone. Then, out of nowhere, their interest cooled too. I later found out from Karl-Heinz Rummenigge, when we played together at Inter Milan, that his compatriot Paul Breitner blocked it because he wanted to play midfield in my position. Breitner was a hugely influential player in Germany, one whose word carried weight. My move was dead.

I had vowed to finish my time at Arsenal as strongly as possible. After a slow start – two wins in the first nine games – that cost us a better run at the title, we'd found form and were a great cup team again. But reaching April, we faced a crazy fixture pile-up – 13 games in just over a month.

It really bit at Easter. Having lost to Norwich in the league on Wednesday, then drawn with Southampton on Saturday, we were due to play Juventus in the European Cup Winners' Cup on Wednesday. Except we were scheduled to play Tottenham in between, on Easter Monday. The club asked for a postponement, on the basis that reaching a European final would benefit England's coefficient. Unsurprisingly, our neighbours refused. Instead, Terry risked a fine and travelled to White Hart Lane without six regulars. Paul Davis made a great debut in a 2–1 victory that was particularly sweet. It was such a makeshift team that Pat Rice played with me in midfield, for the first half at least. I came off at half-time for a rest.

Otherwise, it was the same 15 or 16 players carrying the load every week. Juventus at Highbury was a bruiser that finished 1–1. Marco Tardelli got a red card for a tackle that nearly broke me in two. He'd later introduce himself more politely and we became great friends. Though he has always maintained they would have won the tie if he'd been available to man-mark me in the second leg.

Before that Italian trip, we were at Hillsborough three days later for an FA Cup semi-final with Liverpool, who also looked set to win the league again. A tough goalless draw meant a replay the following Wednesday, this time at Villa Park. Alan Sunderland equalised after David Fairclough put them ahead in a really good game. So the last trip we wanted the following Saturday was Anfield, for a league match. We were sick of each other. It finished in another draw, naturally, 1–1.

Turin, four days later, for the second leg with Juventus, was at least a change of scene – and atmosphere. No English club had ever won at the Stadio Communale. We got a swift insight into how hostile things would be when our team coach was attacked on the way to the ground.

It was another gruelling night against a team full of Italy stars who I'd soon get to know well. We were going out on the away goal rule when Terry and Don sprung young Paul Vaessen, just 18, from the bench late on. In the 88th minute, Graham Rix's run and cross from the left was not unlike the one that had won the cup final. This time Paul was on the back post and he headed confidently past the great Dino Zoff to seal one of the most famous wins in Arsenal's history.

I can't look back on that evening without feeling a great sadness at what happened to Paul. After such a dramatic start to his career he continued to show rich promise and had a real eye for goal. But after a knock in a derby with Tottenham, he suffered a series of injury problems and eventually had to retire in 1982, before he had turned 21.

Something similar happened to my mate Richie Powling, who managed a comeback in the reserves that season, before breaking down again. He could have been my perfect midfield partner but for his degenerative knee condition. Psychologically, to handle all that disappointment must have been so difficult for Paul and Richie. Looking back, they didn't get much support from the club and it was probably the same at all clubs. Nor were they looked after financially. The PFA, the players' union, was nowhere near as powerful then as it is now. And players didn't have the same personal injury insurance. I can honestly say I'm not sure how I'd have coped with being told I would not be able to play football again at that age. Clearly it was so hard for Paul, who lost his way and turned to drugs before he tragically died aged 39. Thankfully, so much more is done these days, mentally and financially, to help players who find themselves in such a situation in what is always a precarious career.

The rest of us were very fortunate with injuries that season. Despite all the games, we kept going. We returned from Italy just in time for a Saturday league game with West Brom. Another draw, we drew too many in the league that year. Then another trip to Sheffield for Liverpool yet again on Monday. More extra time. The second replay finished 1–1 too. This time Sunderland scored more or less from the kickoff, but in an incredible match Kenny Dalglish broke our hearts in the last minute. On it went.

The longest ever FA Cup semi-final was finally settled the following Thursday, at Coventry's Highfield Road, by a powerful Brian Talbot header. Reaching an FA Cup final for a third year in a row was a remarkable achievement. As was outlasting that magnificent Liverpool team of Clemence, Kennedy, Hansen, Thompson, Souness, Dalglish and company.

That win gave us nine days to prepare for a final with West Ham at Wembley – apart from having two league matches to squeeze in first, away to Coventry and at home to Forest. It is a run of matches that still amazes me, when I reflect on it. Here is what it looked like on paper:

2 April: Division 1, Norwich City 2–1 Arsenal
5 April: Division 1, Arsenal 1–1 Southampton
7 April: Division 1, Tottenham 1–2 Arsenal
9 April: ECWC semi-final first leg, Arsenal 1–1 Juventus
12 April: FA Cup semi-final, Arsenal 0–0 Liverpool
16 April: FA Cup semi-final replay, Arsenal 1–1 Liverpool
19 April: Division 1, Liverpool 1–1 Arsenal
23 April: ECWC semi-final second leg, Juventus 0–1 Arsenal
26 April: Division 1, Arsenal 1–1 West Brom
28 April: FA Cup semi-final 2nd replay, Arsenal 1–1 Liverpool
1 May: FA Cup semi-final 3rd replay, Arsenal 1–0 Liverpool
3 May: Division 1, Coventry 0–1 Arsenal
5 May: Division 1, Arsenal 0–0 Nottingham Forest

It was after the Forest game, on my last walk around Highbury as an Arsenal player, that I felt it deeply for the first time, the wrench this was going to be. To leave this club and the place that was home. We had drawn 0–0 on a dreary May Bank Holiday Monday. The Cup Winners' Cup finalists against the European Cup finalists. A dull match played by teams with a lot more on their plates. The supporters didn't seem to mind that we hadn't finished our last league game at home in style. They were satisfied with what so far had been a brilliant season and they had Saturday and Wembley on their minds.

As a team we applauded them for their magnificent support throughout the season. I had plenty to be grateful for. The club and the fans had been so good to me since I broke into the side seven years earlier. I thought of all the people who had helped me since that day in 1969 when I was picked up at Heathrow. It was emotional, but this wasn't a proper goodbye. It wasn't the time. We had two more league games left away from home as well as the two finals. The fans chanted my name and urged me to stay, but my mind was made up.

At Arsenal I saw a club content to consider these cup runs and Wembley appearances as success, with no plans to aim for something more ambitious. In the league, we were only eight points behind Liverpool using just 15 or so players. We had beaten them over four matches in the FA Cup semi-final. The Arsenal board wasn't going to take those performances as proof of what could be achieved if they bought two or three players to strengthen the squad. In their eyes it was evidence that things were fine as they were.

Had the club said to me a year or two earlier that they had plans to challenge for the league title by investing in the team I might have mapped the future differently, and signed a new contract. But there was never any chance of that.

There were seven Irishmen in our Wembley squad this time, with John Devine preferred to Sammy Nelson at left back, though Sammy replaced him in the second half. But this time there was no Irish celebration. West Ham were in the second tier, but had some excellent players and were physically and mentally fresh. Manager John Lyall set them up well and they were very difficult to break down. He dropped forward Stuart

Pearson to midfield to outnumber us and frustrate us and it worked. Paul Allen did a good job man-marking me. Trevor Brooking's header won it.

They deserved their victory, but I have always felt we were just not sharp enough because of all the games we had played and the size of our squad. We were low afterwards, yet lifted by the prospect of another final against Valencia in Brussels just a few days later. Even the Arsenal fans at Wembley sang about going to Heysel at the end. It was inconceivable that we would end the season with nothing having put so much effort in and played so well on so many occasions.

On the coach home from Wembley, Brian Talbot, the only one of us to play in all 70 matches that season, collapsed from exhaustion. But he was declared fit to play by Wednesday. David O'Leary, who had limped out of the cup final with a calf injury, needed a pain-killing injection to start in Belgium. Valencia were not the best team in Spain that season but they had beaten Barcelona over two legs on the way to the final. The legendary Alfredo Di Stéfano was their manager and Mario Kempes, figurehead of Argentina's 1978 World Cup win, was their frontman. We would need to be at our best.

Sadly, we were leggy and it was a game of few chances and no goals. Alan Sunderland, who scored 29 goals that season, had a couple of efforts superbly saved by keeper Carlos Pereira and one disallowed for offside. Pat Jennings and David O'Leary kept Kempes out of the limelight and the penalty shoot-out looked inevitable early in extra time.

This was the first European final to be settled by penalties. We knew it was a possibility and Don Howe had ensured we practised, but it was still a unique event. Looking back at the footage, John Motson gets hugely excited at the novelty – his first shoot-out too. He went up a gear when Big Pat saved the first kick from Kempes. I was up next and Pereira also saved. Motty was adamant it should have been retaken, and when I look back on it now, the keeper had taken a step or two. VAR would have given me another crack. But it never crossed our minds then.

I had been a reliable penalty-taker since I had taken over from Malcolm MacDonald and continued to be throughout my career. But that is a miss that lives with me to this day. For weeks, I'd wake up in a cold sweat thinking about why I didn't put it in the other corner. People talk to me now about a certain game I played in, or a certain goal, and I often have no memory of it. But I've never forgotten that penalty.

Both teams scored until sudden death when it fell on Rixy to keep us in it. Pereira saved again. Graham just slumped over in a tired gesture that summed up how we were all feeling. It was so sad for him, but we all shared the weight of the defeat and knew we should have won it in normal time. There was much debate afterwards about the unfairness of a shoot-out and how there had to be a better way to settle matches. Still nobody has come up with another solution, and I don't think there is one.

Incredibly, we still had two league games to play. Just two days later we were up at Wolverhampton Wanderers. Terry often remarked how he had no idea how we lifted ourselves to beat them 2–1. They were a good side, sitting sixth, having won the League Cup. It meant we had to muster one last effort at Middlesbrough three days later. Liverpool would be champions, ahead of Manchester United, but a win would lift us above Ipswich into third and into a European place. It was a bridge too far. There was nothing left. We lost 5–0. My last game for Arsenal became a scene of utter despair.

We sat in the bath absolutely shattered as it sunk in that our marathon season had given us nothing for our efforts. I just remember Sammy Nelson, double hero and great friend, leaning over and shaking my hand.

'Thanks, Chippy,' he said. 'It was great playing with you.'

'What?' I thought. 'Oh! Thanks.'

It dawned on me then. That was it, that really was my last game for Arsenal. It got a bit emotional.

Was it really the end? As the fog cleared over the next few days, another reality was biting too. I still had nowhere to go. Gigi had let me know about Juventus's interest. The two games against them had put me firmly on their radar. 'Please tell Liam to be patient,' was the message from Juve to Gigi. But I was getting jittery. I might have to eat humble pie.

On 31 May, I married Sarah. We didn't know whether to swap the German Linguaphone tapes for Italian. Arsenal were still publicly saying they wanted me to stay and even though I was out of contract, there was no freedom of movement so I was legally and morally obliged to return for pre-season. It was a touch embarrassing, having said goodbye to everyone after Middlesbrough. Terry was putting his arm around me, still trying to talk me round. Ronnie and Gigi were assuring me that all would work out, advising me to stay as fit as possible for when a top club came in.

It was a strange summer all round at Arsenal. Captain Pat Rice left for Watford, while Clive Allen arrived from QPR, trained a few times, then was exchanged for Kenny Sansom before the season started. Kenny took Sammy's place at left back.

I was waiting for the phone to ring. Then it did. Brian Clough, manager of Nottingham Forest. First thing Clough says is he's heard I'd just got married. 'Well done, young man. I hope you and Sarah will be very happy.' He knew her name? He had done his homework. I was excited to be talking to this strange but brilliant football manager.

'I hear you've bought an apartment in Majorca recently.'

'Yes, Mr Clough.'

'How much did that cost you, young man?'

'Twenty-five thousand, Mr Clough,' I replied.

'I'll buy you five of those if you come to Nottingham Forest.'

Nobody in football had spoken to me like this before. I thanked him and I bought myself some time to think about it. I didn't want to leave Arsenal for another English club. Clough was also quite close to Dennis Roach, so that didn't appeal to me either. I rang him back the next day and told him my ambition was to play in Germany or Italy. 'Good luck, young man.'

Seven years later, after I returned from Italy, I played against Forest at the City Ground in one of my first games for West Ham. As I walked towards the dressing room, there was Brian in his signature green sweatshirt swaggering along the corridor towards me. I hadn't spoken to him since. 'Welcome back, young man. How is Sarah?' I thought, wow, what a memory, this guy is something special.

If I was leaving, Arsenal would have preferred me to go to Manchester United because it would have meant a much bigger transfer fee than a move abroad. I believe the clubs, on the quiet, had agreed a price of one million pounds, about twice as much as Arsenal would get if I moved to Germany or Italy. I met Martin Edwards, the United chairman and owner, at Ronnie Teeman's house in Leeds. A nice man, he told me that United wanted me and gifted me a book on the history of the club. *There's Only One United* by Geoffrey Green, one of the best football writers during my time in England. I accepted it happily but would have had a bet that I knew just as much about the history of United as Martin Edwards did. I told him I was interested but would like to speak to the manager, Dave Sexton. Martin said he would arrange it.

I was back in Dublin enjoying myself with my family, friends and my new wife when I got the call from Ronnie that Dave Sexton was coming over. We arranged to meet at Jury's Hotel in Ballsbridge. I was ushered up to a suite on one of the top floors. 'Call me Dave,' he said. I knew everything about his coaching and managerial career. Assistant to Bertie Mee as Arsenal coach in 1966. Manager of the great Chelsea team of the early 1970s. Manager of QPR, taking them to second in the First Division in 1976, missing out by one point behind Liverpool. He was from a working-class boxing family in Islington, London. Peter Osgood, the brilliant Chelsea striker, once insulted Sexton in the dressing room in front of his teammates and Dave suggested that Ossie 'come round the back of the stand and we'll sort it out'. Ossie wisely decided to have a shower. Generally in football nobody had a bad word to say about Sexton.

I was sitting across from him when the waiter came into the room to take our lunch order. This was a private meeting, nobody was to know anything about it, and the poor man was a nervous wreck. His hand was shaking like a leaf. We ordered Dover sole. When he came back up with the fish we asked for it off the bone. The last thing in the world this man needed, judging by the rattle of the knife and fork against the silver plate.

Dave came across as totally genuine. His quiet manner contrasted with Clough's bullish approach, but he told me he rated me and wanted to make me the biggest signing United had ever made. Same as with Clough, I told Sexton I wanted to go abroad but I would consider his offer. This top-secret meeting quickly became very public and the bookmakers in Dublin soon had United as hot favourites in the market on my next club.

Maybe Juve had just been working their way through a list. I found out later I wasn't the only player on their radar. Kevin

Keegan confirmed to me that he had been approached by Gigi too, but turned Juve down, because his wife was scared off by some high-profile kidnappings and murders taking place in Italy at the time. He reckons they were eyeing Diego Maradona and Michel Platini too.

Finally, Ronnie Teeman called and said we were invited to a meeting to the Mandarin Hotel in Hyde Park – owned by Rocco Forte then – with a senior Fiat executive who had a mandate to negotiate on Juventus's behalf. He had all the papers and there was little thinking time needed. Financially, the contract was life-changing, multiples of what I was earning at Arsenal. I knew Juventus were in the business of winning. I signed that night.

My life changed rapidly. The following morning I was at the Arsenal training ground, to pick up boots and say goodbyes. Embracing and shaking hands with my teammates and with Terry Neill. I choked up as I hugged kitman Tony Donnelly, who made life a pain as an apprentice but had become my mate and card partner. I shook hands with the kids in the youth team I always kept an eye on, who were just starting out on their journey to make it as footballers. The groundsmen, the ladies who made our lunch each day, the whole Arsenal family saw me off.

I walked out onto one of the training pitches to find Don Howe. 'Don, I'm off, I've signed for Juventus.' He was preparing for a session and he could barely bring himself to shake hands. 'See you Liam,' was all he said. It upset me then, how indifferent he was, but later I understood where he was coming from. He was probably hurting too. He wanted to win like me. He was a huge influence on my career, challenging me to become more consistent and more of a team player. I owed him a lot. Terry made a great call bringing him back to Arsenal.

8

Ireland

How do you sum up an international career that lasted 16 years without tasting the one thing you strive to reach – the finals of a World Cup or European Championships?

In the main, I loved it. I was proud of it, was thrilled at the satisfaction it gave my family and friends. The Ireland dressing room was among my favourite places to be. At times it was a happy escape from day-to-day life and the conflict and disillusionment in the Arsenal dressing room. It was like going home. Where a bunch of lads from very similar backgrounds came together and reviewed the lives we were living, over in England.

At other times, it was bitterly frustrating. At the end, it brought heartbreak. Often it made me deeply cynical about the powers that control football and refereeing and whatever dark forces were haunting us. For a spell, in the middle of my career, when results with Ireland were disappointing, a lot of criticism came my way. I could cope. I was used to it in Italy, where the critics could be even more vicious. But it was troubling for my mother and father. Some of us became the focus of wider frustration out there, at this inability to reach the finals of an international tournament.

Even those bad times had something to do with John Giles. Because hopes had been raised and now hopes were being dashed. And it was John Giles who introduced hope and belief to Irish international football.

We have heard an awful lot, over the years, about Ireland's 'philosophy'. It often sounds like putting in place a philosophy is the most complicated thing in the world, a drawn-out process that might involve losing lots of football matches while players work out what it is they're supposed to be doing. But as far as I could see, John had already embedded his philosophy by the time of my first game for Ireland on that magical day at Dalymount against the Soviets.

He mightn't have used the word 'philosophy'. He probably didn't even mention our 'style of play'. But in just his fourth game in charge as player-manager, it was clear everybody already knew what was expected of them. And John knew what he needed from every player to make things fit together. The goalkeeper would throw the ball out to the fullbacks or roll it to the central defenders. Then it was our responsibility, the midfielders, to receive the ball from them. Make yourself available. Don't hide. In possession, we were required to play penetrating passes to our wide men or strikers, in what was essentially a 4-3-3. Bravery in possession was essential.

Our first goal that afternoon epitomised exactly what John was looking for. Right back Joe Kinnear wins the ball in the air, glancing a header back to right-sided centre back Paddy Mulligan. Paddy passes to the other centre back, Terry Mancini, who delivers into midfield to the unmarked Giles. John isn't unmarked through a slice of good fortune; he has done what came so naturally to him and what he has preached all his life – he made himself available. He turns and hits a 30-yard pass to Joe Kinnear, who is now overlapping down the right.

Joe arrows a great ball to the far post, where Don Givens plants a brilliant header into the far corner of the net. Five passes. Every player assured on the ball, fully believing in what we were doing. Jimmy Magee was right. It was a beautiful goal.

It wasn't only on the field that John made a swift impact. The FAI respected him, or at least they knew they couldn't mess with him. One of the things everybody knew about John Giles was that you didn't mess with him. I was new, so had nothing to compare it with, but the other lads made it clear that everything had improved. Facilities, travel arrangements, food. Standards were raised to come close to what we were used to at our clubs. He brought a seriousness to playing for Ireland. We began to meet at training camps in Bisham Abbey in Berkshire, which was used by many professional teams.

Most of this was down to John organising those things himself because the FAI really didn't have any idea about the workings of a professional football environment. They were amateurs, volunteers, with no exposure to the pro game. It wasn't until the late 1980s, when Dr Tony O'Neill became general secretary, that the association began to modernise.

But John's achievements and standing in the game meant he could pick up the phone to anyone. Another friendly in Poland was no longer the only option for Ireland. In 1976, he asked his old Leeds boss Don Revie, then England manager, if they would give us a game. The FA probably wouldn't have given somebody from the FAI a hearing, but John got it on. At that stage of my career, it was a huge thrill. My second time on the pitch at Wembley. First time I was an apprentice, carrying the club banner before the 1972 centenary FA Cup final between Leeds and Arsenal.

John encouraged us to relish the experience but made it clear he wouldn't tolerate anybody being overawed. We weren't here as tourists. 'If every player does his job we can match anyone,' I remember him saying. It was one of his themes. And we played well, certainly didn't go there just to contain them. We drew 1–1, a Gerry Daly penalty, and probably should have won. It was my Arsenal idol Charlie George's only game for England, though he'd left by now for Derby. It was Ray Wilkins' debut too and we were also up against Kevin Keegan and Trevor Brooking. But 10 of us were playing in the First Division, with only goalkeeper Mick Kearns outside it, at Walsall.

It was among John's priorities to eliminate any inferiority complex we brought with us to away matches, because it was our efforts on the road that had cost us qualification for the 1976 Euros. After that win over the Soviets, we also defeated Switzerland in front of 50,000 at Lansdowne Road and took three points from two games with Turkey. Don bagged another four goals in the Dublin win.

But we lost 2–1 in front of 90,000 people in Kiev and fell to a late goal against the Swiss in Berne, missing out on qualification by a point. We played OK in those matches, but there was a nagging sense we could have expected more from ourselves.

It maddened John, Ireland's lack of conviction on away trips, a legacy of decades of misfortune. He can't understand, anyway, why a team might perform better at home than away, when it's still the same football pitch for everybody out there. He often told us, with great comic timing, about the away qualifier in Spain in the 1960s, where Ireland scored a goal but were so bemused that the flag hadn't gone up, that it hadn't been disallowed for some spurious reason, that everybody had been slow to celebrate. Indeed, John reckons this protracted lack of celebration eventually persuaded the officials that some foul play must have taken place and they did disallow the goal.

My good friend Terry Mancini, who was with us at Arsenal during those years, will tell you we'd have qualified if he'd been around. UEFA banned him for four games, eventually reduced to three, for that tangle with Kaplichni at Dalymount. Another indication we got few favours in the corridors of power. He never played for Ireland again.

Terry would not have been slow to celebrate a goal. The one thing he never lacked was belief. A tremendous character in the dressing room, he never tired of telling us about his headed goal at the Maracanã in John's first game as manager, and how, as he was running back to our own half for the restart, Pelé came past him and generously said 'great goal'. A tale only slightly marred by the fact that Pelé had retired from international duty about three years earlier. Never let facts get in the way of a good story.

Whatever was needed, John wanted us to expect more of ourselves and for ourselves. To celebrate our goals and stake our claim properly on the international stage. We were encouraged by the '76 campaign and the growing belief among the supporters too. There was genuine optimism we could qualify for the Argentina World Cup, even when we were drawn in a tough group with France and Bulgaria. Sadly there was only so much even John Giles could control.

In real life I don't think I'm a conspiracy theorist. I don't blame everything that goes wrong on a shady new world order. You won't find me trying to disprove the moon landings. In football, it often frustrates me how players and managers find an easy scapegoat in refereeing decisions. And how fans invariably suspect their team is singled out for unfair treatment. There's far too much criticism and outrage around honest mistakes.

But when it comes to Ireland, and our efforts to qualify for international tournaments, I can't help feeling that there were forces greater than all of us intercepting our best efforts. There were just too many red flags over the years. Or at least too many flags going up.

In my less positive moments, I tend to reduce my Ireland career to four games. Four what-ifs. Four acts of larceny. The first came right away in Paris, in our first qualifier for '78. By now, David O'Leary and Frank Stapleton were with me in the Ireland team. We played very well in the first half, but trailed to a goal early in the second from their star player Michel Platini – not the last time I would come across him. Not long after, I dribbled down the French left and crossed for Frank to head in a brilliant equaliser. Footage doesn't survive from many of these internationals, but this game is out there in full on YouTube. Try to figure out how it could be offside. Frank is behind the ball when I pulled it across, for starters. The French don't even appeal, but sure enough salvation is at hand. The flag is up. Another sorrowful mystery for Irish football. 'It seemed that the linesman had his flag in the air every time we went into their box,' Giles said to the press afterwards. As we chased it late on, France got a second on the counter.

Despite this serious setback in a four-game group, we got back on track by beating France at Lansdowne when I scored early on. Since the French had slipped up in a 2–2 draw in Bulgaria, two wins against the Eastern Europeans would now send us through on top of the group. Alas, what awaited in Sofia was, as reporter Noel Dunne puts it in the *Irish Independent* report of the game, 'one of the most disgraceful displays by a trio of officials I have ever seen'.

Again we had fallen behind early on in front of an hysterical crowd. There was at least one outrageous refusal to give us a penalty when Don Givens was felled in the box. But Don equalised after the break and we pushed for the winner that would put us on the brink of history. Around the hour Steve

Heighway unlocked the Bulgarians down the left and crossed for Gerry Daly, who nodded down for John to hammer into the net. It should have been a rare slice of perfect footballing justice. A valedictory moment of triumph for the man who had done so much for us. But justice and Irish football didn't go hand in hand. Recalling what happened instead still gets the pulse racing too hard for me to be reasonable, so I'll call on the summary of Dunne, a relatively independent witness.

'The referee produced his masterstroke. Having first allowed the goal, he accepted a flag, presumably for offside, from his linesman and only he and his God knows why. Certainly he was the only man in the stadium who had spotted the mysterious infringement.'

Things disintegrated after that. A terrible tackle on Frank went unpunished. A fight broke out that spilled onto the running track round the pitch that I recall being in the middle of, but Mick Martin and Noel Campbell were the two sent off, along with two of theirs. Outrage at decades, maybe centuries, of persecution probably spilled out of us. They got a winner, though Don went through again late on. The flag, naturally, was up.

Afterwards, the Irish media got hold of the great France manager Michel Hidalgo, who had been in the crowd on a scouting mission. 'It is impossible to win here,' he told them, even though the result suited him. 'I thought it was disgusting. Ireland were robbed for I saw nothing wrong at all about the Giles goal and I have no doubt you would have won without the referee.'

There are probably dozens more controversies, but the two other episodes that easily spring to mind came under Eoin Hand's watch, after he took over from John.

The Parc des Princes again. France and Platini. You could easily suffer from déjà vu. Though I recall the elegant Jean

Tigana being their star that night. It had been a good start to qualification for the 1982 World Cup. We had beaten the Netherlands at Lansdowne and drawn with Belgium. In Paris, again we went behind and again it was Heighway on the left who engineered our response. A cross to the back post. Kevin Moran jumps with a defender, the ball drops to Michael Robinson, who thumps it in.

This time it was a Spanish referee observing familiar custom. The only departure from tradition in the officials' vivid imagination was the apparition of a handball, rather than offside.

As Billy George in the *Cork Examiner* tells it: 'The referee cut short Ireland's celebrations after first signaling the goal. He turned after seeing a gesture from his linesman and raced to where Moran had been, beating his wrist as if to indicate handball. It was a decision that mystified the Irish.'

The *Irish Press* ran a sequence of photographs in an effort to solve this mystery. In one, there is indeed an arm up in the vicinity of the ball, before it drops to Robinson. But it is the arm of the marvelous French full back Patrick Battiston, who eventually paid dearly for this qualification when Harald Schumacher nearly killed him with that infamous tackle in the World Cup semi-final.

Mel Moffat wrote in the *Irish Press*: 'Even persistent replays on the video tape later by television reporters failed to spot the hand that only the referee and his linesman saw.'

'Who saw any handball?' asked Eoin afterwards. 'Certainly none of us saw Moran touch the ball and it was a very unsatisfactory decision. It happened just when we looked capable of saving the match.'

'I did not touch the ball with my hand,' confirmed Kevin. 'In fact it hit me full in the face.'

That campaign must still rank among Ireland's best, taking into account the calibre of our opponents. Frank Stapleton, now departed from Arsenal to Manchester United, was a world-class centre forward capable of troubling anyone. We beat France 3–2 in Dublin, drew 2–2 in Rotterdam. But what happened amid thunder and lightning at the Heysel Stadium in Brussels arguably tops all the grievances.

The footage is as ridiculous as I remember. We'd held our own in the first half, despite missing David O'Leary and Mark Lawrenson to injury. Just before the break, I flicked a quick free kick to the near post towards Frank, a move we had often practised, and he arrived just before goalkeeper Michel Preud'homme to divert in. The flag stays down. Frank's arms go up in jubilation, though the Belgians to a man have theirs in the air too, claiming something. Hardly offside – the defensive wall alone was keeping Frank on, not to mind one or two more markers. In the middle of this commotion, the Portuguese referee Raul Nazare seems to be in a bit of a fluster and is signaling something himself. Belatedly, in a generous act of solidarity, the linesman's flag goes up. Nazare's arm follows. Offside, seemingly.

Our protests carried on long after the half-time whistle, until Eoin had to escort us to the dressing room. Though pressure mounted in the second half, we held on reasonably comfortably for what would have been a vital point. But with two minutes to go, under a free kick from our right, their distinguished full back Eric Gerets launched into a comically extravagant leap into the penalty area, which Nazare liked the look of. Gerets's only error was misjudging slightly the diving board from where he made his splash. So it was just a free kick on the 18 yard line. René Vandereycken drilled it in. Crossbar. The ball flies up in the air. Underneath it, maybe Seamus McDonagh is fouled, maybe he's not. But he's on the ground. That powerful predator Jan Ceulemans nods it in. Everywhere, on the bench and in the box, hearts break, heads sink into hands. Protests are muted. After everything, we know it's futile.

Afterwards, rage breaks out everywhere. 'Robbed again – Uproar as referee breaks Irish hearts' was the headline in the *Irish Press*. Mickey Walsh, who was playing for Porto at the time, called the referee a cheat, to his face, in Portuguese. I asked Mickey what was the Portuguese for 'thief'. Much the same as Italian. 'Ladrão, ladrão,' I shouted at him. He just took it all, never pulled out a card. Turns out I went over and above with the research, as Eoin Hand explained afterwards.

'I asked first of all if he understood English and he nodded, I then told him I was the manager of the Irish team and that I thought he was a disgrace and a cheat.'

Eoin went further. 'I said, "You have taken money, you have taken a bribe." That is the most serious thing I have ever said to an official and I should have been reported to UEFA but nothing came of it. Nazare simply stood there motionless as I laid into him. He offered neither defence nor explanation.'

There was a sense within the squad and among the Irish football public that this was a bridge too far, that we had taken this lying down long enough.

'It is more than a coincidence that this sort of thing keeps happening to Ireland – and now we are fed up having the dirty done on us,' Eoin said. 'I will be asking the FAI to make the strongest possible protest to FIFA regarding the vetting of referees for matches at this level.'

FAI president Brendan Menton joined the outrage. 'Bob Beamon's world long jump record of 29 feet 2 inches was beaten by Gerets. It was the most amazing leap I have ever seen.'

Then Sheffield Wednesday manager Jack Charlton was at the match on a scouting mission. 'I was incensed and I am an

Englishman. It was the best goal I have seen this season.' Would we have needed him at all but for that night?

In an amazing interview years later for the *Sunday Tribune*, the sports journalist Paul Howard visited Nazare at his home in Lisbon, armed with a videotape of the match that he had borrowed from Eoin Hand. They watch it together, with Nazare's family. Before the tape rolls, the referee confidently insists the goal had been ruled out for offside, by his linesman. But after watching the images, his tune changes.

'I think I made a mistake when I told you it was offside. Yes, now I remember. I awarded an indirect free-kick. My hand is up to say indirect. And Liam Brady shoots direct. That is why the goal was disallowed. Nobody touches the ball before it goes in the goal.'

Howard rewinds again and it's crystal clear Frank has got a touch. Another version: 'The ball hits off me. It hits off my back and goes in the goal. I remember that is why I disallowed it.' By now, he has lost all credibility. Even his family are questioning him.

We missed out on goal difference for that World Cup. Belgium topped their group in Spain and beat Argentina. France only went out in penalties in the semis. We weren't that far away from the top table.

I wonder how the FAI's complaint to FIFA was received, if it was ever dispatched. There are various theories about why we seemed to be so unfairly treated over the years. No wrongdoing was ever proven against any of the officials who had 'done the dirty' on Ireland, but was there the odd rogue referee on the take? Belgian football was shown to be corrupt when Anderlecht were later proven to have bribed the referee in their 1984 UEFA Cup semi-final win over Nottingham Forest.

Eoin Hand once suggested it was the FAI's famed parsimony haunting us once again. 'Their treatment of visiting referees would have been nothing compared to the way that referees or officials were treated in Belgium or France or England.' Maybe we just didn't show these guys a good enough time when they were on duty in Dublin.

I subscribe to the idea that there was something bigger at play. It's obvious FIFA would prefer certain teams to reach World Cups because of the major sponsorships and television deals hanging on their participation. A World Cup without France, for instance, was in nobody's commercial interest. So might referees sometimes have been given riding instructions, as they might say in racing?

Whatever was behind our misfortune, Ireland's history means you will never find me rowing into any diatribe against VAR. It's not perfect, but it has cleaned up the game. Referees, or whatever dark forces are guiding them, will never have the same power again.

Qualification for that World Cup would have done so much for Eoin Hand. Ireland's players were gutted when John Giles stepped down after the first match of that campaign, a win in Cyrpus. I was very upset. John had already been a huge influence on my life, as a coach and a mentor. I regard him and Giovanni Trapattoni as the best managers I've worked for.

He left the job, ostensibly, over a dispute about wanting to appoint new assistant managers. But he was tired too of fighting those sorts of battles. Of constantly having to drag the FAI along with him.

Eoin did well as his replacement. He had played plenty for John and knew exactly what he wanted. He had the sense not to rock the boat too hard. The routines were the same, the training the same, the tactics similar. But the players were getting better. English-born lads like Michael Robinson, Chris Hughton, Tony Grealish and Mark Lawrenson were lifting standards all the time.

Like John, Eoin had to do a lot of the heavy lifting himself on the organisational front. Making sure the arrangements were right. But he hadn't the clout John carried. You could sense things slipping, the FAI gradually lapsing back into old shambolic ways. Qualification in '82 would have given Eoin the leverage to push back, to make demands.

The tour to South America that summer, that I write about elsewhere, was an utter disaster. It turned the FAI into a joke. For the sake of making a few quid, it undid a lot of the serious-ness John had demanded. If things are not right at the top, it filters down, it affects everything. The atmosphere around the team, the morale. Call-ups were being turned down more often.

Eoin got little help. He had enough on his plate just trying to get the grass cut at Lansdowne. I remember a game in Moscow where he brought his wife with him to do the cooking in the team hotel. All visiting teams were paranoid about the prospects of the local food being tampered with. When we played England again at Wembley in a friendly, we stayed in a budget hotel in Bayswater that was partly a construction site. We walked across the street to the local park to do our training. The FAI hadn't booked anywhere.

Results deteriorated. Crowds of 25,000 were turning up in Dublin, rather than 50,000. Euro '84 results were so-so. We needed to beat Spain at home, but drew 3–3. A 3–2 home defeat by the Netherlands, when we'd been 2–0 up, finished us. Two promising kids called Gullit and van Basten did the damage.

Despite a welcome win over the Soviet Union in front of a half-full Lansdowne in 1984, the World Cup '86 journey never got off the ground. Defeats in Denmark and Norway followed, though the Danes were emerging as a class side, with the Laudrups and Preben Elkjær. By now the fans and the media were fed up with hard-luck stories and became fiercely critical of Eoin. I was getting it too, and Frank Stapleton to some extent. I was playing in Serie A with Inter Milan. Frank was leading the line for Manchester United. A lot was expected – it came with the territory. And we were getting it in the neck. I thought it was unfair. I always turned up, always tried my best. But towards the end of the Euro '84 road, it got me down. I'd been captain under John, when he stopped playing himself, and Eoin had kept things that way. But I went to him and said I wanted to give it up. I guess I was feeling the pressure. He gave it to Tony Grealish first, then Frank.

A lot of the heat was being conducted through the pen of the former international Eamon Dunphy, who was writing savage columns about the team in the Sunday papers. Dunphy became preoccupied by the idea that I'd gone soft and complacent in Italy, that I was swaggering in on Ireland duty as if doing everybody a favour and producing nothing, while having too much influence in the dressing room. He once described my efforts as a 'monument to conceit'. It was garbage and wouldn't have bothered me too much, except it was upsetting my mother and father.

All you can do is keep the head down and get on with it. A long football career is bound to bring spells where you're not everyone's cup of tea. But when we lost 4–1 at home to the Danes in November 1985, our final World Cup qualifier played in front of just 14,000 fans, the top table never felt further away.

To my mind, there were two other things preventing Irish football from achieving its potential – history and politics.

I would love to have played on an all-Ireland team. I enjoy rugby anyway, never miss a Six Nations game, but that's what I'm most envious of, that they represent the whole island.

The prospect looked possible, at times, in the 1970s. In 1973, John Giles and Martin O'Neill played together in midfield on a cross-border team in a friendly for charity against Brazil. Derek Dougan got the northern lads to buy into it. What a side. Top-class midfield, a world-class goalkeeper in Pat Jennings, with Dougan and Terry Conroy and Don Givens up front. The only pity is George Best wasn't available.

But the will never seemed to be there in the FAI or IFA to make it work. Rugby never split, but once soccer did it was always going to be extremely difficult to put things back together. Two sets of jobs, two sets of blazers, and two sets of political beliefs. Very difficult to overcome.

I've never doubted the players could make it work. We came close enough, at Highbury, to putting one into practice, with seven of us in the squad, straddling the supposed divide. We never had an argument over politics. Am I naive to think footballers could have played a role in building bridges between our communities if given a chance? Surely some agreement could have been reached over the anthem and the flag. Now, I can't ever see it happening unless the north and the south come to some agreement politically over a united Ireland.

I played in the Republic's first competitive fixture against Northern Ireland in 1978 and found it a sad and strange occasion. It was a scoreless draw played in excellent spirit on the pitch, but surrounded by an odd kind of tension, with the Troubles at their height. The return match in Belfast the following year was worse and the abuse we took at Windsor Park was pretty severe in that 1–0 defeat.

I was injured, but made sure to travel with the squad, so I couldn't be accused of chickening out. At one stage Gerry Daly, beside me on the bench, got hit on the head by something thrown from the crowd and was dazed. Over came my pal Sammy Nelson from their bench, ever the opportunist and the joker. 'Fucking hell, Gerry, you've been shot!'

9

The Italian Job

I SAID MY ARSENAL goodbyes in the morning and was on a British Airways flight to Turin that afternoon, accompanied only by two Italian journalists Gigi Peronace had set up to get the inside story. Sarah was going to follow in a few weeks, after pre-season camp. I was excited but apprehensive. New country, new language, new kind of football. I'd watched the 1980 Euros closely, back in Dublin. It was Italy's home championship and the team was built around seven Juve stars, who would mostly grow into the core of the '82 world champions. I'd seen them up close in our European semi-final too. Players like Dino Zoff in goal, similar to Pat Jennings in ability and temperament. The elegant Roberto Bettega in attack, a complete striker. Marco Tardelli, Claudio Gentile, Antonio Cabrini, Franco Causio and Gaetano Scirea. Some of the finest players in world football. It was exciting the club wanted me as their foreign player, but there would be pressure in such company.

The plane was half empty. Turin is an industrial city that doesn't attract many holidaymakers. Nobody had recognised me on the flight. After all the speculation and anticipation, this was all nicely low-key. We landed after a 90-minute flight. My stomach was churning. As the plane taxied towards the terminal I heard loud cheering from a large crowd on the balcony of the airport. Everyone on the flight turned around to see who on the plane was commanding this attention. I kept looking out the window. There must have been a thousand Juventus fans and the black and white colours were everywhere. A banner read 'Welcome Brady'. I was carried shoulder-high through arrivals, no passport control needed. My state of mind was flipping from fear to excitement and back. It fully dawned on me, the size of this club and the level of expectation around it.

Giovanni Trapattoni, the coach, stepped forward to shake my hand, flanked by club officials and an interpreter, Cinzia Bizotto, daughter of Trap's assistant Romulo Bizotto. She would become a great friend. Cinzia translated Trap's Italian to tell me Juve had made up their minds to sign me after my performance against them in the semi-final. Which mightn't have been strictly true, I learned later, but it probably got me on a shortlist. I would have the number 10 shirt, he said. Numbers meant little in England but wearing 10 in Italy would bring scrutiny from media and fans. It was the club's way too of sending a message that I would be their playmaker. It was a vote of confidence.

Before we could leave the airport, there was a press conference, with dozens of journalists firing questions in Italian. I'd never seen anything like the frenzy, and even Cinzia seemed rattled. I would, over time, become used to the madness and intensity of the Italian football press, and learn that whatever words I managed might not make it accurately onto the page. On that summer evening, it was another reminder of how much adjusting I'd need to do.

I wonder if Pep Guardiola or Jürgen Klopp do the airport run. Trap drove us for a half hour or so up into the Alpine hills outside Turin to a hotel in Villar Perosa near Fiat President and Juventus owner Gianni Agnelli's imposing 18th-century country retreat.

My new teammates had finished eating but were waiting in the dining room and they all stood up and applauded me in. I picked out faces I'd played against a few months before. Friendlier now. Captain Giuseppe Furino presented me with the 10 shirt and I was told Roberto Bettega would be my roommate during the training camp, as he could speak some English. I didn't bring up how he nearly broke David O'Leary's leg a few months previous. But we struck up an early deal. As well as being a truly great player, Roberto had an eye on the future. He figured English would be a great help to him when his career was over. He promised if I gave him a lesson or two, he'd help me *parlare Italiano*. He wasn't wrong, because he ended up vice-chairman of the club.

No chips on the menu that night but I had broadened my palate by then thanks to an Italian restaurant in North London that had become my regular place on a Saturday evening after matches. It was spaghetti bolognese and veal Milanese that first evening. I was offered wine but thought I had better pass since we were in pre-season training. The next night I noticed most of the players had a couple of glasses of red, so was happy to follow suit.

I picked up a few of the nicknames. Tardelli was *schizo*, or psycho, which was very appropriate, and Franco Causio was *il Barone*, the Baron. Franco was fond of himself and arrived to training every day in a different suit and tie. He also had a taste for expensive silk pyjamas. In fact they all wore pyjamas, as I found out on one of the first evenings, when we were summoned to Franco's room. He had just signed a new contract and wanted to celebrate. No cans of beer, but a couple of bottles of champagne on ice. Franco also had a cigarette on the go as we toasted him. They all smoked. Me, Trap and Romolo Bizzotto the assistant coach were about the only people at the club who didn't.

It felt slightly surreal. These top players I watched closely at the Euros now sitting around me in their pyjamas in this smokey bedroom. God knows what they made of me, in my vest and underpants. A bloke who needed smartening up, no doubt. But they seemed to be a good bunch of lads who made me feel very welcome.

My first encounter with Gianni Agnelli came on a Sunday morning during the training camp, when his helicopter landed in the estate. This would become the routine whenever we played at home on Sunday afternoons. We'd stay here the night before our games and he'd join us on a morning walk around the grounds. We'd gather around him and he'd address us, usually Trap first, then a question or two for a couple of players.

This morning, he definitely wanted to hear from me. I knew a bit about him. That he was Italy's richest man. That he was regarded as an international playboy, who might breakfast in Rome, lunch in Paris and have one or two in New York before the night was out. For an industrialist who'd built one of Europe's biggest manufacturing empires, but had been grappling with economic depression and the rise of union-led protest, he still spared plenty of time for skiing in the Alps, or racing around Italy in a Ferrari-powered Fiat, or entertaining the world's most glamorous women on his yacht, moored somewhere off the Amalfi coast.

In Turin he was revered, the closest thing to royalty. The saying went: 'Agnelli is Fiat, Fiat is Turin, and Turin is Italy'. Hundreds of thousands of workers migrated from southern Italy to work for Fiat in Turin. The Agnelli family wanted to give their workers an outlet from all the hard work, and what better than a winning football team to entertain them? He was highly educated and spoke to me in a posh English accent, and like many with posh English accents he had difficulty pronouncing his Rs.

'Bwady. How are we getting on?'

'Very well, sir, everything is fine.'

'Excellent, that's what I like to hear.'

If I closed my eyes, I might have been speaking to the old Etonian Denis Hill-Wood, the chairman of Arsenal. Apart from Bettega, nobody would have understood what was being said. I doubt if Agnelli really knew much about me. I hadn't played in a World Cup or Euros. I later found out I was down the list of players Juve wanted as their first big foreign signing for 14 years. He would have liked Platini or Keegan or Rummenigge but luckily for me he couldn't get them at the time.

Giampiero Boniperti, a great ex-player of the club who played with John Charles in the late 1950s, was the Juve president. He looked after the club day to day and made most of the football decisions, but Agnelli took a keen interest and phoned him early every morning. It might be comparable to when Roman Abramovich owned Chelsea. When it came to the big decisions, Boniperti deferred to the guy whose money financed the club, as I learned to my cost less than two years later.

That training camp was tough. The heat was intense, and despite Bettega's help it was hard going not being able to understand or speak the language. I couldn't wait for Sarah to arrive and start our life in Turin. Juve arranged a month in a comfortable hotel so we could find an apartment. It was the third week in August and the city was practically empty, with offices, shops and factories closed so workers could get away to the seaside, mountains and lakes. We got an Italian teacher for some evening classes and slowly a few phrases sunk in. Having studied French at St Aidan's until I was 15 was a help.

My first official games were in the Italian Cup. A seeded group format two weeks before the league season. The big Serie A clubs used it as part of pre-season and it held nothing like the importance of the FA Cup in England. It was a bit of a money-spinner for the Serie B or C sides we usually played. We easily topped our group to move on to the knockout stages and I scored my first goal for the club. But it was no preparation for the real thing and certainly no preparation for my Serie A bow at 3pm on the island of Sardinia. It was baking, surely 40 degrees, and I couldn't raise a gallop. We drew 1–1 with Cagliari thanks to a Tardelli goal, but it was far from the result or standard expected of us if we were to challenge champions Inter, who had strengthened their side with the signing of Austria's midfield playmaker Herbert Prohaska.

I was gutted, knew I had played poorly and struggled to cope at all with the conditions. The coach ride away from the stadium was quiet and the mood was low. One of the directors, Doctor Giuliano, sat a few rows in front of me. The radio was on and reports were coming in from games around the country. By now I could pick up a few basic phrases and I heard him talking to the driver.

'How did Inter get on?'

'They won 4–0!'

'Prohaska? Play any good?'

'They just said he was the best player on the pitch.'

'*Cazzo*', in Italian. Fuck in English.

'Looks like we have signed the wrong foreigner.'

He had no idea I could make out what he was saying. You don't forget those things, and his remark stuck with me. I was always a harsh judge of myself and I knew I hadn't played well. Being the only foreign player, I accepted that I was under a microscope. Italian people are impulsive but I felt Giuliano was a little premature with his judgement. Come the end of the season he would be hugging and kissing me.

On the way back to Turin by plane from Cagliari it dawned on me properly for the first time that I could fail here. I knew now I was in at at the deep end. Expectancy levels were different. At Arsenal, under Terry Neill and Don Howe, we expected to challenge for a place in Europe and compete in the League and FA cups. In Turin nothing other than the title was acceptable.

In England, before I left, the papers had been full of scepticism. Didn't players as good as Jimmy Greaves and Denis Law fail to crack Italy? Would the Irishman cope with playing 'abroad'? Plenty of journalists and players were of the opinion it was only going to end one way – failure and back to English football with my tail between my legs.

I always had confidence in myself. Going to England at 15, my first game against Shankly's Liverpool at Anfield and my first cap for Ireland at Dalymount against the Soviet Union. I had taken all that in my stride, but after that first Serie A game a little of that fear crept in, the same doubts I felt that first afternoon in an Irish shirt at Dalymount. Maybe I had been a little naive about how different Italian football would be.

Besides any tactical adjustments, it was quickly clear the lifestyle was different. That hit home after one of the cup games in the middle of August, played in the extreme heat. I was still living in the hotel and Tardelli, who was becoming a good friend, dropped me off. 'Come in for a beer,' I said. He came in. It was a boiling August evening and we'd probably lost a kilo or two in sweat. 'But only one, Liam.' 'No, Marco,' I said, 'I'm parched, we are going to have a few beers, you'll enjoy it.' He was adamant. 'No, no, no. I only drink one or else I get a bad head.'

And that was it, something I had to come to terms with. My other teammates were just the same. Alcohol didn't go hand in hand with being a professional footballer. My drinking days were over. It was a lifestyle change for the better. Before long, I was the fittest I'd been in my career and I began to really enjoy this new life.

Trap's training was interesting, with the emphasis on the tactical and technical side. On Thursdays, we'd play a practice match against the youth team or a small club who was asked to play in the formation of our next opponents. Attention was paid to every detail. It was a high-performance culture, long before that kind of terminology was used.

Life in a new city and culture was stimulating too. Sarah and I got on well with the other players and their families. Everybody went out of their way to help us settle in. And something clicked with the Italian lessons. We didn't find it a chore getting to grips with this new language. We found it an interesting challenge. I'd always done OK in school, despite leaving at 15. Looking back, I wish I'd used all that spare time at Arsenal more productively than in my ambition to master the game of snooker. In a way, speaking Italian felt like I was making up for ending my education early.

We found a beautiful unfurnished apartment on the edge of the city and Marco organised a contact of his to help us make it a home. We were soon living in tasteful comfort, a step up from my flat in Palmers Green. My immersion in Italian life didn't quite extend to their TV, which beyond news and football seemed to consist of terrible game shows or cabaret. So our friends in London and Dublin were soon pestered for VHS recordings.

And as a huge music lover we needed a hi-fi. Life wasn't worth living if Bob Dylan, the Eagles or Van Morrison weren't blasting out of the stereo. The players seemed to have contacts in every line of business, but this time it was Trap who suggested a friend of his at Sony HQ in Milan and offered to drive me. His friend picked out some of the latest kit for me, at a Trap price, all to be delivered to the apartment. No Bluetooth, alas, in those days, so it arrived in a forest of wires. I was clueless and still am when it comes to assembling anything. I rang Trap and asked if he knew a technician. 'No problem, I'll do it, Liam.' He was round to us after training later in the week to put it all together. I know Arsène Wenger was pretty attentive around helping players settle in at Arsenal and most clubs have to be in this day and age. But I can't picture too many managers lying on the floor of an apartment, screwdriver in hand, knee deep in cables. It was soon good to go. 'Listen to classical,' was his parting advice. 'Much more relaxing.' He wanted me to settle quickly. A happy player was a more productive one.

However, Inter and Roma were setting the early pace. My form had improved, I was sure, but I hadn't delivered what was expected of a Juventus number 10. The whole team was suffering from carrying the load for Italy in the Euros. We were beaten at home by Bologna, a really bad result. We went out of the UEFA Cup on penalties to Polish side Widzew Łódź, featuring Zbigniew Boniek, a name that would crop up again. And when we lost the city derby to Torino, we were mired in mid-table and the flak was flying.

I was getting plenty of it in the papers. With three dailies devoted only to sport the journalists were busy filling their columns. Players in Italy were expected to talk to the writers most days. And as the foreign player, I was in particular demand. For the first few months I had my friend Cinzia interpreting. I did my fair share of interviews but I would read my quotes next day and notice quite a bit of embroidery. I'd ask Cinzia, 'I didn't say that, did I?' I'd been wary of the press in England but this was far worse. There was unbelievable exaggeration and often plain invention.

The turning point in my fortunes came when Inter visited in November. This was the equivalent of Manchester United v Liverpool. Before the game, the president, Bonoperti, visited the dressing room. He was a calm guy, who'd done everything to support me and try to relieve any pressure, even though the results were bringing heat on him. But today he was agitated. After the usual rousing words, he suddenly became quiet and serious.

'Who is taking penalties today?'

Our regular taker, Franco Causio, had missed against Łódź, and afterwards said I should take them from now on.

'Me, Mr President, it's me now,' I said, from the far corner of the dressing room.

'*Preparati*, Liam. Prepare yourself,' he said, looking me right in the eye. 'I have a strong feeling we will get a penalty today.'

Bonoperti's premonition came to pass in the 50th minute when an Inter full back mistimed a tackle on Antonio Cabrini. I put it away for my first goal in Serie A. I made the second when my shot from outside the box crashed down off the crossbar in front of our sweeper Gaetano Scirea, who forced it in. Inter pulled a late goal back but the victory triggered a 14-match unbeaten run that took us to the top of the league.

I often think about that penalty, which proved so valuable for me. Unlike in England then, in Italy every match was televised, so the footage is out there. For me, it's a stonewall penalty, but there is no escaping the rumours that surrounded Italian football in that era and beyond. Players and officials had been suspended for match-fixing, so there was often a cloud of suspicion. The bigger teams, including Juventus, did appear to enjoy more favourable treatment from referees, though the same could be said of all the top leagues. Only once, later at Sampdoria, did anyone hint at anything dubious in my company, when a teammate asked if we might be content with a draw at the weekend. I told him to go away.

In any case, that win was like a blood transfusion for our season. My form improved massively and I began to score goals regularly and contribute much more to the team. Before long, the narrative in the papers was all about how I'd got to grips with the Italian game.

Before leaving London, I'd asked John Giles for advice. 'You will be OK in Italy,' he said, 'because you will get time on the ball. I've played against them for Leeds. They sit back and with your ability to take players on you'll be fine. In the last third, you'll be able to beat players and get past them.'

And John, not for the first or last time, was right. That's exactly what I tried to do and things started falling into place.

At Arsenal, Pat Jennings would kick the ball out, Frank Stapleton would jump for it and we would see what we could get from the bits and pieces. That rarely happened in Italy. The goalkeeper threw the ball out to his defenders because the opposition would have dropped back to the halfway line. Sometimes I would be man-marked, but getting rid of the marker was not too difficult if you went deeper to get on the ball because they wouldn't follow you. Most teams wanted to drop off and make it very tight in the last third of the pitch. So I began to drift deeper, get on the ball, and run at teams from there.

And I found the game less physical than in England. The English media had tended to label Italian football and players as dirty. When Juve played Arsenal in that Cup Winners' Cup

116

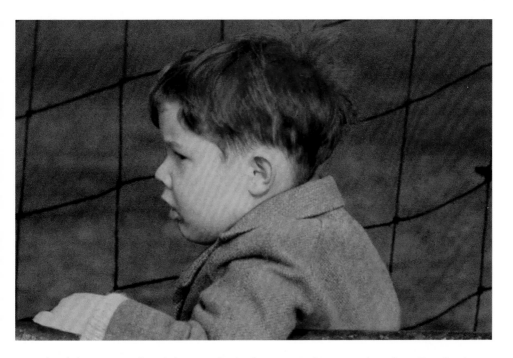

Back of the net: Behind the goal, I believe watching my brother Frank play. I must be five or six and it's probably at Stella Maris, one of the few grounds then in Dublin schoolboy football that had nets.

On yer bike, son: Bringing the corner flags back to the pavilion at St Kevin's Ellenfield Park. St Kevin's is very much a community club and if there was another game on we'd all watch and help out. In the background, The Church of the Holy Child also had a big say on what went on in the community.

Above: Double bubble: Nice introduction to Highbury. One of my first acts as an apprentice was carrying the league and FA Cup trophies behind a pipe band before the first home game of the 71–72 season.

Right: Good, better, best: Looks like homesickness is kicking in. Youth team coach Ian Crawford setting us straight in a London Colney dressing room in 1971.

Above: Four green Gunners: Johnny Murphy, David O'Leary, Frank Stapleton and myself in front of the Garden of Remembrance in Dublin in 1973. Johnny couldn't stand being away from Dublin and went home after six months, going on to become an international for Ireland at rugby.

Left: First team: A photo from 1975. By now, you can see Ian Crawford was out of my hair.

Record collection: A picture taken for the Arsenal match programme at my lodgings in Winchmore Hill, north London. I'm holding *Blonde on Blonde* by Bob Dylan, one of my favourite albums.

Seven heaven: Celebrating one of my favourite Arsenal goals in a 2-2 draw with Leeds United with the North Bank at Highbury in the first |game of the 1978-79 season.

Wembley joy: My best assist, with the right peg, for Frank to put us 2-0 up against Manchester United in the 1979 FA Cup final. Frank was one of the great headers of a ball.

Street party: Next day at Islington Town Hall, celebrating the Cup win with the Arsenal fans.

Celebrating in Islington

Silverware: December 1979, receiving the club player of the year award from Arsenal supporters. I was thrilled to win three of those from the fans.

Above: Debut day: With two of the greats of Irish football, John Giles and Steve Heighway, before my first cap for Ireland at Dalymount Park against the USSR in 1974, sporting the perm that went wrong.

Left: Midfield battle: In action during that game which brought one of Ireland's most famous wins.

Above: Familiar foe: Swapping pennants with the great Michel Platini before Ireland's 3-2 win over France at Lansdowne Road in 1981. I was playing for Juventus, the following year Platini came to take my place.

Right: My way or …: Jack Charlton laying down the law ahead of our qualifier against Belgium in Brussels on the way to Euro '88. I scored a last-minute penalty in a 2-2 draw.

Big Paul: Celebrating with the magnificent Paul McGrath after he opened the scoring against Bulgaria in our 2-0 win at Lansdowne in the final game of that '88 qualifying campaign.

Consoled by Jack after I was sent off late in that game against Bulgaria. We had no idea the red card would have such significance.

Me and Jack, our differences behind us, at my testimonial.

Welcome to Italy: Gigi Peronace greeting me at Turin Airport as Arsenal arrive to play Juventus in the 1980 Cup Winners' Cup semi-final. There's Frank behind. At this stage Gigi was keen for me to go to Italy and was working to arrange a move.

Done deal: Back at Turin Airport a few months later as a Juve player. No passport needed as I was carried through arrivals by fanatical supporters.

Left: New home: In Juventus training kit during my first season.

Below: Scudetto shower: Me and Antonio Cabrini, with Juventus president Giampiero Boniperti, after we clinched the 1981 title by beating Fiorentina. Boniperti had to change his suit after he was drenched with champagne.

Roommate: My dear friend Trevor Francis, one of the best strikers I've played with, at a Sampdoria pre-season training camp in the Dolomite Mountains, where they took us to escape the heat.

Flying start: Samp beat Juve, Inter and then Roma here to kick off the 82–83 season. What a start for a newly promoted team. That's Bruno Conti, their number 7, with Falcao trying to block the pass. Francesco Casagrande, my minder, is behind.

An Irishman and a German speaking Italian: Celebrating at Inter Milan with my neighbour in Como, Karl Heinz Rummenigge, the best player I've played with and a friend for life.

Diego the greatest: In Inter colours at a testimonial for Ossie Ardiles at White Hart Lane with the great Diego Maradona lining up for Spurs. There has been nobody better.

Inswinger: Taking a corner for West Ham. I thoroughly enjoyed my three years at Upton Park.

Hot seat: Outside the doors at Celtic Park having just been announced as the new Celtic manager. I didn't need reminding, but the media scrum showed what a huge club I'd joined.

The dream panel: On RTÉ duty ahead of the 2014 World Cup. A midfield trio of Giles, Dunphy and Brady, with the great Bill O'Herlihy ready to pull the strings. We had arguments and laughs galore.

Hanging up the mic: My last appearance with RTÉ Sport this year, with another good pal, Didi Hamann, in the background. I was fortunate to have 25 years as a pundit and it was nice to sign off with an Ireland win at Lansdowne Road.

Brady bunch: Pat, Ray, Breda, Eamonn, Frank and myself. A Christmas get-together at the Carpenter's Arms in Kent, a pub run by my nephew Jamie, Ray's son.

Back home: Mam and Dad outside our front door at Glenshesk Road in 1985. My father Ned was a keen gardener and was very proud of that creeper at the front.

semi-final, a lot was made of tackles by Bettega and Tardelli. But I barely got injured there. I don't think I ever got hurt from a tackle. There were hard players but they rarely went over the top. There were plenty of cynical fouls, tripping you up or pulling your shirt. And there were players who'd do anything to gain an advantage, enthusiastic exponents of the arts of diving and feigning injury, which wasn't as widespread then in England.

But there was nothing like the aggression you encountered against the likes of Liverpool, with Souness, Case or my friend Tommy Smith. Nearly every team had a real hard man whose job was to stop the creative players. Perryman or Pratt at Spurs, Harris at Chelsea, Hunter at Leeds. I played with Peter Storey at Arsenal. He was that type of player. In England, if you weren't smart you'd get broken up. The Italians wouldn't do that to you. Forwards might have suffered a little more, treated to the odd reducer from behind from the likes of Gentile. But that was not my game. If I missed a game in Italy, it was down to a muscle injury.

Inter fell away and with three games to go in the season, we sat a point ahead of Roma at the top, with Napoli just behind, seeking their first title. But we still had both contenders to play. First, it was Roma in Turin. The brilliant Brazilian midfielder Falcão was their foreign signing and the media billed it as me against him: Brady v Falcão. But they also had Carlo Ancelotti in midfield, who went on to become a serial winner as a manager. He was a top player too, a bit like Graeme Souness in style. Strong, forceful and an excellent passer. I had Tardelli alongside me and we were braced for a hell of a battle to control midfield. I'd never experienced that level of tension before. There was nothing between the sides for an hour and then our captain Furino hit Falcão with a crunching late tackle. Furino had already been booked. The referee sent him off. We had to play the last 30 minutes with 10 men. Roma got on top and we were hanging on.

In the last few minutes, their pressure told. Their centre back Turone pushed up from the back, got on the end of a cross from the right, and finished with a diving header past Zoff. It would have been a famous goal, putting Roma in line for their first title since 1942. Instead, it became an infamous decision, because the flag was up for offside, curtailing Turone's celebrations but not Roma's protests, which went on for several minutes. And 40-odd years.

When the game eventually restarted, we held on and stayed a point ahead. Roma's fans have never really got this game or that goal out of their heads. It is still brought up 40 years later. They call it the great Juventus robbery. They insist the referee was bent. I still hear it plenty on my travels. 'Robbers! Turone's goal was good.' I've watched it back many times on old footage of the game. It's hard to call from the camera angle. VAR would certainly have spent some time drawing the lines. My feeling is that offside was given in good faith. If the referee was bent, would he really have sent off our captain?

Two to go. In Naples, the fans have always been crazy. This was pre-Maradona, and their foreigner was the great Dutch defender Rudi Krol. This time they were in a frenzy. They still had a chance of the title if they beat us. Their supporters tried to play their part by pitching up outside our hotel the night before the game until the very early hours of the morning, tooting their horns and chanting, hoping to deprive us of sleep. The Stadio San Paolo – now the Diego Maradona Stadium – was a cauldron. But that was the afternoon when I fully appreciated up close the utter winning mentality of men like Zoff, Tardelli, Gentile and Scirea. 'We need a result and we are not going to concede.' The same mentality that would see

Italy win the World Cup in Spain a year later. We handled the pressure and kept the crowd quiet by keeping possession of the ball. We nicked a goal with 20 minutes to go and that was enough. Two huge examinations had been passed.

A win over Fiorentina at home would secure the title. Ronnie Teeman flew in from Leeds. The Stadio Communale was jam-packed. We dominated the game and if it wasn't for their Italian international goalkeeper Giovanni Galli we would have won comfortably. It finished 1–0, a Cabrini volley enough to win us the Scudetto. It was an emotional day. I felt a sense of relief and satisfaction at showing I could play at this level and I had proven a few people wrong, both in England and Italy, who felt I wouldn't be able to handle Italian football. We had achieved our aims and I even ended up the team's leading goalscorer. That I only scored eight league goals in 30 matches demonstrates how mean we were in defence.

In the jubilation of the moment, there was a cloud of sadness. Gigi Peronace died that Christmas. The man who played such a part in taking me to Turin never got to see me fulfil his hopes. He was just 55 and had been in Uruguay as general manager to the Italian national side for a tour during the Serie A Christmas break. He suffered a heart attack in the team hotel. That news had hit me very hard. I was close to Gigi and his family. He had four young children so to see them lose their dad like that was shocking.

I truly saw Turin as home now. Praise was coming my way. My teammates had my back earlier in the season when they knew I was feeling the pressure and they were happy for me now. The club was on a high. Boniperti told us to get ready for the European Cup next season. It felt like I'd be here for the foreseeable future. Who could predict what was going to happen nine months later?

10

Platini In, Brady Out

THERE IS ONE SHAMEFUL blot on my copybook in Turin, that should have had me deported really, for cultural treason against my adopted home. One afternoon the club president's secretary called me from the office.

'Hello, Brady. Sorry to trouble you but the club is hosting a reception for Luciano Pavarotti this evening and we hoped you would like to join us.'

As my wheels turned, she waited reasonably patiently.

'Would you like to come, Brady?'

'Luciano who?' I eventually mustered.

'Pavarotti, the opera singer.'

'Oh, opera. *No grazie.*'

Back in London, I'd have put my LP collection up against any of the lads. I loved a Saturday night with a band at the Hammersmith Palais or the Rainbow Rooms in Finsbury Park. The *NME* was my paper of choice. But classical was a no-go area. And in fairness, you'd have struggled to find knowledgeable appreciation of anything classical in the Highbury dressing room. But there went my chance to spend an evening hobnobbing with an icon. Blown in blissful ignorance. If only Italia

'90 and his rendition of 'Nessun dorma' had come along a little earlier.

Otherwise, I felt more Torinese by the day. We'd holidayed that summer in Alassio on the Riviera, as the people of Turin do, as well as going back to England and Ireland to see family and friends. Marco and his wife's friends were our friends. I loved the city and I got on well with my teammates. I appreciated the way they had stuck by me when I struggled and could sense I was now trusted. Big Dino Zoff, such a calming, authoritative figure on the pitch, was a generous and kind person off it. I remember him taking me aside for a quiet word after training, early in that first season. 'Shoot more,' was all he said, in Italian basic enough for me to grasp, 'you have a bomb in that left foot.' That encouragement from somebody with his aura meant a lot.

Antonio Cabrini, Claudio Gentile and Gaetano Scirea were magnificent defenders and great characters. Cabrini was a slightly smaller version of Paolo Maldini. Gentile possessed that crucial quality in a man-marker that I'd never seen in England: the humility to be content to play absolutely no part in the game himself as long as his man – invariably the opposition's best player – didn't score or create anything. While Scirea was a Rolls-Royce, the Italian Beckenbauer. The two were chalk and cheese together at the back, silk and steel. Scirea left his mark on the game with panache and sportsmanship. Gentile left his mark mainly on star players. But he was a good guy and will tell you he was never sent off for a foul, just once for handball.

Franco Causio – the Baron – was a proud southern Italian, who started out convinced all the northerners were looking down on him, and so became more sophisticated than any of them, with his sharp suits and cigarette holders. He became another great friend. In midfield, Beppe Furino, our captain, and Marco, who earned that *schizo* nickname at times, largely absolved me of responsibility for winning the ball back and urged me to concentrate on stuff I was good at.

My first Italian teacher, Roberto Bettega, told me one day they had all found it extremely funny when, before my very first game, the bell went to summon us from the dressing room and I stood up and shook everyone's hand. But they also sort of liked it. It was something I felt I should do as the newcomer, but it was completely alien to the Italians, where everybody tended to go into their shells before kickoff and focus on their own jobs. Italian football could be quite individualistic in that way, where you looked after your patch first. But while there weren't the same showy demonstrations of team spirit that you might get in an English dressing room, I could tell from that first night in Causio's bedroom that Trap had forged a special bond among these guys. And it was even tighter 12 months on.

Retain the title and win the European Cup was the straightforward target for the 1981–82 season. The president, Giampiero Boniperti, skipped the 'one game at a time' clichés to reiterate that message in the dressing room before the first game, at home to Cesena. From across the room, Bettega, whose voice carried the weight of a serious pro who'd been around the place since he was a kid, had a proposal. 'Let's get off to a good start. How about you double our bonus for winning and we get nothing for a draw?' This was unheard of at Arsenal, where bonuses were locked down in black and white on your contract. But Boniperti agreed without hesitation. We won 6–1, with Roberto scoring a hat-trick, and we reeled off five more victories on the spin. No slow start this year. Roberto was a shrewd negotiator and maybe the president was a master psychologist.

I'll always remember my first European Cup game. It was a defeat to Celtic in Parkhead, with Murdo MacLeod's goal sending 60,000 fans into delirium. I'll never forget the generosity of the reception they gave me that night. To be sure, 1–0 was a dangerous deficit, but we were better back at the Stadio Comunale, where goals from Pietro Paolo Virdis and Bettega turned the tie around. A youthful Packie Bonner kept the score down and one of his best saves prevented me from scoring from 20 yards.

So things were going well. There was a new face in the group too, though he couldn't be on the pitch with us. The great Italian striker Paolo Rossi arrived from Perugia that summer, though he had begun his football life at Juve, before his career took an unfortunate turn. His signing was a surprise, mainly because he still had almost a year left to serve on a two-year ban for alleged involvement in the Totonero match-fixing scandal that had rocked Italian football. Two Roman restaurateurs were discovered to be cooking up a betting ring that had been fixing matches. Milan and Lazio were relegated and a host of clubs copped points deductions, while several players were banned.

Paolo always denied his involvement. Fully fit, he trained with us all the time, trained as if he was priming himself for Sunday. And it was instantly obvious he had all the tricks of the great strikers. It must have been a difficult time for him. He came to all the games and sat in the stand. But he was forever cheerful, always smiling, a down-to-earth lad who quickly became part of the group. Marco was his good friend from Italy duty, so after the matches we'd go out for a meal. Myself, Marco and him, a few friends from outside football, our wives. After, we'd go back to someone's house and watch the Italian *Match of the Day* where Paolo might have a cigarette and one or two glasses of wine. But like Marco, he was another man for moderation.

For all our class and camaraderie, we could surrender to a dip in form like anyone else. That run of six wins gave way to a sequence of one win in the next six, with three defeats. There was no panic, no crisis meetings. The dressing room was full of wise heads and experience that had pulled through slumps before. But the problem for me was I hadn't quite recaptured the form of the year before, certainly the second half of that season. Opponents knew my game now. Italians take great personal pride in making life difficult for attacking players and I was singled out by man-markers in most games. And they were very good at it. It was in their DNA. One or two grumbles about my performances started to reach the papers.

And in the middle of that difficult spell came two matches that may well have changed the course of my life again. We had a bad night in Brussels, losing 3–1 to a strong Anderlecht side in the second round of the European Cup. We were still confident of pulling through in Turin, but Bettega ruptured his cruciate early in the game and we laboured to a 1–1 draw. Winning a first European Cup was Agnelli's big project. Was that the night he decided improvements would be needed next season?

Those wise old heads steadied the ship. We trailed a fine Fiorentina side – Pietro Vierchowod, Giovanni Galli, Giancarlo Antognoni – by a point at the halfway stage of the season, but then clicked into gear with a run of seven wins. I was escaping the clutches of my minders, scoring goals. With about six weeks left in the season, there was a meeting with Boniperti. Everyone was happy. I'd be staying for the third year of my deal, he assured me. And I assured him that's what I wanted. I saw myself in Turin for years. The rules on foreign players had been loosened to allow two. The club wanted to bring in the classy Polish striker Zbigniew Boniek from Widzew Łódź, he told me. That made sense, with Roberto now 32 and facing a long recovery.

On 25 April, I scored the only goal – a late penalty – to beat Inter and take us top of the table. Neck and neck with Fiorentina, three matches to play. The Friday before the first of those, away at Udinese, I was awoken early by the phone. It was my former agent Dennis Roach, just about the last person I expected, since we hadn't parted on the best of terms.

'How can I help you, Dennis?'

'It's more a case of how I can help you, Liam.'

'Right.' Didn't we have this conversation around four years ago?

'Where are you planning on playing next season?'

'What are you on about Dennis? I've signed here for three years, I'm happy, I've no plans to play anywhere else.'

'Well, it's just that I know Juventus are going to sign Michel Platini and they want Boniek as their second foreigner. Haven't they told you? I know it's true because I had him lined up to go to Arsenal but he pulled out at the last minute and said he was signing for Juve.'

I was on the back foot. Shocked, confused. Didn't know what to say. Dennis, though, appeared to be enjoying himself.

'But don't worry, Liam. I can sort you out with another club. I can even bring you back to England, if you fancy?'

'We'll see, Dennis.' I got off the phone as politely as I could manage.

Could it be true? It didn't add up, after what Bonaperti had told me. But Dennis sounded sure of his information. Platini was a special player, among the most sought-after in Europe. The French captain. A regular goalscorer from midfield at

Saint-Étienne. I decided I would go to see Trapattoni after training that morning.

'Excuse me, Mister' – the Italians used the English word as their version of 'gaffer' – 'can I have a word?'

I knew, just from Giovanni's reaction, that something was up. He was ill at ease, uncomfortable. I spilled it, told him about the call. Told him I'd heard Platini was coming.

'I don't know anything, Liam, that's news to me.'

But his face was bright red. I knew.

While I was in the shower, the physio took a call from the club offices. I was wanted to meet with Boniperti's right-hand man, Franco Barettini. He spoke perfect English and explained calmly that Platini had arrived in Turin earlier that morning to sign for Juventus. He then brought me in to see Boniperti. Had he just spirited the Frenchman out the back door?

The president was sheepish, embarrassed. He thought he could keep all this a secret until the season had finished. He said the club had already finalised the Boniek deal but the owner, Gianni Agnelli, had decided he wanted Platini too. So I would have to go.

It was a punch in the guts. My first true brush with rejection, in football anyhow.

'You want me out?'

'I wouldn't put it like that. It's not me. It's Mr Agnelli's decision. What can I do?'

I liked the guy and could see he was suffering, but I was boiling.

'Well you can forget about me for the rest of the games. My season is over. I'm never playing for Juventus again.'

That sent him into full central casting Italian mode, waving his hands, pale with anguish, pleading, beseeching me to see sense.

'Please, Liam, don't be like that. We have just three games left. We must win the league.'

But I wasn't listening. Just stormed out, venting my hurt and shock. I was out, gone. *Finito*. It was sadness as much as anger. There's almost a self-delusion that comes with being a footballer. All around you can plainly see what a ruthless business it is, yet when you're doing well and are part of something successful, you feel indispensable, bullet-proof. Every footballer loves to see a world-class player coming in, welcomes the team improving and growing, until he's the one being replaced.

Back home, Sarah was upset too. She was as happy in Turin as I was, and we just hadn't seen this coming. I rang Ronnie Teeman back in Leeds. Anytime I had a problem, Ronnie was never short of an answer. He listened carefully to my account and delivered his calm prescription on how to handle this.

'OK, no problem. This is the world you're living in now. It probably happens in Italy all the time. You have to do things right. Be really professional about it. Train well, play the games, finish the season and win the league. And you'll come out of this in a much better situation than you're in now.'

It was just what I needed to hear. I'd have dismounted my high horse eventually anyway, I'd imagine. I'd never really have gone on strike. But Ronnie was right, it was better to knuckle down straight away. The phone rang all evening. Tardelli and Cabrini were first up, then many of the others. Word had spread. They were sympathetic. The words of comfort were genuine. But they all wanted to know too if I'd be on the coach with them to Udine the next day. I told them I'd be there.

And I was, in body anyway. After not much sleep, I reported for training to find the news already splashed across the front pages. 'Platini in, Brady out' screamed the headlines. It was an awkward bus trip. The lads didn't really know what to say.

Trap's way of handling things was to focus completely on the match. But his tactical instructions were barely sinking in.

If that game against Udinese was the beginning of my ending, it was the start for Paolo Rossi. His ban was up and Trap didn't hesitate to throw him straight in. That's how well he had been training all season. Maybe Giovanni figured too that we needed a lift amid the strain of all this unscheduled drama. Paolo's smile, back out there where he belonged, and his darting runs, were a fresh energy source. On an afternoon when emotions churned, I'm proud to have done the spadework for his first goal back. A clipped free kick that he headed in expertly at the near post. The work of a smooth penalty box predator the world would soon see much more of. We were thrilled for him. We won 5–1, having gone behind inside two minutes. The day got better with news that Fiorentina had drawn.

Next up was a farewell. Napoli in my final home game. Nil–nil. We couldn't break them down. Bettega's injury was still costing us and goalkeeper Luciano Castellini was outstanding. A few tears rolled afterwards during a slow walk around the Comunale. The supporters were generous. A giant banner read 'Grazie'. I addressed the crowd and told them I would never forget them. Fiorentina won. The race was level heading to the final day.

Catanzaro is a small city on the sole of Italy. It sits on the Med but is overlooked by mountains, making the tiny Stadio Nicola Ceravolo feel even more claustrophobic. Its football club has spent seven seasons in Serie A in its history, and this was its best one. They lay seventh. The place was stuffed to see if mighty Juve could be denied the title, and the atmosphere was febrile. Rossi was the main target. *Guappo. Guappo.* Crook. Crook. When we landed at the local airport the night before, he'd been struck by a local, and we'd been pelted with coins.

Claudio Ranieri was the Catanzaro captain but had fallen out with the manager, Bruno Pace, and had been dropped. So the guy who'd go on to manage both Juventus and Fiorentina would play no part in deciding the two clubs' fates that day.

In the first half, the Ceravolo crowd howled for a penalty when Sergio Brio knocked over their striker, Carlo Borghi, in the box. The ref wasn't having it. Another decision that still gets mentioned on my Italian travels. The penalty we got, with 15 minutes to go, was clear-cut. Handball on the line. No Old Lady conspiracies needed around this one.

It was the one proper conversation I'd had with Trap, since my departure was confirmed. Whatever about playing, I wouldn't be taking any more penalties. It wouldn't be fair, the added layer of pressure given all the media talk around my exit and my frame of mind. Pietro Paolo Virdis had been given the job for the last three games.

But by now, the big man was sitting on the bench, subbed off. There seemed a long moment of hesitation. Everyone was celebrating the decision but nobody was picking up the ball. I looked towards the bench and Trap looked towards me. The hands were going but his gestures weren't as assertive as usual. He was asking, not demanding. Will you take it, please?

In one sense, I wish there wasn't so much fuss made about that penalty. Two of the best years of my life get reduced to this supposed act of great professionalism. Where I park my hurt pride to do my job. It's stupid. What would I possibly have had to gain from knocking it wide? It's almost insulting that there was so much commentary out there that I might miss it as an act of revenge.

And yet, at the same time, it's the most nervous I've ever been from 12 yards. The heart was really going. Even after Valencia, it has rarely crossed my mind that I might miss a penalty. The goal always looks pretty big, walking up. But it had shrunk a touch in the Ceravolo that afternoon. The scene awaiting in the box was hardly an oasis of calm. Some of the Catanzaro players were still badgering the ref, others were rotavating the penalty spot. All sorts were being pelted onto the pitch and the goalkeeper, Alessandro Zaninelli, had turned litter warden and was taking his sweet time in a thorough clean-up operation. I didn't notice it then, but if you watch back the video you can just make out a large Fiorentina flag among the home banners in the crowd.

It wasn't a great penalty. It was a bit careful. Not in the corner, but enough disguise to send Zaninelli the other way. The celebration was manic, more aggressive than usual. A lot of punching the air. A release of relief and joy and hurt and anger. Rossi was first to join me. His support and empathy, at a time when he had a lot on his own plate, meant a lot during those weeks.

Fiorentina had their own tale of woe. They drew at Cagliari. A goal disallowed for a foul on the goalkeeper. A decision they probably won't forget until they win the Scudetto again. Instead, it was ours. The 20th. The second golden star. We found out in the dressing room, having sprinted off to escape a mutinous pitch invasion.

My teammates were grateful I had taken the responsibility and were kind in their tributes when talking to the media. But at some point in the celebrations it hit me properly that this was all over. That I wasn't part of this group anymore. There was a public hug with Boniperti, there were more tears and I mostly said the right things, wished Boniek and Platini well. But I couldn't bottle all my disappointment at how things had been done. 'La classe non è acqua,' I said in one interview. Class isn't water, it's not everywhere. Still, when we stepped off the plane in Turin, ready for the party to start, I was still holding onto the match ball. Forty years later, I dropped it back to the club museum.

There was still an exit to be negotiated. Ronnie flew over from England for a meeting at Boniperti's house in the hills above Turin. I was surprised to find Agnelli there. I hadn't expected that. 'Thank you, Bwady.' He told me he was grateful for my professionalism, my service, my contribution to two title wins. He instructed Boniperti that everything was to be sorted that day regarding the financial side of our divorce. Ronnie didn't have to do much negotiating.

Did I have a go at Agnelli? Don't be ridiculous. You don't take on a guy that influential. In any case, when I was working on this book, I found an old diary where I had scribbled some thoughts during that season. There's a telling entry from February 1982: 'Watched Italy play France in Paris. Platini was brilliant. Agnelli was there.'

Ultimately, he was proved right with Platini. He took time to settle, as I had, but then he was on a different level to me, to everyone. Where I had scored eight goals a season, he would get 19 or 20. He was wonderful at arriving in the box at exactly the right time. Juventus got themselves a truly great player and three years later Agnelli got his European Cup.

I watched the World Cup final that summer in Gibney's pub in Malahide, watched my friends become legends in their country by beating West Germany. Zoff, Cabrini, Gentile, Scirea. Tardelli and that *schizo* celebration we will never let him forget. Rossi and his goals and his redemption. I was delighted for them, but it was bittersweet. I missed them.

It is so sad that two of them are gone. Gaetano died just seven years later, in a dreadful car accident in Poland, on scouting duty for Juve, the year after he retired from playing.

He played with such class and grace and lived that way too. He was loved by everyone. Dino was his great friend. When they roomed together, the place was so calm that Marco used to call it Switzerland.

News of Paolo's death in 2020 was heartbreaking. We stayed friends and often met up whenever our paths brought us to the same city. I'm glad we had those three matches together, but more glad that he stayed in my life. In his later years, he became a hugely popular TV pundit. And Italy fell in love with him all over again when he starred on *Ballando con le Stelle*, their version of *Strictly*. Still on the toes. And still smiling.

11

Samp and Inter

As an Irish footballer, you accepted the FAI was genuinely in need of money and was invariably scratching round to either cut costs or make a few quid. It was a given. Even allowing for that, it doesn't rank high among their great ideas, a trip to Buenos Aires to play Argentina during the Falklands War – or the Malvinas War, depending on how you look at it. Unfortunately, the FAI didn't appear to have looked at it at all. We're neutral, we're not at war with Argentina, was the association's view.

But of course the majority of our players played in England and several had British passports. They could literally be considered enemies of the Argentinian state. The reaction from English clubs was predictable. Keith Burkinshaw at Tottenham called the prospect 'comical' and ruled out Chris Hughton and Tony Galvin. Manchester United boss Ron Atkinson, normally pretty good about releasing players, simply told Eoin Hand, the team manager, to 'jump off a cliff'. Eoin recalls asking for an official response and being told to officially 'fuck off'. That was Frank Stapleton, Kevin Moran and Ashley Grimes gone.

The lads at Liverpool and Arsenal went the same way. No Lawrenson, Whelan, O'Leary, Devine. Even if the clubs allowed it, how many players would have been comfortable playing? Sharing a pitch with Argentina wouldn't have gone down well with their clubs or their fans. Ossie Ardiles had to go on loan from Tottenham to PSG to get away from the backlash against Argentinians not long after. Ironically, Ossie, whom I got to know much better after we retired, was very much against the military junta running Argentina.

Despite all this, the FAI was putting the squeeze on Eoin to come up with a squad to travel. On paper – and in an alternate universe where there wasn't a war on – it was a decent tour. We'd play Chile and Brazil too. All three countries had qualified for the World Cup, and our selection as credible warm-up opponents reflected our improving status in the international game.

Probably more important, from their side, the players heard the FAI stood to make around £50,000. However, the Argentinians were apparently becoming unhappy with the calibre of the travelling squad. So Eoin was under pressure, making dozens of phone calls, and getting increasingly desperate. I read in Eoin's autobiography that one of the bright sparks in the FAI suggested he bring Tony Ward, a good League of Ireland player, who might provide the glamour the Argentinians had wanted since he'd been European Player of the Year, albeit at rugby.

Since I didn't see my Ireland teammates too often anymore, I always looked forward to international trips. Though I could have done without this one. My club future was undecided. I had no idea where I'd be playing, or living, the following season. And Sarah and I had just learnt she was expecting our first child. But Eoin was desperate for me to travel and the idea of playing Brazil at the Maracanã was exciting. Another of those boyhood dreams.

Eventually, even the FAI had to face up to the lunacy of the plan, and the Argentina game was pulled four days before we were due to leave. Too late for most of the missing players, who'd made other arrangements or were gone on club tours. Liverpool had just won the league for the 13th time and were off to Benidorm.

When I arrived at Heathrow, for the first leg to Madrid, I learnt that Eoin had managed to gather 14 players – including a few newcomers from England and some League of Ireland lads – and was still on the phone to others. It was obviously a shambles, even before we learned we'd still be travelling on to Chile via Buenos Aires because that's what the FAI had originally booked.

There were a few sweating on that flight when we landed in Buenos Aries. The late Michael Robinson, one of our English-born players, was convinced he'd be arrested. A long 10 hours followed hanging around Ezeiza International Airport as FAI officials tried to explain our business in the country to Argentinian security. It wasn't clear if we were going to be detained or deported before we were finally allowed to board a connecting flight to Santiago.

The day after landing, we lost 1–0 to Chile in a tight game, caught cold in the heat by a goal in the first minute. Michael Robinson picked up an injury, but with a makeshift side we did pretty well against a team that had qualified for the World Cup.

It was one of the strangest atmospheres I've played in. I knew little about the place at the time, though there were plenty of signs of the oppressive General Pinochet dictatorship in the soldiers lining most of the streets and visible in the national stadium where we played. I knew the stadium had been turned into a place of torture and execution during the USA-backed coup in 1973, and though this was seven years later you could detect fear among the people. However, there was a friendliness about them, and it was such a beautiful city.

There was another surprise waiting in Rio. Another blow. Another farce. The match was going to be played not in the Maracanã, but nearly 500 miles away in Uberlândia, which none of us had heard of. We were based in Rio and actually flew to the venue with the Brazil team, then the World Cup favourites. The likes of Socrates, Junior, Eder and Zico were on board, and Falcão, who I knew well from playing against him at Roma.

All things considered (we were further depleted when Michael Robinson went home injured – I think his nerves were shattered going through Buenos Aires) we produced a remarkable effort for 45 minutes to go in just trailing to a Falcão goal. We were very pleased in the dressing room, which I haven't often seen at one–nil down. If we could keep it like that, we'd be entitled to a lap of honour. Instead, our mistake was to try to score one ourselves, which was a little ambitious in the circumstances. Given space in the second half, they put on a show for 80,000 delirious fans who had never seen the national team in their city.

It became embarrassing. And the heat was steaming. I distinctly remember running back from midfield at one stage, as this band of superstars poured through us, and hearing Mick Martin, who was filling in at the back, shout: 'Don't worry, I'll pick up these four.' Gerry Ryan told me that when Eoin looked down his bench for options everybody ducked out of his line of vision. It finished 7–0 and we slunk off the field too humiliated to swap our sodden shirts. It still stands in the record books as Ireland's worst defeat.

We shared the flight back to Rio with the Brazilian players again. They danced the samba in the aisle while their music played. We sat in our seats and watched them enjoying themselves. Though Mick Martin bagged Zico's number 10 shirt. I was convinced we'd seen the world champions. Though a few weeks later in Spain, my mates from Juventus, especially Paolo Rossi, had other ideas.

The farce wasn't over yet. There was one more little twist in the FAI's tale. They had been frantically trying to organise a short-notice replacement for the Argentina game, to recoup the lost revenue. And the solution arrived at was Trinidad and Tobago, and another four flights, at least on the route the FAI had plotted to the Caribbean.

By now, I had had enough with it all. The Maracanã dream had turned into a nightmare. I tried to buy my own ticket back to Italy, but it proved impossible to get a flight. I'm not sure if it was Eoin or Mick Martin who turned travel agent but one of them at least managed to find a quicker way to Trinidad via San Diego.

There was one more moment of tragicomedy on the team bus. Tony Grealish, another of my mates taken too young, chucked a boot bag at somebody on the bus and hit our physio Trevor in the face, knocking his false front teeth down his throat. Tony apologised, but Trevor had to wait a day or two to recover his teeth!

We played two games on the island of Trinidad, against a club side and the national team. To tell the truth, we were never sure which game was which. There were no journalists on the trip so the matches were barely documented. I actually scored in the first, which we lost 2–1, and we won the second 3–0. Eoin believes we beat the national team but the locals switched the results. So the defeat stands as another blot on Ireland's international record.

By then it hardly mattered. After a farcical schedule with a patchwork team, no wonder the players were fed up with the

FAI. Back home, Peadar O'Driscoll, the FAI's General Secretary, declared the tour an outstanding success. In truth it had been a joke, a Mickey Mouse affair that set us and Eoin back. There had been disappointment at just failing to qualify for the World Cup, but also positivity around our performances and a sense that Irish football was on the up. We had beaten France and Holland. But the tour to South America undid all that. This was a return to the bad old days. The professional progress made under John and then in Eoin's first couple of years was gone. Club managers in England were already putting players under pressure to drop international football. The FAI and the poor judgement the tour to South America demonstrated made it easier for them.

Back in Turin, I had to sort out my next chapter. Arsenal would have had me back and Ron Atkinson had been on the phone to me too, but he was close to Dennis Roach and I didn't like that aspect of doing a deal with United.

I began to consider staying in Italy. I'd done the hardest part of settling in a new country by learning the language and Sarah and I enjoyed the lifestyle, even though Italy was a violent and divided country. There was a class war going on. By that point we could follow the news and had a better understanding of what was happening. You couldn't escape it, because the coverage was so graphic. The TV and newspapers constantly carried photos of bloodied dead bodies or cars blown to pieces. A bombing by a fascist organisation at Bologna station killed 85 people a few weeks after I arrived.

It was the Marxist Red Brigades on the left against the neo-fascist groups on the right. Fascism never really died in Italy. In conversation with older people, Mussolini was still getting plenty of credit, with claims that the country was better when he was in charge. 'At least the trains ran on time when he was in control' was said to me plenty of times. The older generation would complain it was chaos now, no discipline, no respect for life. The socialists and unions had too much power and were taking over.

The government was usually a coalition of three or four parties that seemed to collapse every few months. Politicians and industrialists were assassination targets. None more so than Juve owner Gianni Agnelli, the head of Fiat. He was under heavy protection. Considering the Mafia's presence too, Italy was a pretty scary place to live. Yet as footballers we seemed to be isolated from all that, and it never really entered our lives.

What surprised me about Italy was how liberal the people were. For a very Catholic country, there was little of the repression and control by the Church I associated with the Ireland I grew up in. Divorce and contraception weren't too difficult to come by in Italy. Football seemed to be the main religion. And Agnelli and Giampiero Boniperti still had a say in where I would be going to Mass. Both Roma and Inter Milan wanted to talk to me, but Juve wouldn't entertain selling to a rival for the Scudetto.

Which is when Sampdoria and their president Paolo Mantovani came on the scene. Mantovani was an oil mogul obsessed with putting Genoa's second club among Italy's elite. We met in Geneva as he had to live abroad while fighting a fraud and tax case, in which he was later acquitted. Renowned for his passionate support of the team, he was also discouraged by his doctors from attending any more Samp matches, after suffering serious heart problems during a Coppa Italia game that March.

But his enthusiasm was infectious. He sold me and my lawyer Ronnie Teeman on his vision, and gave his word he'd sign another top-class foreigner to join me. It would undoubtedly be a step down from Juventus, a gamble. Sampdoria had just been promoted to Serie A, no European football, realistically a title challenge would be impossible. But I instantly liked Mantovani. The financial terms were generous and I did my homework too. A good friend who lived in Genoa backed my positive impression of the owner. He had a reputation for keeping his promises and had already built the club a new training complex. My friend couldn't say enough about the wonderful city and climate and assured me we would be happy living in Genoa.

We weren't disappointed on that score. Living there, you had no need to take a holiday. The club arranged an apartment in a beautiful villa in Nervi, facing onto the bay, with a garden full of palm and lemon trees running right down to the Mediterranean. I soon had a new neighbour. Trevor Francis, famously England's first million-pound player, arrived from Manchester City with his wife Helen and their son Matthew.

Mantovani also gave Bologna 2.5 billion lira (£1.5 million then) plus four players for 17-year-old Roberto Mancini, who was tipped to be Italian football's next superstar. The press christened him 'Il Bambino D'Oro'. The Golden Boy. The city was beside itself with excitement at this statement of intent from a newly promoted club.

It was a new front two with me behind in the number 10 role. Though it took time to come together. Roberto and I didn't always get on. He was a kid who'd had a lot of praise before he had actually achieved anything. I saw it many times later in life in my work at the Arsenal Academy – young lads burdened with that kind of expectation can't always carry it instantly.

He needed the odd reminder, let's say, about when to release the ball, when to pass rather than shoot. And he didn't always appreciate that sort of advice coming from me, though the boss, Renzo Ulivieri, encouraged me to keep delivering it. Mancini also got off to a rocky start with Francis, when the two of them fought over taking a penalty in a pre-season game and carried their dispute into the dressing room, where a few punches were thrown. Ulivieri sorted that one in his usual calm way. I liked playing under him, a serious guy but with a sense of humour. Everyone was treated the same, no favourites, but he also understood, like all good managers, that he was dealing with very different personalities. His way of sorting out that argument was making me penalty-taker.

Very quickly, a rebuilt team became a real tight family. The atmosphere was good around the dressing room and the attitude was right on the pitch. Thanks to Ulivieri but also the captain Alessandro Scanziani, who always set the right example in workrate. And guys like Francesco Casagrande, one of my best pals in Genoa, a selfless midfielder with an winning attitude like Furino, my captain at Juve.

And playing behind a front two that talented was a thrill. Trevor became a good friend, with me in the interpreter role during his first few months. At his best, he was among the most exciting players I've played with. It was a terrible shock when we got news of his death this year. And what a footballer Mancini became. A goal against Roma early in the season typified his instinctive genius. Scanziani knocked it to me inside our half and Roberto faced up to me, showing for the ball into feet. I knew he was kidding on the defender. He spins, collects the 40-yard floater in his stride, holds off the centre half, and rolls in the winner.

Our start to the season was another for that old 'you couldn't write the script' category. First game, Juve visit Genoa. The upstarts against the champions. And the press was full of 'Platini v Brady'. My revenge mission, all that stuff. But there was never anything personal between us. It was the business of football and I admired him hugely as a player, a better player

141

than me. I got to know him a little bit socially when I'd return to Turin to visit friends who lived in the same apartment block. He was always kind and respectful about me whenever the press probed for a supposed rivalry.

Of course, there was a little bit of an edge that afternoon, in a buoyant Marassi stadium. I knew the opposition better than my teammates but I was desperate to play well and get a result against the club that had discarded me. We kept them quiet and with about 20 minutes to go Maura Ferroni, our full back, drove forward to drill one of only three goals he scored in his life. I sprinted to be among the first celebrating with him. What a start.

The following week, away at Inter Milan, our brilliant strike pairing showed they had learned to get along. Francis was far from an old-fashioned number 9. A very skilful player with lightning speed, he glided across the ground. At the San Siro, he picked the ball up in our half, dropped a shoulder and eased past a couple of defenders. After a one-two with Mancini on the edge of the area, Trevor picked out the corner of the net. In the second half, he picked out Mancini just as accurately with a cross and the kid volleyed the winner.

Next came the win over Roma – an incredible start against the three top teams. In exile, Mantovani was in raptures. For the sake of his heart, it was probably just as well that he had to have videotapes of the matches driven to Geneva. It was often Tuesday before he got to watch them in full. Then the phone calls would come to find out how I was settling in. I told him I couldn't have been happier.

For a man living 400km away, Mantovani was very hands-on. Constantly in touch, checking on the well-being of the squad, making sure everything was professionally done. Even to the extent of organising for the Irish tricolour and the Union Jack to fly above the stadium on match days. The Sampdoria fans fell in love with the team. Full houses every time we played at home. The city buzzed with football talk. And we often got 5,000 fans at the training ground to watch our sessions.

Unfortunately, in that win over Roma, a heavy tackle by Pietro Vierchowod, a Sampdoria player bought by Mantovani and loaned to Roma and a defender rarely described without use of the word 'rugged', crocked Trevor and he missed a couple of months of the season. Trevor was so important to our chances. The fans loved him. He produced spectacular moments, and to operate without him wasn't easy. It knocked the team's rhythm and our performances dropped a little in the second half of the season, having been among the front runners in the table at Christmas. We finished seventh, very creditable for a promoted team.

There was one other special weekend in Turin. A decent 1–1 with Juve on my return to the city on the weekend our daughter Ella was born. Juve probably suffered a World Cup hangover that season, with so many involved in Italy's success. Roma stopped them winning a third title in a row and Hamburg beat them in the European Cup final. I'm often asked if I was happy they didn't seamlessly move on without me. When I watched the European final I still had the feeling I should have been out there with them. But when they lost, I wasn't upset. A little sad for my friends, sure, but not for Agnelli. Human nature I suppose.

I consider the two seasons at Sampdoria to be among the best of my career, and it was an enormously happy time in my life. I felt strong, sure of my role in the team and totally appreciated by the club, my teammates and the supporters. There was a limit to what we could achieve against the big boys – we came seventh again the following season – but it was a club building something great and building it properly.

The summer I left, the late great Gianluca Vialli arrived, and he and Mancini became the 'goal twins'. Roberto dropped a bit deeper, got that number 10 shirt he probably wanted and, with the likes of Attilio Lombardo, Gianluca Pagliuca and the rugged Vierchowod, who came back from Rome, they drove the team to several cup successes over the following seasons. Eventually, Mantovani's ultimate promise was kept when the club won its only Scudetto in 1991. Reaching the European Cup final at Wembley the following season, narrowly losing to Barcelona, demonstrated how far he had taken the club.

I was delighted for the man. He died just two years later, at 63, of cancer, prompting an incredible outpouring of emotion in the city. When he was cleared by the authorities he was able to watch the team he built. His stamp is all over Genoa, in the street named after him and the training ground he provided.

Roberto Mancini dedicated his European Championship win with Italy to Mantovani. The assured kid became one of the great Italian players, and then one of the most respected managers in the world. We met in Florence after that Euros success and reminisced about those happy days and laughed about our teething problems. We talked a lot about a rare club owner who, as Roberto puts it, managed to touch the heart of all his players.

My form at Sampdoria gave me choices. At the end of my two-year contract, Mantovani tried to talk me into staying. I loved my time in Genoa, but I missed playing for a club that could compete at the very highest level.

I met the sporting director of AC Milan. Don Howe, by now Arsenal manager, came with a delegation on a private plane to see me play in Florence. Don, chairman Peter Hill-Wood, and directors Richard Carr and Ken Friar. It was tempting, but I wasn't ready to go 'home'.

I definitely wasn't ready to go to Tottenham. Chairman Irving Scholar was a tax exile in Monaco, and as it was only an hour's drive away he started coming to Sampdoria games on Sundays. Eventually, he persuaded me to drive up to Monaco for a chat. He tried to convince me that Spurs would be a good move but I had to tell him that even in the business of football, there are some things you just can't do.

The successful Milanese businessman Ernesto Pellegrini had just taken over at Inter Milan and was promising to bring back trophies to the club he loved. Inter had a host of national team players. Zenga the goalkeeper. Defenders Collovati and Bergomi, World Cup winners in '82. The prolific goalscorer Alessandro Altobelli, who got the third goal in that final. Pellegrini told me he was going to sign Karl-Heinz Rummenigge from Bayern Munich. Up-and-coming coach Ilario Castagner had been given the responsibility of making this team title winners. I signed, thinking I'm back in the big time. We were moving house again.

Mantovani had a hand in one funny episode that followed me to Inter. We parted on good terms and he asked me to help my replacement, a certain Graeme Souness, settle in. No problem, though me and Graeme had had a few clashes back in England, when Arsenal played Liverpool. In a moment of probably unnecessary frankness, I'd called him the dirtiest player in the First Division.

It turned out I was away with the Inter squad when he arrived, but Sarah showed him the apartment he was going to move into, and showed him the ropes. Where to buy furniture, where to eat. All very amicable.

Next time we met was in a pre-season friendly back in Genoa, arranged as part of my transfer deal. Inter kicked off with Altobelli knocking it to Rummenigge, who passed back to me on the edge of the centre circle. As I was looking up to pass,

I heard this animal roar and glimpsed the shadow of something flying towards me. It was Souness in mid-air, flying feet first like a maniacal kamikaze pilot. Eyes wild and wide with only me in his sights. Thankfully, I just managed to swerve away from his landing before I became the wreckage. He was still growling and snarling at me from the floor. This was a friendly. A few moments later, I managed to collar Trevor.

'What the fuck was that all about?'

'Well, he says you left him in the dark . . .'

Turned out, there had been a misunderstanding over the apartment. We didn't know the removal men had literally stripped the place bare of all fixtures and fittings, right down to the lamps. So when Graeme and his wife came back from their dinner at a local restaurant, he flicked the switch and there was no light to be had.

We had some fierce battles down through the years on the field but, in fairness, when Graeme became manager of Glasgow Rangers, tongue in cheek he asked me if I fancied being the first Catholic to play for the club. I said no thanks. I recalled the reception I'd got at Ibrox Park. Whistled at every time I got the ball. 'Fenian bastard'. Like I was back in Belfast as a kid with my dad.

Later, when we were pundits together on RTÉ, we had some good nights out and put all the midfield battles properly behind us. We even laughed about the still beauty of a dark night on Genoa bay.

Inter was meant to be my return to the battle for big prizes. The season started well and we went the first six games unbeaten, though a loss in the Milan derby halted our momentum. I faced up to Ray Wilkins and Mark Hateley, AC Milan's new foreign duo, in the San Siro in front of 80,000 fans. The biggest derby I had played in by far. Hateley scored

the winner and became an instant hero. We were hugely disappointed but we recovered well.

At the halfway stage, we were level with Verona, the surprise
of the season, who had the German Hans-Peter Briegel and
the Dane Preben Elkjær. Nobody gave them a chance of going
all the way. We visited their stadium in a decisive match with
the two clubs neck and neck. This was when we were supposed
to deliver the psychological blow that would finish off the
underdogs. We took the lead but Briegel equalised in the
second half. A bit like Leicester City in 2016 in the Premier
League, Verona were really consistent and held on against all
the odds and predictions.

I couldn't put a finger on exactly what was missing. It wasn't
evident on paper, in the individual qualities of our players. Or
in the pretty ideal mix of youth and know-how. Throughout
my career, I've always hated blaming the coach. Given half a
chance by the set-up, I figured experienced quality footballers
should usually be able to work things out, when they cross the
white line. But ultimately Ilario Castagner got the blame for
failing to get the best out of us. He didn't gel us, you could
say. He was a rookie coach and maybe lacked a certain authority
around star players.

There was just something in the delicate mix of a successful
team that wasn't right. Maybe you could call it a softness, a
lack of determination to become a title-winning side. I could
tell we didn't quite have what Juventus had. That desire to
have each other's backs, that refusal to accept that it wasn't
your day. We eventually fell away to third late in the campaign.
Verona were a team with less talent that us, but they were full
of belief and commitment.

The inconsistency of those two years at Inter could probably
be summed up by four games: the two-legged UEFA Cup

semi-finals with Real Madrid. Both times, we brought a two-goal lead away from the San Siro. In 1985, I scored a penalty in a convincing 2–0 win. Without an away goal conceded, Italian teams didn't get beat often from that position. On those two occasions I learnt there is something mystical about the Bernabéu on a major European night, whatever the deficit. The Remontada – their heritage of stirring comebacks. Our first contribution to that heritage came in the second leg that we lost 3–0. You could point to moments of bad luck – Altobelli had one cleared off the line at 2–0 that would have settled it – but ultimately we hadn't the togetherness to cope when the tide was around our waists. We sank.

The following season, I had one of my best games for Inter as we led 3–1 this time, after the San Siro leg. I was back playing with my great mate Marco Tardelli, who'd signed from Juve, and he got two, though Jorge Valdano's late away goal was annoying and dangerous. By then Castagner had been replaced by Mario Corso and our title hopes were long gone. I scored a penalty in the second half at the Bernabéu. It finished 3–1 to Madrid and eventually we went out 5–1 after extra time.

An episode at half-time in that game indicated another side of the Italian mindset that I became accustomed to. Win at all costs. Bergomi had been hit by a coin from the crowd, but was fine to carry on. In the dressing room at half-time, with us 2–0 down, Altobelli was shouting 'cut him, cut him', urging the team doctor to slice his head open to make the injury look worse, so we could go to the referee and have the game called off. Altobelli was serious. I couldn't believe it. But it was something in a lot of the Italian lads' makeup, a readiness to take advantage. Whether that was of a missile from the crowd or an outstretched leg in the box.

I look back with so much regret. The players have to take responsibility for Inter's underperformance in those two seasons. I joined at 28, hitting my peak, and had plenty of good matches, but I didn't repeat the consistency I'd shown at Sampdoria. It might have been that the pressure was too great on a squad at a club where second was nowhere, never mind third. Or perhaps the culture of the club was wrong. There was always talk of change around the place. The dressing room never seemed settled. I was never targeted by the fans, but equally I sensed they never quite warmed to me like the supporters at my other clubs. That first season we should have won the title. Unbeaten at home, we lost it on the road.

Still, there were plenty of enjoyable moments too, when a talented team clicked. I met the best player I've played with and made a friend for life. Karl-Heinz, in both cases. A German and an Irishman communicating in Italian. We lived close together, on beautiful Lake Como, half an hour from the training ground. A kind, funny yet serious man, and what a giant of the game. The perfect striker, who could beat you with one touch and a dip of the shoulder. And could finish whatever way was needed. A special blend of creativity and efficiency. Runner-up in two World Cup finals. A very intelligent man, and it was no surprise to me that he made a fine career after finishing the game, as Executive Chairman of Bayern Munich.

We keep in touch, and like me he looks back on those seasons with regret. He stayed for one more campaign, though he began to struggle with injury. My time was up, as the club enlisted the great Argentinian Daniel Passarella, the 1978 World Cup-winning captain, from Fiorentina, as their second foreigner.

I was moving on again, 30 now. Perhaps it was time to return to England.

12

The Great Escape –
Ascoli to Inter

IT'S THE DECISION I regret most in my playing career – moving for money. It wasn't a logical decision. It wasn't a football decision. It wasn't a lifestyle decision. I joined Ascoli because of the contract I was offered.

Inter were keen for me to make up my mind quickly so they could get Passarella signed. And for the first time in my career, there weren't a pile of options stacking up. And I got jittery. I jumped the gun. There were, in fairness, plenty of arguments for staying in Italy. It was the place to play, for footballing reasons as much as anything. It was the country a lot of the best players in the world were heading for, except maybe Spain, for Barcelona and Real Madrid.

The top tier was here – Maradona, Platini, Zico. British players were stepping off the plane every week – Joe Jordan, Trevor Francis, Graeme Souness, Ray Wilkins, Mark Hateley, Gordon Cowans and Des Walker.

And I felt at home there. I had lots of friends in football but also from outside the game. I could speak Italian fluently, loved the food. And the style of football suited me, especially gone 30. It was less frantic, and I had six seasons under my belt. However, the two-foreigner rule was still in place, so my options in Italy might have been limited. I figured more attractive offers might come from England, but I was wrong.

I didn't have an agent. I still used a lawyer, Ronnie Teeman, a great friend of John Giles and now my great friend too. Ronnie was brilliant on the contracts and legal stuff, but I didn't expect him to be contacting clubs and managers on my behalf. For that, I turned to Reg Drury, a journalist with the *News of the World*, who was a good friend. Reg was hugely respected and knew everybody in the game.

In one sense, I was still that eight-year-old dreamer about football. When the Italian adventure was over, I'd return to Arsenal, where the fans would welcome me back and I'd give them the last few years of my career. George Graham had recently taken over as manager. The club had endured a lean time after I left, and Terry Neill and Don Howe had lost their positions. I knew George from my days as a kid at Highbury and was hopeful he'd give me the fairy-tale ending.

The phone didn't ring, however. So I got Reg to put the feelers out with George. It maybe took a week for Reg to phone the house in Como. 'The answer is no, Liam. George wants to go with young and hungry players.' Of course that stung a little. You always figure your appetite is still as sharp as anyone's. But the game quickly teaches you not to take other people's judgements too personally. It's the footballing life. No two managers see the game the same.

And I admired George for sticking to his plan. Over the course of his first two seasons at Highbury the veterans left – Sansom, Woodcock, Nicholas, my mate Graham Rix. Only David O'Leary survived the cull. George was true to his beliefs. He pinned his own rise as a manager on lads fighting their way up in the game: Lee Dixon, Nigel Winterburn,

Steve Bould, Alan Smith, even Ian Wright. Along with the hugely talented youngsters already at Arsenal such as Tony Adams, David Rocastle, Michael Thomas and Paul Merson. It worked brilliantly for him. He won six trophies in his years as Arsenal manager.

John Hollins, my former teammate, was now manager at Chelsea. He came to visit my house and said he wanted to sign me. I did like the idea of returning to live in London so I told John as long as the financial side could be sorted with Ronnie, I would be very willing to sign for Chelsea. Ken Bates was the owner and chairman and he wasn't as keen as John. John was under some pressure at the time and Bates didn't want to back him. The move was off.

With no transfer window then, I could have waited until the season started. Invariably one or two big clubs start poorly and that makes their minds up about moving in the transfer market. But that would mean no pre-season preparation.

The only option I had in Italy was Ascoli, a small provincial club. Mr Ascoli was Costantino Rozzi, club owner and president who'd made his money in construction and wine. A larger-than-life figure, you'd probably call him, which is often a warning sign.

He was always on TV, wearing his signature red socks, causing controversy, usually moaning about referees or some other outrage that meant the small provincial clubs never got a fair crack of the whip.

To the people of Ascoli he was a hero. The club had just been promoted again to Serie A and Mr Ascoli insisted I would be the catalyst for other big signings to follow. They were going to take on the big boys. Mantovani at Sampdoria had been honest with his project. Rozzi, as I suspected and later discovered, was talking guff.

He offered to match my wages at Inter. And while the two-for-eigner rule could see you squeezed out of a club a little unfairly, it also put you in a privileged position where the wages were generous. Still, everything in my gut told me this guy was a spoofer, but the wallet overruled the brain. Reluctantly, I signed.

Things actually started off OK. We beat AC Milan at the San Siro in our first game of the season. Another win at Torino followed and I was playing well. Everyone was happy, Rozzi's red socks were getting plenty of outings on the telly. However, there were no more signings. That set some alarm bells going. The deadline for an upfront image rights payment I had been promised had come and gone. This wasn't what I signed up to.

I started asking questions of a couple of the players I became friends with and the answers weren't encouraging. 'You didn't really believe Rozzi would actually pay you that?' They'd seen plenty of players come and go, having been short-changed. I knew I had made a huge mistake. Results invariably started to worsen.

After we lost 5–0 at home to Juventus I experienced something I'd never seen in my football life before. Rozzi was in the dressing room ranting and raving. Our wages were stopped until results improved. It was becoming clear I'd joined a madhouse.

I was still playing every game, but I was annoyed with myself, more than anyone. The irony wasn't lost on me. In chasing money, I'd lost money. And I knew, after three or four months, things had to come to a head. So I headed into the club's offices off one of the elegant Renaissance squares in the small town.

I'd set up a casual catch-up with the club secretary – Mr Armalei to the players – who seemed a decent guy and carried no blame for my predicament. But I knew he'd have the documents I needed.

I played it cool, all smiles, very civilised. Something about needing to check contract details for my accountant back home. No problem. He produced the papers from a filing cabinet in the corner of his office and handed them over. A quick glance confirmed the detail on image rights was there, in black and white, then I folded the papers, slipped them in my pocket and headed for the door. Cue a swift change in room temperature and a ridiculous comedy capers chase around his office.

'Where are you going? Give that back . . .'

'Tell the president I want every penny I'm owed – or I'm going to the newspapers.'

Armalei gets to the office door before me and locks it so I duck back towards his large office window. A good time to recall I was three floors up. Still, there was no backing down now.

'I'm going out this way if I have to.'

'You'll break your legs,' pointed out Armalei, accurately enough.

'I'm jumping unless you open the door and if I get injured you can explain it to the press.'

Thankfully he didn't call my bluff and relented and unlocked the door. I had my proof. In a very heated meeting with Rozzi I told him I wanted to leave on a free transfer and he could keep his money, but I'd be going to the Italian Federation if he didn't let me leave on my terms.

All I needed now was somewhere to go.

I hadn't given up entirely on Arsenal, but George's young team was going well and Reg confirmed there would be no change of heart. I was still playing for Ascoli in February when I left for Ireland duty and the famous European Championship qualifier win over Scotland. Reg had been in contact with West

Ham manager John Lyall, who was in Hampden that night and was impressed with what he saw.

A few days later, word came through that the Hammers would take me, and Rozzi, for once, was in no position to shout the odds. Reg got his exclusive in the *News of the World*. John Lyall said it was the easiest deal he'd ever done. He maybe didn't realise how desperate I was to get away.

Celtic manager David Hay also watched the match in Hampden and made a late approach. That would have given me a genuine dilemma, with European football as good as guaranteed every year. However, I'd given my word to John and was soon back in London with my wife and daughter in the old apartment I'd held on to in North London.

Despite my relief to be back, it was quickly obvious how much English football had changed while I was away. They sometimes say you need wing mirrors to play in midfield. Those days a sunroof came in handy too. The ball was up in the sky a lot. Some games passed me by completely. Managers like Graham Taylor and Howard Wilkinson were going direct. Even top sides like Everton and Arsenal preferred to start playing in the opposition half, a bit like Jack.

And it was a rough league now. The middle of the park was a bit of a jungle, full of intimidation – my first visit to play Wimbledon at Plough Lane a case in point. They had Vinnie Jones, John Fashanu, Dennis Wise, and they were in your ear all the time. 'We're going to kill you. We're going to break you up.'

I remember trying to organise our marking at a corner and Fashanu was giving it the usual: 'Listen to the little fucking Paddy bastard.' Fashanu and Jones were always trying to intimidate. I thought I'd give Fash a bit of his own treatment. 'You're not fit to lace my fucking boots. You're useless. You couldn't trap a bag of cement.' I could see him boiling over, wound up, smoke coming out of his ears.

A few minutes later I had the ball on the halfway line out on the left, up against the touchline with very little space, waiting for an option. Plough Lane was a small pitch, so he was never far away, and I could hear him shouting he was going to kill me. Built like a light heavyweight boxer, sprinting towards me he was like a charging rhino. I always wanted to get on the ball in my career but this was one time I'd gladly have done without it. He came steaming in. He was going to do me and smash me over the hoardings a yard behind me. I tried to keep my cool. Wait, wait. I pretended to pass but at the last second rolled the ball through his legs and he ploughed straight into the advertising boards.

'I told you you couldn't fucking lace my boots.'

The rest of the game I made sure I never got myself in such a precarious position again. And at the final whistle, I was straight over to our captain Alvin Martin – physically our biggest player – to walk with me off the pitch. Fash never did get me.

I got on very well with the lads at West Ham. It was a good dressing room and I felt at home immediately. Alvin, Billy Bonds, Tony Gale, Phil Parkes, Alan Devonshire, Frank McAvennie, Mark Ward, they were characters in the best sense of the word. And some very good youngsters like Tony Cottee, a tremendous goalscorer, the young midfielder Paul Ince, destined to become the guvnor at Manchester United and Inter Milan, Stewart Robson, recently signed from Arsenal.

John – a softly spoken Scottish gentleman with a London accent – was the ideal manager for me too. Although the trend in the game at the time was leaning towards long ball, John was of the belief that the ball was for passing and the game was about creativity. The fans at Upton Park wanted to see that. Never mind what anyone else was doing, he wanted to play. Out from Tony Gale and Alvin Martin at the back through myself or Alan Devonshire. Get it down and get it wide, rely on skill and flair, not physical force.

The season, however, wasn't going well and my arrival didn't turn things around. We lost my first three games with the club and were well and truly in a relegation battle when Arsenal came to Upton Park for one of those midweek derbies that stirred something in the East End blood. When the lights were on, that place was plugged in. It was always a ground with atmosphere, but a big match under floodlights at Upton Park is where you wanted to be. It was the club of Moore, Hurst and Peters, and the fans were proud of their history.

This night was about my own history too. It did feel strange, lining up against the club that had looked after me since I was 13. I respected what George Graham was doing at Arsenal, but I wanted to show him I could still play. And I was even more keen to prove to the Hammers fans that they hadn't signed a player who couldn't cope in the English game I had returned to.

Stewart Robson was with me in midfield. He had left Arsenal a few months previously, as he never really got on with George. George was in the process of turning Arsenal into a highly organised team. They had beaten Liverpool in the League Cup final at Wembley a few days earlier and were on a high. The toughness George demanded from his players was very evident. Tony Adams at centre back. Michael Thomas in midfield. Viv Anderson at right back was still very athletic. Steve Williams had a bit of everything about him in the middle of the park. Dave O'Leary and Paul Davis were the two remaining from when I left in 1980.

John picked me to play on the left, where I was up against a young David Rocastle, a skilful, dynamic player. An exciting youngster who would become a huge fan favourite. Everybody at Arsenal loved him. He was later taken from us so tragically young.

We were well and truly in a relegation scrap and needed the points badly. We started the match very well and Tony Cottee gave us the lead but Arsenal drew level with a penalty scored by one of their youngsters, Martin Hayes. We got a break we badly needed when the referee awarded us a penalty in the second half. Cottee slammed it home.

Around 10 minutes from the end, I won a challenge with Rocastle near the halfway line, and drove at their defence. My mate David O'Leary was backing off, ready to stick out one of those long legs to block any shot, but I managed to send an outside-of-the-foot bender around him into the far corner. One of my better goals, and the place went berserk.

Many of the Arsenal fans behind that goal applauded, which was a real compliment. But let's just say the era of not celebrating against your former club wasn't yet upon us. I veered away and jumped into the old 'Chicken Run' East Stand, home of the real hardline Hammers, even getting booked for the celebration. It finished 3–1, a much-needed win.

After the game George was asked by the press if he regretted not bringing me back to Highbury. I don't think he appreciated that. When Arsenal beat us early the following season, he made a point of noting afterwards that Steve Williams ran the game and was by far the best midfielder on the pitch. He had a good memory.

But this was a special night that bedded me in at West Ham. It gave us the confidence to get some very good results, especially at home. In our last six home games we won four and drew two and relegation was no longer an issue. We finished off the season with a flourish. I got my second goal for the club in the last game of the season, in a win that sent Manchester City down. The fans were relieved a difficult season was over.

How was that tremendous Hammers team in a relegation fight? The season before they'd finished third, staying with Liverpool and Everton well down the home straight. In John the club had a top manager, who'd won two FA Cups (one against my Arsenal team) and reached the Cup Winners' Cup final.

West Ham could never realistically win the title. The club just didn't have the money to compete with the very biggest English clubs on wages and transfer fees. John was already grappling with a problem nearly every West Ham boss has encountered – trying to hold on to his best players.

Other clubs were constantly 'getting into them', as they say in the game. It was the talk of the dressing room, with lads openly discussing the deals on offer elsewhere. Frank McAvennie was adamant he was off to Celtic and that's what happened. That broke up a wonderful partnership with Tony Cottee. A goal machine like Cottee was inevitably being tapped up as well, and Mark Ward was in demand.

In that sense, John was a victim of his own success. He'd fish gems like McAvennie and Ward from St Mirren and Oldham and before long they'd want to take the next step. He developed youngsters like Cottee and Ince and before long they were looking to move.

It was disappointing for me, hoping we were capable of doing well in the league and had a fair chance of winning a cup. In reality, we were sliding in the opposite direction.

My own contribution was limited by the one bad injury of my career, which caused me to miss big chunks of the next two seasons, including Euro '88.

Sometimes when the knee groans and crunches, I can nearly feel the dry mud at Derby's Baseball Ground. The studs stick, the leg twists, that stab of pain. And the horrible moment when you know it's bad. We had to play on some rubbish pitches in those days. I often get asked about the money today's players earn, and I never begrudge them a penny. But I do envy them the perfect pitches they play on week in, week out.

The cruciate isn't ever an injury you want, but especially then. Mine was ruptured, there was an operation, but nothing like the reconstruction the surgeons are able to perform now. They sewed it back together as best they could and told me to concentrate on building up my thigh muscles. It took me the best part of a year to get back playing.

In truth, I was never quite the same player. At 32 it's difficult to recover after such a serious injury. You hear pundits and fans saying players have lost that yard of pace and that is exactly what happened to me. On top of that I began to have trouble with back pain and groin problems.

You could still put together a decent highlights reel from the West Ham days. But following that injury I never made the contribution I had hoped to. I'd like to have scored a few more goals for the club, but at least there were some decent ones in there. A top-corner curler past Peter Shilton at least gave me a happier memory of the Baseball Ground to hold on to.

Players continued to leave or wanted to leave. Injuries plagued us. I had been out for 10 months and Phil Parkes, our best goalkeeper, was hardly ever fit. Stewart Robson and Alvin Martin – two crucial players for us – missed a lot of games.

We struggled to win on Saturday afternoons. We weren't great in daylight, but there were a few more magical nights. A 4–1 League Cup win over Liverpool was especially memorable. Paul Ince was brilliant in that game and truly put himself in the shop window with two great goals. Liverpool were the best team in England but couldn't cope with our quick passing game that night.

We lost twice in the League Cup semi-final, both times on those dreadful plastic pitches, to Luton and Oldham, which, looking back, was grossly unfair. Both home teams knew exactly how to play on the artificial surface.

Despite going on a winning run very late in the season we needed to go to Anfield and win in our last game. Liverpool thrashed us 5–1 and we were relegated. That win made Liverpool racing certainties for the league. It set up the famous Michael Thomas finale at Anfield, the decider delayed by the Hillsborough tragedy, when Arsenal had to win by two goals.

I watched that game in a Dublin hotel room, on international duty for the World Cup qualifier with Malta. It was the night everything about George Graham's management style and team-building was vindicated. I was thrilled, especially as the team was packed with lads brought through the youth system. Including, of course, David O'Leary, who got his hands on the First Division championship trophy for the first time.

West Ham sacked John Lyall that summer, which I felt was very wrong and I know it deeply hurt him. They hired Lou Macari on the back of successive promotions at Swindon Town but he just never fitted in. Lou had been getting the best out of ordinary players and to achieve two promotions in two years was no mean feat. He was in his element with lads who looked up to him who he could really influence. At West Ham, he had good players who were also experienced in the ways of the football world and probably needed to be impressed by a new manager and his coaching methods. But with Lou it was all very basic.

His training seemed to be based solely around fitness. He increased the physical work dramatically and the players didn't buy into it. As a player he could run all day. I remembered well he would be my man-marker whenever Arsenal played United, including in the '79 Cup final.

And he employed some strange motivational ideas. It was actually Lou in charge for that League Cup semi at Oldham's Boundary Park astro, on 14 February 1990, when his pre-match speech took an unusual turn.

'Oldham at Wembley just doesn't sound right to me. Can you imagine a headline "Oldham are at Wembley?" I just can't see it.'

I suppose he was trying to boost our confidence, but even someone relatively sceptical about superstitions like me was rattled. In Italy, it was drummed into us never to tempt fate. If you heard somebody say 'nothing can go wrong now', the Italian antidote was to squeeze your own balls. I did that night, but it didn't work.

Oldham, under Joe Royle, were a decent, up-and-coming side with Denis Irwin and other very good players like Warhurst, Marshall and Barrett. While the pitch gave them a massive advantage. They knew exactly the pace a pass needed to be played at. At every opportunity, their wingers put the ball into our box. And they could always read the bounce. It ranks as one of the most embarrassing defeats of my career and in the story of West Ham United. 6–0. Next day the papers called it the Valentine's Day Massacre.

To Lou's credit, he brought in good players like Ian Bishop, Martin Allen, Trevor Morley and Ludo Mikloško, who would become a hero between the posts at the club. But he was soon gone himself, in February that first season, after a newspaper made allegations about football betting irregularities when he'd been at Swindon.

Lou's departure gave the club the opportunity to turn to a true West Ham legend in Billy Bonds. The mood changed instantly. Bill was so popular his appointment rallied everyone, lifted spirits and made the rest of that campaign a pleasure.

Meeting Bill for the first time at West Ham made me question if I'd really worked hard enough throughout my career, if I had actually been as professional as I needed to be to get the best out of my talent. Nobody trained better or harder than Bill.

In the days before players were properly educated on nutrition – at West Ham, we had sausage, egg, chips and beans in the club canteen on Fridays, the day before a game – Bill was skipping those favourite meals. He stood out as someone who prepared himself properly and left nothing to chance. He was a phenomenal athlete who gave 100% in everything he did. He played 799 games for West Ham and rightly has a stand in his name at West Ham's new ground at the London Stadium.

He proved to be a fine manager as well, though I suspected he was never comfortable in that position. The game was changing dramatically. Agents were heavily involved in the transfer market. I know Billy would have hated the wheeling and dealing that had become a big part of the game. Under his watch the club was travelling in the right direction again and he would achieve promotion the following season.

But I knew my journey was almost over.

With the Irish team, Jack had moved on. After my injury, I couldn't offer him the physicality midfield players like Andy

Townsend, Ronnie Whelan and Kevin Sheedy were capable of. And when the 1990 World Cup was off the table, I sort of knew it was the right time to call it a day.

There were a few interesting offers to play on, but I wouldn't really have been doing myself or a new club justice. I was honest with myself. I'd had enough.

It had been frustrating those last couple of years, the cruciate ligament injury triggering lots of smaller ones, but I'd had little to complain about. From 15 to 32, there were 17 years more or less injury-free, which was a remarkably fortunate run. In this game you take the good with the bad, and I'd had an awful lot of good.

I was going to do some punditry work for the BBC at Italia '90 – I had a plan to go into sports management as a players' representative, and there would be a testimonial with Ireland.

So I began to contemplate my exit. In a discussion with Billy I told him I had no problem with him playing the up-and-coming kids in those last few games, to give them vital experience for the following season. Typical of Billy, he offered me a start on the last day of the season: 5 May 1990 against Wolves. I told him to stick with young Kevin Keen, son of Mike, who had played with my brothers at QPR in the 1960s. The wheel turns.

There was a presentation and guard of honour beforehand and it was a pretty emotional day for me. The reception I got from the West Ham fans is a cherished memory. There was a full house at Upton Park even though there was nothing on the game. The fans were there for Billy and their enthusiasm for next season.

He put me on late in the second half. We were already three up and it was very nearly full time when I picked up Stewart Robson's precise pass. Now I had space in front of me I began to eye the goal. A Wolves defender came to close me down and I dropped my shoulder to the right and went past him on the left. Now I'm within range and I let go. It went in like a rocket. Oh man, what a feeling. Last game, last minute, you couldn't write the script. There are not many things sweeter than the ones that fly in like an arrow.

I was heading for the Chicken Run again, to celebrate, but this time it met me halfway. The pitch invasion encouraged the referee to blow up a few seconds early and football had given me one parting gift. A goal with my last kick of the ball as a professional footballer.

Thank you West Ham, thank you John Lyall, and thank you Billy Bonds for that happy ending.

13

Big Jack

IN THE WEEKS AFTER he became Republic of Ireland manager, Jack Charlton was a guest at a wedding. He sat at a football table with Billy Bremner and Alex Smith – then St Mirren manager – among others. At some point in the night, Jack began holding court on his plans for the Irish. One of the urgent items on his to-do list, Jack revealed, was to 'bomb out Brady' (dispense with my services). Billy, who I knew reasonably well through John Giles, and who had been well accustomed to challenging Jack's ideas from their Leeds days together, thought this was ridiculous. But Jack was adamant, as he was about most things.

Naturally, the way football is, this story eventually wound its way back to me. Who had been in his ear, I've always wondered. As I first noticed at the Player of the Year dinner in 1979, Jack was close to lots of journalists. Eamon Dunphy was my chief suspect, though I've never asked him. Eamon had been my number one critic in the latter days of Eoin Hand's era. And around that time, he and Jack had been friendly. The view was, led by Eamon, that I had far too much influence in the Irish dressing room and had essentially been picking Eoin's team for him. Frank Stapleton was accused of much the same. Codswallop, of course, but I suppose it was the kind of conspiracy that made for entertaining reading, at a time when the team wasn't delivering.

Whoever it was, it sounded like Jack's view of me was compromised before I'd even met him properly. The dogs on the streets were barking that I was going to be out of his plans. Even though, by my reckoning, he'd seen me play once in six seasons – and that was in that controversial Ireland defeat in Belgium in 1981. Not much evidence to bomb someone out.

To be fair, maybe Jack wouldn't have needed anyone to warn him about me. I wasn't his type, you could say. I'd played against his Sheffield Wednesday team and his Middlesbrough team and both favoured more direct methods of transferring the ball from one end to the other. Jack, like a clutch of managers in the English game at that time, was a disciple of Charles Hughes, the FA coaching director who famously concluded that most goals were scored from three passes or fewer. So it was seemingly a fool's errand to consider keeping the ball for a fourth pass or, God forbid, anything that might be described as a passing move.

It was a philosophy Jack had believed in since he was a player, John Giles often told me. At Leeds, when John or Billy Bremner looked for the ball from Jack he would refuse to give it to them and would want to launch it himself, up to Allan Clarke. Until Don Revie eventually told Jack that he wouldn't be playing if he didn't play ball and play through his midfield.

John had also been in for the Ireland job again, at that time, ready to give it another go with the FAI. And Bob Paisley had been a surprise candidate. Jack's approach wasn't an appetising prospect for most of us. It was fresh in our minds that Newcastle United's fans hadn't been too impressed with his style of play.

I was in Jack's squad for his first game, a friendly against Wales at Lansdowne Road in March 1986. The match didn't go great. A terrible affair in front of a small crowd on a bumpy pitch, typically wrecked by rugby at that time of year. Wales won 1–0 and nobody seemed impressed. The Irish football public needed a bit of convincing, anyway, that an Englishman should be managing the national team. There was even the odd protest banner in the ground. 'Go home, Union Jack.' There were a few mutters too among the players. Jack had gone in strong, as you can imagine, in the days before, and made it clear how we'd be playing. And advised anyone who didn't like that as to what they could do.

The game was probably most notable for the debuts of John Aldridge and Ray Houghton, Jack's first bits of recruitment. I think Davy Langan had tipped off Eoin Hand that both were eligible, and that info made its way to Jack. But I remember flying out of Dublin that week even less sure about my future in green.

I actually missed the next three matches, through club commitments with Inter Milan. And Dave O'Leary's problems with Jack began when he pulled out of the friendly with Uruguay – George Graham was never a huge fan of releasing players for international duty. Jack duly left Dave out of his squad for a summer tournament in Iceland. But when a host of players pulled out, including all the Liverpool contingent, Dave was recalled, but then opted not to travel because he'd already booked his family holiday. Was it saying no to Jack that cost him three years in exile? Or was it Dave's natural tendency to play out from the back? A convenient mixture of both, perhaps.

So Dave wasn't in the squad for Jack's first competitive game, against Belgium in Brussels. And I didn't expect to be either, having missed three of his four preparation matches. But I was there. And as it happened, I'd just gone to Ascoli, had been worked hard in pre-season by their renowned coach Aldo Sensibile, and was arguably in the best shape of my life.

I trained well but still didn't hold out much expectation of playing. He called us in on the training pitch the day before the match to tell us the team. He pointed to me. 'You're number six, Ian.' As he carried on with the rest, I stopped him. 'My name is Liam, Jack. Ian Brady was the Moors murderer.'

I played well. We got a great result (2–2 against the World Cup semi-finalists) and I knocked in the last-minute penalty, given for a foul on Frank by the goalkeeper Jean-Marie Pfaff so obvious that the referee more or less had to give it. Nor was there any way of flagging offside from the spot, so we got our away point. The Jack regime was up and running and somehow, far from being bombed out, I was part of it.

People tend to boil down my relationship with Jack to one heated episode towards the end, but it was a lot more complicated, with plenty of contradictions. Overall, we got on really well during that qualification campaign. I played all eight matches and probably put in some of my best performances for Ireland. No doubt, I had to adapt, as we all did. Essentially, Jack did a reverse Revie and made it crystal clear to Kevin Moran and Mick McCarthy at the back that if they or anyone else in midfield gave me the ball, they wouldn't be playing for him again. Nor would I, if I kept looking for it.

It was a simple game plan. He felt that continental defenders weren't comfortable when turned around so he wanted the ball knocked in behind them whenever possible. We could play when we won it in their half. Putting opposition defenders under pressure – pressing – wasn't a miraculous cure that Jack had discovered. John Giles had been preaching it since the early 1970s. But to be fair to Jack, this game plan was so simplified that at least everybody was on the same page. Because there weren't too many pages in this manual. There were no special plans for the opposition. In Brussels, he didn't even mention their star player Enzo Scifo before the game.

169

But we were good at set pieces, under Jack. He did have us practise those. And mainly our style was about imposing – 'inflicting', Jack would say – our game on the opposition. That meant getting the ball into the channels, where Aldo's tongue would be hanging out from chasing it. Ray Houghton was ideal for what Jack wanted to do. He could play, but he was also like a bumblebee with a relentless knack of buzzing to wherever a ball might drop.

It was hard for me to change completely. I gave up looking for the ball from the centre halves or full backs, but if I got it in midfield, I might sometimes look to play a crossfield pass, or thread one into Frank's feet, or bring a full back into play. Things Jack didn't want. If it came off, you'd hear nothing from him, he'd just sit there on the bench, as if he hadn't noticed anything. If it didn't, he'd be on his feet bawling, throwing his cap on the ground in rage.

I always had the nagging sense he was putting up with me, that I was a reluctant selection. Little things. Times I'd think, 'What did you have to say that for?' Out in Sofia, for instance, where we all played well again, but lost late on when Kevin gave away a penalty. 'You played well,' he said to me after, 'but I wish I'd taken you off with 20 minutes to go. We might have held on.' As if it was all my fault.

But that result was the only blemish, really, on a great campaign. And I enjoyed it, overall. I found myself getting on the ball further up the pitch, maybe from knockdowns from Frank, or off hasty clearances Aldo had forced with his harrying. And here's another contradiction. I know Jack, if he were alive today, would still make the case that he got the best out of me, that I played some of my most efficient football for Ireland under him, that I was certainly better than in the last few years under Eoin, and that he got me using my ability in the right areas of the pitch. And even though almost everything about his style goes against how I like the game played, it's an argument I'd struggle to win. Because it was hard to win any argument with Jack.

There can't have been many more stubborn men. On one trip, we were playing cards on the bus. A points game, where you had to remember the cards that had gone and play in sequence. Jack played the wrong card and we all piled in, penalising him. He wasn't having it. 'What's going on?' 'You played the wrong card, Jack.' 'No, I didn't.' I wasn't letting him off the hook. 'Yes, you did.' Next thing, he gathers the cards, slides open the little window above us and chucks the whole lot onto the road. Next morning, I'm leaving my room in the hotel when he collars me. 'Come here, you, I've been thinking, you were right, I did play the wrong card.' When I told John Giles this story, he'd seen it all before. They'd lost a deck or two on the bus with Leeds.

Jack's stubbornness was most obvious in his treatment of Dave O'Leary, who he simply refused to pick, no matter how much journalists wrote about it. It was disgraceful really, given how classy a player Dave was and the service he'd given to Ireland.

But for all his idiosyncrasies, Jack was a great character to be around. The organisation and the facilities and the training were no better than they ever had been. Details weren't Jack's thing. Nor names. Paul McGrath was always John, because Jack had played against John McGrath. Niall Quinn was 'Arsenal' and Tony Cascarino was 'the ice cream man'. But he let us have a drink and a game of golf and he made it a happy camp, created an atmosphere where everybody looked forward to landing in Dublin on a Sunday evening.

There was strength in the clarity of his message. Nobody was under any illusions about what was expected. He also had a very human side and an instinctive way with people. Everyone knew Paul McGrath had his problems around that time. He had a tendency to go AWOL. But Jack turned a blind eye in a way he wouldn't have for any other player. Paul was a superstar, in many ways, brilliant centre back, could play midfield, score goals from set pieces. All the players were 100% in agreement with the slack Jack cut Paul.

The win in Hampden over Scotland, when Mark Lawrenson scored, opened up the group for us. The teamsheet also serves as exhibit A for the prosecution who argue Jack could have played more ambitiously with the quality of player he had. Pound for pound the best Irish team I've played in. Jack working a formation on the back of his cigarette packet that shoehorned all his best players in. Mark Lawrenson with me in midfield. Paul McGrath and Ronnie Whelan repurposed as full backs. Packie, Mick, Kevin. Tony Galvin and Ray Houghton wide. Aldo and Frank up front. Ronnie was confused when the team was announced. 'You've me at left back, Jack.' 'Yeah, have you a problem with that?' 'No, no problem.' And it wasn't to Ronnie, or Paul, who could play anywhere.

Not long after, we beat Brazil in Dublin, with one of the goals I remember most fondly. It didn't make up for the battering we got in Uberlândia, but beating Brazil was an incredible feather in our cap. Will we ever see that again from an Irish team? No doubt Jack would point out that I picked up the ball just outside the box after it came back off John Byrne. And he'd probably choose to ignore the string of passes in midfield just before. As I remember it, we actually played a bit that day. Jack tended to relax the leash sometimes for a friendly. I'm sure I even got a pass or two off Mick. Though I remember John Anderson, who played full back, playing it strictly by the book. Down the line every time. I think John, who knew Jack from Newcastle, was more afraid of him than the rest of us.

Beating the Brazilians certainly contributed to the feel-good factor building around the squad. We rounded off a fine qualification effort that October with a 2–0 win over Bulgaria at home, their only defeat, with Moran and McGrath scoring. I played well again, though I spoiled things with one of the stupidest moments of my career, five minutes from the end. A draw suited the Bulgarians, so they had spent most of the game wasting time. Other than when they were kicking us. This lad Sadakov had paid particularly close attention to me, his studs getting to know my calves well. When he rattled into me one last time, I snapped, and lashed out with an elbow, flooring him. Wily old pros are often lauded for taking their revenge quietly. This belonged at the opposite end of that scale. I couldn't have been more conspicuous.

But walking off the field, I didn't feel that bad. It wasn't going to cost us. Jack came over for a pat on the back in a very public show of support that was appreciated. And there was a strong ovation from the fans. It was the same inside. 'Don't worry about it. No harm done.' He was in rallying mood, congratulating the lads on a great effort. Something to build on for a proper crack at the World Cup. Bulgaria now just needed a draw at home to Scotland to top the group and take the one qualification spot. Scotland's form had been indifferent. Everyone presumed that was a formality.

I didn't dwell on it at all, even when word came a couple of weeks later that I'd been handed a four-match ban for violent conduct. At my age, the next World Cup campaign seemed a long time away and there was no guarantee Jack would still be putting up with me by then. So on a Wednesday afternoon that November, on a day off at my new club West Ham, I was playing golf with Pat Jennings, just the two of us. Pat was a very tasty player then, off about six.

Back in the clubhouse after, I asked the barman, 'Do you know the Scotland score?' 'Oh yeah,' he says casually, as if he was telling me what the soup was, 'they beat them alright, you've qualified for the Euros, Liam. Congratulations.' 'You're kidding me!' And that's when it dawned. Oh fuck. What have I done? How could I have been so idiotic? A four-game ban would rule me out of the competition unless Ireland made the final. There's no way I could go. I didn't know whether to celebrate or cry.

And so as Ireland was melting down in celebration at a first tournament qualification, and Scotland's goalscorer Gary Mackay was becoming an instant national hero, I was stewing back home and trying to pull my thoughts together. Was there any way out of this one? By some point of the evening, I had convinced myself there might just be and got on the phone to Des Casey at the FAI. 'Des, can we appeal?'

Des was too diplomatic to say it straight, but you could read between the lines of his hesitation. 'Liam, you flattened the guy in full view of the referee and TV cameras. This isn't one of the great miscarriages of justice of our time. They're not going to change their minds at UEFA. Do you really think there would be any point in appealing?'

'What about leniency?'

Four games seemed harsh. I'd been provoked. Had never been sent off for Ireland before. I can't remember if I'd even been booked. Maybe we could get it reduced. Des wasn't terribly convinced about our prospects, but promised to give it a go. In the meantime, over the next few days, I pestered every decent contact I had in football, to see what my chances might be. I rang Giampiero Boniperti, the Juventus president, who was a mover and shaker across the European game. Ken Friar at Arsenal, who mixed with UEFA delegates. And Gordon Taylor, the chairman of the PFA, sent what was essentially a character reference to UEFA. A plea for mercy, that I was coming to the end of my career, and this was totally out of character.

The message we got from everywhere was to prepare our case well, make a convincing appeal at my personal UEFA hearing, and there might be a chance. So I set out for Zurich that December with Des and FAI president Pat O'Brien, a Corkman. By now Des, who was a delegate on UEFA committees, was confident. Full of beans. But I could see Pat was apprehensive. When he stood up to speak, between his nerves and the Cork accent, nobody could understand what he was saying. I always found Cork people speak very quickly anyway. I saw a couple of interpreters looking bewildered.

I was starting to panic. Don't worry, Des was assuring me. 'It will be OK.' He was an old pro at this, a trade union man, used to holding court. And he launched into an impassioned plea for clemency. 'To Irish football, Liam Brady is what Michel Platini is to French football and what Diego Maradona is to . . . Brazilian football.'

My head was literally in my hands in despair.

Thankfully, the match referee Jan Keizer was quite conciliatory in his testimony. He accepted he had had no option but to send me off, but he wasn't convinced it had been truly violent conduct, which is what I'd been charged with. It was a rare break for Ireland from the men in the middle. Though I'd always found Keizer to be a top referee in both club and international football. Whatever the reason, my offence was downgraded to unsporting behaviour, and the ban halved from four matches to two.

I was grateful to the FAI for listening to me and for their efforts in taking things to UEFA. And later that evening Jack confirmed he would now be bringing me to Germany. Though he did throw in, when talking to the media, that it might be difficult to change a winning team for the third match.

As it turned out, that sense of anticipation at a lifetime's ambition about to be fulfilled lasted only a couple of months, until one Saturday in February at Derby County's Baseball Ground, where the knee caved in. Euro '88 just wasn't to be. Unbelievably, my midfield partner, Mark Lawrenson, suffered the same fate, with an Achilles injury, and never played for Ireland again. Mark later told me he couldn't even watch the finals on TV, he was so gutted. I felt the same, for a while, but in the end was glad to be in Germany as a pundit, and grateful to Jack for letting me accompany the squad.

Why wasn't that the end? The thing I never quite understood about Jack is why he brought me back into the squad after the Euros. Maybe he felt obligated due to my injury misfortune. But I know Jack felt things had moved on without me. By the time I got fit, Paul McGrath was in midfield, with Ronnie, while Andy Townsend was finalising his switch to the green.

Yet I was just back in the West Ham team a couple of months when Jack recalled me for the friendly with France in Dalymount, in February 1989. Bats, Amoros, Battiston, Papin. Laurent Blanc in midfield. Michel Platini the manager. It was my 68th appearance for Ireland, a record, and I played OK in a nil–nil draw. Maybe Jack was just getting that land-mark out of the way. There was probably a hint to his thinking in Andy Townsend's debut in the middle, while he moved me out to the left.

When we travelled to Budapest in the next qualifier – another nil–nil – he left me on the bench until the last 10 minutes. And afterwards, in the media, it all came spilling out, the beginnings of a classic 'war of words'.

'The pace and the work rate which our style now demands does not permit Liam Brady at 33 to give me a full 90 minutes' play, so I will not be including him in my original lineups from now on. I only intend to use him as a substitute and bring him on late in games.'

I'm not sure why Jack needed to tell everyone this. He hadn't told me. But my response was diplomacy personified: 'Jack Charlton is the boss and he makes the decisions and whatever he asks me to do for Ireland I will be happy to do my bit.' Or at least it started out that way. 'I have proved with West Ham and also for the Republic of Ireland against France at Dalymount that I can stick out the pace as well as anyone, but Jack Charlton's memory doesn't appear to stretch back as far as that.'

That exchange was a mistake on both our parts, because from then on, Jack's 'treatment of Brady', like his 'treatment of O'Leary' became a topic of huge interest to the press. And as we saw with Dave, the press telling Jack what to do was only going to bring out his stubborn streak. I was still in the squad for the qualifier with Spain at Lansdowne in April – that famous 1–0 win – though I didn't get on. And back at the Airport Hotel afterwards, frustrations came spilling out again, this time from Jack's side.

The issue of money was always bubbling under the surface in the Irish squad. We felt short-changed at Euro '88. A commercial bandwagon had taken off around the Irish team and in our naivety, we never hitched ourselves to it. Jack had his own deals and the FAI cashed in through its sponsorship with Opel, but there was nothing in that for us. So for the World Cup campaign, we set up a players' pool. Kevin Moran's brother recommended Drury Communications, a PR company run by Fintan Drury and Billy Murphy. Their job was to maximise the revenue we could make through lining up gigs and deals with sponsors. An agency was lining up gigs and deals with sponsors. I was one of the players at the forefront, with Kevin, Frank, Ray and Packie. I don't think that went in my favour with Jack. He had no problem with us making a few quid, but he was getting it in the ear from the FAI and Arnold O'Byrne, the Opel Ireland chief, was really annoyed. I reckon O'Byrne felt he played a key part in our qualification. And he and Jack were tight.

It would get messier as qualification for Italy became more likely. The players got our own deal with Irish Permanent. We made a TV ad with myself and Kevin Moran walking into a branch to swap our punts for lira. It went down well with the public and I don't think O'Byrne liked it. That episode eventually ended up on the steps of the High Court, with Opel insisting their rights around the team had been breached.

But after that Spain match, the players had taken a first stand, and refused to attend the usual post-match function for sponsors, heading straight back to our hotel. That caused a stand-up row in the lobby, in front of a sizeable audience, with Jack pointing the finger at myself and Frank, more or less accusing us of leading the rest of the squad astray. That was probably when Jack decided it finally was time to 'bomb out Brady'.

I reported to the squad for the September friendly with West Germany. Jack's assistant Maurice Setters had watched me, up north somewhere, playing for West Ham, where I'd had a nightmare. So I wasn't expecting to play. Then the day before the game, to my amazement, Jack picked me in the team. Where did that come from?

I've watched it back, the 35 minutes. The infamous half hour people boil down my relationship with Jack Charlton to. I wasn't terrible, but I wasn't great. I cringe at a lot of old footage of my playing days. At my efforts to tackle, especially. There's an embarrassing moment early in the game against the Germans. Thomas Häßler shapes to cross and I sell myself cheaply. Lunge on the floor and he sweeps past. Jack would have hated that. Afterwards, he said he knew after 15 minutes I couldn't hack it at this level any more.

That was harsh. I was still on the road back from serious injury. In one sense, he had a point. It was going to be difficult for me to become the same player I was during the Euro 88 campaign. A yard of pace had evaporated. I was sure I could still play at this level but maybe I couldn't play the football he wanted to play. But I still think he was wrong to do it, to haul me off after 35 minutes. I'd had a hand in Frank's goal. He didn't have to make a big deal of it. I would have understood if he wanted to make changes at half-time, but the way it was done made me angry.

I took it badly. A shouting match at half-time. Jack giving it back. Players getting between us. 'We've got to play the second half.' I went in the showers and made up my mind that it was over. Frank tried to talk me out of it. 'Don't make it easy for him.' But I went out afterwards and told the media I was retiring from international football.

Sixteen years after the innocence and magic of Dalymount and the USSR, it was a terribly sore way to wrap things up with Ireland. It caused a storm. A huge debate. Frank was convinced it was all a setup. He and Tony Galvin had played too, Jack's other two veterans, and neither featured much again. He'd made up his mind we were finished and wanted to prove it. Jack seemed to confirm as much later in quotes I've read. 'With Ireland, they don't give up on their fucking heroes easily, so you've really got to show 'em.' I'm happy I didn't get involved in a slagging match.

The letter arrived a few weeks later. It had a Northumberland postcode.

'Dear Liam. I'm sorry the way things worked out after the Germany game. I wish to thank you for what you did during my time with the Republic. I never intended to hurt you, believe that. You would be very welcome to come to Italy should we get there. In your testimonial I will do all I can to help.

'I hope the next time we meet you will still have a little time for me and we might find time to repair some of the damage. This is just a quick note I felt I had to send you. All the best Liam, I hope things work out for you. Jack.'

It was a demonstration of sentiment that I didn't expect from Jack. He could be as gruff and abrupt as they come, but there was an empathy to him too, in there somewhere. It was very sincere and I appreciated it. It was the kind of note you put away safely. I wrote back telling him we were fine, forget about it, we move on.

We never had another cross word. I told the press the chapter was closed, I was happy with my decision to retire, which calmed things down a bit. Jack was a great help with my testimonial before the World Cup and made me welcome around the camp in Italy. Our paths often crossed, long after he finished with Ireland, and we could always have a laugh.

Was he right, I'm often asked, to get Ireland playing like we did? When you consider what Italia '90 did for football in the country, it's hard to build a strong case against him. Could we have done even better with the quality of players Jack had? Or, to put it another way, would John Giles have done better with that group? In my opinion, yes. But it's something I'll never be able to prove.

Should I have gone to that World Cup as a player? The way I look at it, I probably still could have contributed something, but maybe only under a different manager, who played a different way. People often say, you could have come on with 15 minutes to go against Egypt, on that dull afternoon in Palermo when we laboured to a nil–nil draw. Funnily enough, Jack even mentioned it, at the hotel that night, the camp a little deflated after the high of the draw against England. 'I could have done with you today, Liam . . .' But Jack being Jack, he wasn't finished. '. . . if you were two or three years younger.'

14

Celtic

BECOMING A FOOTBALL MANAGER was never in my mind when I decided to retire in 1990. I was set on taking time out from the routine of being a player for the best part of 20 years. No more hotels, airports, buses up and down motorways to play games. Ronnie Teeman continued to advise me and I came out of my professional career with property and savings to give myself and my family a solid platform to make the next decision without pressure.

I had become friends with Fintan Drury, whose company Drury Communications had advised the Irish squad and had done a great job for the players. Fintan and I started to think about a sports agency to look after individual players. By then, agents had well and truly arrived on the scene, but many players were still naive when it came to career management. We decided to go into business together with an agency called Brady Drury Sports Management.

One of our first clients was Packie Bonner and one of my first assignments was to speak to Billy McNeill, then Celtic manager, and chairman Jack McGinn, about Packie's contract. On the back of his performances in the Italy World Cup,

Celtic were keen to renew his contract. He'd had a great tournament and was hot property after that save from Romania's Daniel Timofte. Celtić wanted to reward his service anyway and Packie wanted to stay, so we concluded our business without a problem. We came out with Packie getting a much-improved contract that matched his status in the game and he was very happy. It was a pleasure to deal with Billy and Jack.

Towards the end of that 1990–91 season, Packie asked me if I had any interest in management. By this time Celtic had confirmed they were letting Billy go at the end of the season. Over the previous three seasons, Rangers had become the dominant force in Scotland. Who wouldn't have thrown their hat in? The idea that I could walk off the field and straight into one of the great clubs was very enticing.

In the interview process, strangely, there were few candidates. Frank Stapleton, as it happens, was also in the hunt. Though no established managers with track records seemed to be on the shortlist. Maybe that was a clue I should have taken into account. But I interviewed, presented my ideas, and the offer came. I spent little time assessing the reality of what I was getting into. There was another meeting to talk about the future, where the club was going. I'd have around a million to spend in the first season. Rangers had pulled well ahead, but I believed that budget gave me a fighting shot. I took everybody and everything at face value.

I should have done my due diligence. I should have rung Billy. It was awkward, as I was taking his job, but I should have been forthright enough to pick up the phone. I could have rung David Hay, who had been interested in bringing me to Celtic as a player a few years earlier. Either would have given me a steer on the goings-on at the club.

I was a failure as Celtic manager. It is better to get that stark admission out of the way. Because this account of 28 months in that job is likely to venture into territory that could be interpreted as excuses, as a case for the defence. It is not. I didn't deliver. I failed, in my estimation, for two fundamental reasons. I was a novice, the first manager of Celtic since the 1800s with no experience, I was told. And I found it hard to deal with many of the problems I encountered. Furthermore, while I thought I knew plenty about the club, in reality I didn't have any idea. I hadn't done my homework on the board and its problems with debt and upgrading the stadium. There were things I should have known about and things I could never have known about.

Perhaps more importantly, I hadn't properly realised that at Celtic you're not managing a club or even a team; you're the leader of a community. It is a heavy load to carry, especially for a rookie. I'm not sure when that first dawned on me. Maybe on the afternoon, early on, when a Catholic priest from the local diocese arrived uninvited to bless my house, and marched past my bewilderment with his thurible of incense swinging. Or when one of the neighbours on the road knocked on the door and asked why my son was going to the local Church of Scotland school. 'What's it got to do with you?' I asked him. That's probably when I figured out what people meant when they described football life in Glasgow as being a goldfish bowl.

My first week after accepting the job, I got word that Paul Elliott, Celtic's top-class centre back, was being transferred to Chelsea. I hadn't spoken to Paul. The players hadn't even reported back for pre-season. This was a huge shock because I'd been told by the board I'd be in charge of all football matters. The fee would be around £1.2 million, which was more or less my budget, except I'd now have to replace one of my best players with that money too. That's when I first began to get a bad vibe. What have I signed up to? I rang Jack McGinn. 'What's going on? Why wasn't I told?' His reaction was a concern. 'You're not going to resign over this, are you?' That would have been embarrassing for him and the club. It's probably what I should have done, but then I'd always have wondered. Even though he was chairman, I knew Jack hadn't made the decision about Elliott. It had been chief executive Terry Cassidy. It was a stark warning we'd have a difficult relationship.

I knew the job wouldn't be easy. I saw how much Rangers were spending on the playing staff and the stadium. There was ongoing talk of expanding Parkhead or moving lock stock, but nothing seemed likely to happen. Rangers' Ibrox Park, meanwhile, seemed to be in a constant process of modernisation. It was a club restless for improvement since David Murray bought it. And with money somehow always available. Indeed in recent years we learned that Rangers would go to great and illegal lengths to ensure money was always available.

During Graeme Souness's era as manager, that money had been used to take advantage of the English ban from European football and tempt the best players north of the border. It is unthinkable now, an age where we saw a constant stream of the top English talent heading north to Glasgow. Trevor Steven. Terry Butcher. Mark Hateley. Ray Wilkins. Trevor Francis. And ultimately England's best player of that era, Paul Gascoigne. It wasn't just England – they were able to lure Oleksiy Mykhaylychenko from Sampdoria, when he'd just been part of the side that won my old club's only Serie A title. Rangers were shopping in Harrods, I was down the local shop.

Now led by Walter Smith, who'd been Graeme's assistant until he left for Liverpool the previous season, Rangers had won four of the last five Scottish titles. Billy McNeill's magnificent double in 1988 – the club's centenary year – was Celtic's last show of defiance. Walter would win the next six too, spending over £50 million on transfer fees – more than any other club in Britain in that time.

In sharp contrast, Celtic's board never had much money available and were not in a position to invest in the team. The directors had little wealth behind them besides the shares they owned in the club. Yet they constantly resisted approaches for those shares from people who might actually have money to put in. So there was always a power struggle going on. And a fragile board as concerned with fighting their own corner as taking the club forward. Many of them were there simply because their families had always run the club.

You often hear it said that the most important relationship at a club is owner and manager. At Celtic there were six board members to deal with.

The White and Kelly families who had controlled the club since its foundation provided three, the Kelly brothers Michael and Kevin and Christopher White. There was Tom Grant, who had a significant shareholding through family contacts. And then Jack McGinn and Jimmy Farrell, who had a long history of serving the club in senior positions.

I soon learned the six weren't necessarily sharing a hymn sheet. Michael Kelly sang loudest. He thought he was chairman and was constantly pushing agendas. He had risen in political circles, having previously served as Glasgow's Lord Provost, the mayoral figure heading the city council. But being first citizen was no preparation for the cut and thrust of political life at Celtic. This was another ball game.

Kelly was busy and forever wanting to know what he didn't need to know. He knew nothing about football but wanted to be privy to team matters. I'd come into the dressing room before a match and he'd be sitting there while players were getting changed. He was told often enough it wasn't his place, but it was water off a duck's back. It didn't take me long to decide he wasn't my cup of tea.

Celtic's first ever chief executive had been appointed around six months before, an acceptance of sorts by the board that it was struggling to get to grips with the financial state of the club. Or maybe they just needed a frontman to take the flak. Terry Cassidy was Michael Kelly's choice. An executive in the news-paper business from Middlesbrough who, in his opinion at least, had turned around the fortunes of the *Irish Times* in Dublin.

He was controversial from day one of his appointment and he was already causing problems for the board. Cassidy had been all over the removal of Billy McNeill. Whatever your views on whether Billy's time was up, this should have been a most delicate situation. A parting of ways with a legend, the club's greatest captain. Instead, Cassidy charged in on his ego and drafted a memo which outlined the club's plans to swing the axe. It made the papers and swiftly earned him the disgust of the supporters.

Billy summed him up as a 'thoroughly unpleasant, untrust-worthy, overbearing, offensive individual'. From my experience, that was Billy's charitable side talking. I had a meeting in his office one day and he just slipped me a piece of paper with his team on it for that weekend's match. I threw the paper back at him and walked out.

This is what I was dealing with. He was adamant he could have made it as a footballer. He was on the books of Nottingham Forest when he was 17 but injury wrecked his career. I'd be doing very well if I had a fiver for every businessman who told me they could have been a footballer but for injury or their parents insisting they concentrated on their studies.

We had more than a few stand-up rows until he was eventually kicked out of the job after two years, after making an enemy of almost everybody. Celtic were arguably worse off financially than when he arrived and had managed to lose their shirt sponsor, partly because Cassidy had upset the people at long-time sponsors C R Smith.

He then became a writer for the *Sunday Mail* and one of his first columns argued that football managers were worthless and unnecessary. I didn't need to read it. He'd never concealed that opinion in my presence. Michael Kelly and Cassidy should have been helping me, lightening the load on an inexperienced manager learning the ropes. In reality, they were a hindrance. They didn't have a clue.

I was nervous, taking a team for the first time. I desperately wanted to do well. But perhaps deep down I wondered if I was really ready for it. There was enjoyment too. I had Tommy Craig and Mick Martin with me as coaches. And although the facilities were pretty basic, I loved being on the training ground. Well away from the nonsense upstairs. The players seemed to respond to what we wanted, certainly at the beginning. And the fans were generous. Liked how we tried to play. They gave me every chance, backed me until I wasn't backable any more.

But I made mistakes. And big Tony Cascarino was a conspicuous one. We still talk about it now when we meet. Who made the bigger gaffe? Me signing him or him agreeing to come? But neither of us was laughing at the time. It came between us, I suppose, as friends, how things didn't work out for him. I was probably hard on him, at times. I didn't know he was having problems settling in Glasgow. An experienced manager would have factored all this in.

I just thought we needed a different type of striker. We had Charlie Nicholas, Andy Walker, Tommy Coyne, good technical players. But in Scotland, when you face a lot of lesser teams who sit deep behind the ball, I felt we needed a direct option, an aerial threat. And I bet £1.1 million – a club record fee – on that judgement.

But Cas has described vividly himself how confidence drained away from him in Glasgow. To the point where he stopped making certain runs in case he had the great misfortune of somebody presenting him with a chance to score. Every game where he didn't score loaded more pressure on the next one.

Again, it probably came down to me underestimating the claustrophobia of the Glasgow goldfish bowl. I just didn't take that into account, how a London lad like Cas, a happy-go-lucky character, would handle the responsibility of being Celtic's number 9. The pressure, I would say, is as great as in Manchester or Liverpool. And Tony was a fish out of water. He hated the scrutiny, even if it was just fans telling him on the street that 'the goal will come, big mon'. He hated the Celtic–Rangers stuff, didn't get the rivalry, couldn't understand why he shouldn't be seen hanging around at night with the Rangers lads like his old mate Terry Hurlock. His first Old Firm game at Celtic Park, he turned up in a royal-blue jacket. He had no idea what I had got him into.

And I got the impression his wife struggled with the move so far from London. Which probably didn't do anything for Tony's resolve to make things work out. He was still a good player, as he showed later in France, where he scored so freely that the Marseilles supporters called him 'Tony Goal'. It underlined what is the case with many footballers – a happy domestic situation goes a long way to helping you produce the goods.

Towards the end of that first season I managed to find a solution and arranged a swap for Cas with Tommy Boyd at Chelsea, who turned out to be a great servant for Celtic. Tony was thrilled. I'd imagine he hit the road to London without collecting his post.

But his time at Celtic put some doubts around my reputation as a recruiter of talent. And the worse thing is, I repeated that mistake. At the start of my second season I paid £1.5 million to West Ham for Stuart Slater. Sometimes when you've played with a guy, maybe you can be seduced by their pure ability. You know them intimately, have witnessed what they can do when testing the very limits of their talent in training. I knew Stuart had all the tools to be a top player and he was a very good player for West Ham. I felt he'd provide assists and score his fair share. But was he ready to handle the expectation of being Celtic's most expensive signing? A quiet, decent lad from Suffolk? He just didn't progress as I thought and left for Ipswich a year later, having managed just three goals.

There was one Old Firm game where it might have turned for him, if fate had been interested in helping him out. Instead, Andy Goram made three or four brilliant saves and grabbed Stuart's headlines. But the fault was mine, for misjudging what was needed to shoulder responsibility for Celtic's goals. I should have made mental toughness a priority. You must be a certain type of character to succeed at one of the Old Firm clubs.

I bought Tony Mowbray and Gary Gillespie, fine defenders and good lads. But both were dogged by injury misfortune and tended to be unavailable whenever they were most needed. Frank McAvennie and Andy Payton from Middlesbrough did

OK, while Tommy Craig recommended me Gordon Marshall and he came in and was a good keeper for the club.

That handed me one of my toughest decisions, when I had to drop Packie after a poor spell. I just felt he needed time out of the team. Packie understood and accepted it as the good professional he was. But for a rookie manager it was another difficult part of the baptism.

That's another thing I admire about John Giles, how he so comfortably handled managing players he'd played with and been friends with. With John, he could be manager, teammate and pal during the 90 minutes and juggle all the hats easily. I think he achieved it mainly because everybody knew there were never any agendas or favours with him. He simply gave it to you straight all the time. Good or bad, but never cruel. I tried to make that my approach, but I found it awkward, with both Packie and Tony.

Things were never hopeless, at least in the first two years. We had top players like Paul McStay and John Collins in the team. It clicked at times. Sometimes the football was great. But we'd go on a run, then hit bad patches. Consistency was elusive. While Walter had a team for the long haul, able to withstand whatever came their way over a winding campaign. We finished 10 points behind them in the league the first year and when we clashed in the Scottish Cup semi-final there was a perfect illustration of their ability to tough things out. They were down to 10 men inside 10 minutes. We shook every bit of woodwork second half, but Ally McCoist's goal gave them a win they celebrated deliriously. Walter charged across the pitch at the end to mark one of his first big statements as the boss.

Despite the bitterness between the clubs' fans, I liked Walter and we got on fine. Tommy Craig, who had also been Billy's assistant, told me the city expected the two managers to set a good example, to be civil to one another. So we had a few lunches together. He was a good man, dignified. And when he occasionally lost the rag on Old Firm day, it was never with me.

But I needed that trophy badly. Any trophy. I had a rotten 5–1 UEFA Cup defeat at Neuchâtel Xamax on my rap sheet too, though that really came too early to be properly my fault. It just underlined the size of the job ahead. In the second season, an early cup exit to Falkirk was a disaster and essentially ended the season in February. We finished 13 points behind Rangers in third.

The fans were raging, though most of the anger was directed upstairs. 'Sack the board' became a common chant and banner. There were always protests outside Parkhead on matchdays. It only triggered the defence mechanisms of the people in charge. Behind the scenes stuff appeared in the papers and I found out one board member had leaked it. I confronted him at a board meeting. 'Why are you being underhand? Why don't you just front me up?' I was baffled by all this business, had no experience in handling it.

It probably says much about the inertia and indecision that gripped Celtic that they gave me a third season. Rangers were still high-rolling, financing their dreams of the European Cup. They spent big again on Duncan Ferguson and Gordon Durie.

After two years without putting any dent in our rivals, I made a decision to bring in Joe Jordan to take the coaching. Joe had become a friend during our time in Italy and had done well managing Hearts. The problem for me was Joe wanted to bring in his number two at Hearts, Frank Connor. The board gave the go-ahead but only if I got rid of somebody else from the staff. By now, I wasn't in a position of strength and didn't have much of a negotiating hand. So I had to let Mick Martin go, who was a great friend. Mick hadn't done anything wrong and looking back over my career, it's one of the things I can't reflect on with any pride. Thankfully it never upset our friendship.

The idea with Joe was we'd be a partnership, more than boss and assistant. Maybe he'd do for me what Don Howe had unlocked in Terry Neill's time at Arsenal. But 10 games in we'd won just twice and after a defeat by St Johnstone in October I went to Kevin Kelly and resigned. They were probably thankful somebody had made a decision.

I presumed they'd give Joe the job, but having not enjoyed any beginner's luck with me, now they wanted somebody with a track record. Lou Macari had history as a Celtic player and came up from Stoke. It didn't work out for him either, and didn't work for several more seasons. The Scottish title wasn't reclaimed for another five years. With that board in control, there was never credibility the club could move forward. It wasn't until Fergus McCann took control that the turnaround began. He had the money and business acumen to make things happen.

It's still raw with me, that failure. I didn't go back to Celtic for a long time. If I had my time over, I'd start at a smaller club. Or take a job as an assistant. Learn my trade. Find a place where the board could at least agree to disagree. But I plunged in at the deep end and sank.

I'd love to have even one trophy to show for that time. There were one or two great nights, when I felt very happy in the job. The European turnaround against Cologne; 2–0 down away, we beat them 3–0 at home. A late John Collins winner under the lights. That was living. There is nothing like the noise at Celtic Park on those nights.

Ibrox isn't a library either. Standing in front of the bench there is an experience that will always remain with me. North

London, Turin, Milan – nothing compares. It was vitriolic. Fenian this, Catholic that. The place constantly on a knife edge. One tackle, one gesture from the dugout, could generate as much noise as a goal anywhere else. You can feel this wall of aggression behind you and you certainly couldn't celebrate a goal, in case you incited a riot.

When looking back over a long football life, I love the fact I've experienced it. And did get to celebrate a goal or two, internally at least. A win at Ibrox in 1992 sticks in my mind, when Charlie Nicholas and Gerry Creaney scored, and we briefly gave Celtic fans hope, playing in a style they enjoyed. I even belatedly met Pavarotti in Glasgow, to make up for my ignorance back in Turin. He came to help with an event for a multiple sclerosis charity. My daughter was with me and we went to a church where he sang, along with just a violin and cello. It was beautiful, spine-tingling.

It didn't work out, but I don't regret my time living in Glasgow at all. When you stripped away the divisions, people were people. Most with sense, some without. Our next-door neighbours became great friends, became the people we left our keys with. They were Rangers diehards.

15

Brighton

THE CALL CAME FROM the Witch Inn, a lovely country pub in Lindfield, West Sussex. It was October 1993, the timing just off for Halloween trick or treat. Though the treat was Gerry Ryan's voice on the line, my old Ireland teammate, one of my best mates and one of the nicest guys I've known in football. A great player for Brighton and Hove Albion before a broken leg ended his career early, he now ran the pub with his wife Simeon. Living in Sussex, he was still friendly with some of the Brighton directors and in a discussion about hiring a new manager, he'd thrown in my name. It's one of the funny quirks of football that you're rarely approached directly about anything. Clubs tend to keep a little distance in case things don't work out. So Gerry was on the line as the middleman charged with seeing if I'd be interested.

It would be a step down. But I felt scarred, I suppose, that Celtic hadn't worked out and I wanted to prove myself better than that. I wasn't in a huge hurry but was well aware that in the eyes of a lot of football people I had failed. There wouldn't be a queue for my services. I had to say I was interested.

My memories of Brighton were good, having played against Gerry at the Goldstone Ground during a great time in the history of the club. Arsenal were the visitors after the club gained promotion to the First Division for the first time in 1979. Alan Mullery was their manager and the ground was heaving. The town buzzing as the Arsenal supporters made a seaside weekend of the trip. Ex-Spurs and no lover of Arsenal, Mullery was telling the press that they would make us suffer. We beat them 4–0 and spoiled that party – Frank Stapleton scored the first top-flight goal at the Goldstone. But they held their own for four years and made an FA Cup final in 1983 and were unlucky not to win the first game at Wembley, drawing 2–2 against Manchester United.

Ten years later the club was in dire straits – second from bottom of the third tier, Division 2. Barry Lloyd had been let go as manager and they looked certs for another drop to the basement of the English League. Financially, there were all sorts of problems. Everybody seemed to be owed money by the club. There had been winding-up orders and High Court hearings.

So did I not hear alarm bells ringing? I suppose I did, to some extent. If you were taking a young manager aside and advising him of a promising opportunity where he could cut his teeth properly and make steady progress, Brighton would have been a long way from your top recommendation. I wasn't naive about the size of the task, but in my mind was the idea of reviving a club where I knew there was a big following and a deep passion among the supporters. And I figured the quicker I got back into management the better.

I had an interview with Bill Archer and David Bellotti, the guys running the club. I was initially taken by the candid assessment of Archer, when I met him at a hotel off the M6 near Preston. This man is telling it straight, I thought. His business partner Greg Stanley ran a chain of DIY shops and supposedly had put a lot of money into the club over the years.

Archer hadn't put anything in of his own. He was there to salvage what he could of Stanley's money. As it turned out, he would become probably the most divisive figure in Brighton's history, but he was quite persuasive. He told me there was no money now, but if I could spark any momentum and get them up the table, he'd find the funds to back me. It seemed fair, but ultimately he was spinning me a yarn. He never had any intention of backing me.

So I accepted the job. A two-year contract. Gerry agreed to be my assistant, and George Petchey, a great football man who set Laurie Cunningham on his way to stardom at Orient, came on board to look after the youth set-up, where we would need to be productive, given the lack of money for signings.

My initial enthusiasm took a knock that first afternoon I pushed open the doors to the Goldstone. This wasn't the vibrant place I remembered. It was a tattered shell that smelt of disappointment. Where people had evidently given up. It was in a bad state of disrepair. The stands, the dressing rooms. The terraces were full of weeds. How could you ask a player to change in a run-down dressing room then run out and play with pride?

I got in any staff we could find, along with the young apprentices, and mounted a clean-up operation. I got stuck in myself, painting walls, cleaning carpets, reapplying some dignity. I wanted people to appreciate that this is a proper football club. A club that had found hard times, but would work its way out of this dire situation.

There was an instant glimpse of the potential that first Saturday, 18 December, at home to Bradford. The attendance was more than 6,500, double the usual, sucked back in by a glimmer of hope, the way supporters are when it comes to football. Football's scriptwriters were working overtime too, because there in the opposite dugout was my old pal Frank Stapleton. Still a great friend now. We were both 37, though Frank was fitter than me and still registered to play for the visitors. The old fire still burned for Frank and I admired him for that and couldn't argue that Bradford didn't deserve their win, 1–0 from the penalty spot.

Afterwards, we caught up briefly and I remember Frank summed up better than I could myself why I was doing this, what brought us both to a wet and windy Goldstone the week before Christmas. It was part of our make-up. It was our lives. What else could we do? Deny us the rhythm of a football week for a few months and we were adrift. We just couldn't easily walk away from the game.

I really enjoyed becoming immersed in the game again. Relished the routine. I understood right away this wasn't a place where shouting the odds would work. There was little point making demands of lads who weren't even sure what they had to give. They needed encouraging and their confidence rebuilt. There were senior players who needed motivating and youngsters who needed educating. We could have got something from that Bradford game but for a young lad, Stuart Munday, diving into a tackle to give away a penalty. I could already see he was a good kid who just needed that rashness coached out of him. He was receptive. All the youngsters were. Several were raw but keen to learn.

The great bonus was the attitude of the experienced lads. Steve Foster, of the famous headband, was a club hero who had seen the rise and fall. But Fossie was 36. I feared he might be going through the motions at this stage of his career and it would have been hard to blame him. Colin Pates was a few years younger but he'd been at Chelsea and Arsenal and could have been winding down. I appealed to them to give me a dig out, to lead this rescue mission. And they responded just as I hoped.

And then I went and signed someone even older. Free transfers and loans were our only means of recruiting players and Gerry noticed another local hero was still playing non-league for Sittingbourne. The great Jimmy Case, who won two European Cups with Liverpool before becoming a key part of Brighton's early 1980s success story.

Jimmy was nearly 40 but what he'd lost in energy, he kept topping up with know-how. Every pass still driven to its destination. Every tackle still a dangerous crash scene. And his enthusiasm rubbed off on the youngsters. If Jimmy was closing opponents down, what excuse had the kids? He got involved in the coaching too and we got on great. Except for one afternoon against Rotherham, I think.

I was in the dugout and Jimmy was just in front of me near the halfway line. The Rotherham left back, a kid starting out, took a heavy touch and as the ball ran away from him, he stretched his left leg out to regain control. Jimmy had seen players naively leave themselves in this vulnerable scenario many times and arrived at just the right moment to plant his studs below the lad's knee. A classic over-the-ball tackle. All too familiar in my playing days. I heard a crack and a scream and jumped off the bench. 'Jimmy, what are you doing, he's just a kid, he's done nothing to you.' And to be fair to Jimmy, he was instantly apologetic. Regret in his eyes. 'Sorry, Liam, I just couldn't resist it.'

The tackle was ingrained in him. Nothing personal, just a way of life growing up working the 1970s engine rooms. Handling yourself, they'd call it. He had been transported back to the days when Graeme Souness and Terry McDermott were beside him in Liverpool's menacing midfield. You picked your battles then and I learned many years ago that you leave a 50/50 alone when Jimmy Case is on the other end of it. That Rotherham youngster was probably never as innocent again. It was a relatively cheap lesson, it turned out, since the crack I'd heard was just his shin pad breaking.

Jimmy, Fossie and Colin Pates brought the younger players on in those early weeks and months. And we started to play. We had a couple of very talented players. Robert Codner, a midfielder from London, who I didn't see for my first three weeks in the job as he was in Lewes prison for driving offences. Welsh striker Kurt Nogan was a very good finisher but he was another youngster who just needed more guidance. A little more structure, I think. To be told what runs to make and how much effort was expected. And when he scored one or two, a surge in confidence made his contribution invaluable.

Confidence and belief is so vital to a team. There was a lack of both with a lot of the players. With morale on the floor, they'd stopped working hard enough and weren't doing themselves justice. But with Kurt scoring we pieced together a run of results and started to climb the table.

It's funny the things that stick in your mind. My memories of the next eight or nine months are probably selective. The vignettes I can recall are largely happy ones. There must have been frustrations. The club was still broke. The board was a mess. Results weren't perfect. But I just remember thoroughly enjoying the work and the place.

New Year's Day and this livewire on loan from Arsenal, Mark Flatts, heats up a freezing Goldstone. He's a lovely young kid off the field but on the park there's a strut about him. That's exactly what we need. He's full of tricks and we thrash Cambridge 4–1. A Nogan hat-trick. Mark loved his time with us and his cameo probably opened a few doors at Arsenal.

It's February and I'm walking along the dingy corridors of the old Leeds Road stadium ahead of a meeting with Huddersfield. Their manager, Neil Warnock, is approaching. I've just been named Manager of the Month in recognition of our rise from the relegation mire. Warnock is shoving out a hand. 'Oh, here he comes, the Manager of the Month. It's not what you know, it's who you know.' I shake his hand and ignore the jibe. But I can picture the look on his face too after we win 3–1. He is sick. I've never warmed to Warnock.

I can see the Goldstone filling up week by week – 8,000, 10,000, 16,000 by the end of the season. They're enjoying the football again. There is a good feeling round the place again.

I'm sitting at home watching Arsenal win the European Cup Winners' Cup final against Parma, thrilled the club has gone one better than our team did in 1980. And proud to see Paul Dickov out there revelling in the Copenhagen celebrations, just a few weeks after we said goodbye to him. George Graham was pleased with how Mark Flatts got on and did me a huge favour by sending Paul to us too. He was superb, scoring five goals in a couple of months and would have stayed longer but Arsenal suffered a few injuries and he was called back to Highbury.

Himself and Nogan were a real handful for defences. Having some connections in the game was proving a help even if I didn't have a chequebook. We finished 14th and everyone was pretty happy. I hoped Archer would now back me with some money for wages and transfers but it wasn't forthcoming. I smelt a rat then and should have walked away. I had regained some credibility as a manager.

However, I was happy in the job, so I carried on. Rolled up my sleeves for the same kind of season. At least I could change some of the players I didn't fancy. I signed two kids from Spurs on free transfers, Junior Campbell and Jeff Minton. I get in on loan a youngster from Norwich City, Ade Akinbiyi. He's electric, bullying defenders, scores four goals in seven games. Gerry Ryan, Jimmy Case and I were watching a lot of reserve football at the time.

We lose just twice in the first 10. There's promotion talk. After beating Wycombe Wanderers over two legs in the League Cup, we get a plum draw with Premier League Leicester City. Kurt Nogan scores in a 1–0 win at the Goldstone but it's a two-legged affair. A large Brighton crowd trek with us to Filbert Street, more in hope than expectation, while Kurt is in the shop window, with rumours that big guns are sniffing around.

There are spells where we pass it around like the Premier League team and other times when we refuse to wilt under pressure. And then the kid who dived in that first afternoon, Stuart Munday, pings in a rocket from 35 yards. A stunner. His coming-of-age moment. Nogan adds a second in a win Brighton fans of that generation still mention. And only partly because of the comical late drama, when Jimmy Case is sent off for being deaf. Jimmy, who always struggled with deafness, had left his hearing aid in the dressing room. And with the furious home fans screaming for every decision, he can't hear the referee whistling urgently to hurry him on taking a late corner. His face is a picture of amazement when the ref pulls out his second yellow card.

It's one of the most enjoyable nights of my managerial career. Surely Archer and Stanley will support me now. Management is incredibly satisfying when you have a dressing room on a roll. Training is great. People have each other's backs. There's banter and mickey-taking, but when the whistle goes the players are together. I'd experienced it under Terry Neill and Don Howe at Arsenal, John Giles with the Irish team and Giovanni Trapattoni with Juventus. Whatever is going on in the boardroom doesn't matter. Setbacks are processed as learning experiences. Sleeves are rolled up. We go again. We're together.

And then, as mysteriously as a group bonds and grows, things can unravel. The glue bringing people together is confidence. Belief. And when it hisses away, cracks appear. Blame is thrown around. Even the maths of football is fickle. 'Unbeaten in three' overnight becomes 'one win in five'.

Steve Foster breaks a cheekbone and we go out to Swindon in the next round of the League Cup. The club has earned a lot of money with our little run. We lose 3–0 at Huddersfield's brand new McAlpine Stadium. Warnock is beaming afterwards. We briefly gain the status of giants when we are killed by Kingstonian in the FA Cup. Kurt Nogan never scores for the club again. Four months of blanks and he pisses off the fans by telling the press about his plans to get a big move. Eventually he is getting booed and departs for £250,000 to Burnley. Not that any of the fee comes my way. Frank Stapleton, who also sees the fickle side of football when he is sacked by Bradford, helps us out but only stays a couple of games.

We go a dozen games without a win, talk of promotion long forgotten. And one Friday reality truly bites when the coach driver turns up for a trip north. Except he has no plans to drive us anywhere. He hasn't been paid for three months and can't take the hit any longer. He's just there out of courtesy to give us time to make alternative plans. I give him my own credit card to pay for the journey and make promises about the rest of the bill that I can't be sure the club will keep. Not long after, a minibus is donated for the youth team, but the club won't even pay the insurance on it. The supporters' club eventually give me a cheque.

We finished the season 16th. Not what we wanted. But when things got sticky, we needed help. A signing or two. Gillingham signed Akinbiyi a couple of seasons later for two hundred grand and sold him after a season for over a million. I could have got him. The kid loved his time playing for us. We had shown enough, as a management team and a dressing room, to deserve backing. We couldn't keep pulling rabbits out of a magic hat. Investment nearly always determines a club's ceiling. It was time to call in that early promise Bill Archer made.

We rarely saw him. He lived up north near Crewe and very rarely came to Brighton. I remember meeting him when we played Wrexham away. David Bellotti, the chief executive, had given me the impression that this was going to be a productive meeting. A few hundred grand to spend was mentioned. Though I gradually learned that David tended to tell people what they wanted to hear.

After pleasantries, I recall setting my stall out. 'I've proved I can get the fans in the door. We're going in the right direction. But with a bit of money we can do so much more.' His reply should have brought an end to this episode. 'Liam, I actually need you to cut the wage bill further.'

I should have walked. I wanted to. But I felt a responsibility to Gerry and George, as well as to some of the young players I had brought to the club that season. In the end, the three of us took a pay cut rather than lose a coach or a player. But I knew, deep down, this was a dead end. These people weren't serious about the football club. We started the 1995–96 season with a patchwork squad, another old Seagulls hero, Ireland international John Byrne, back for a swansong. I brought some famous players to the club but unfortunately they were near to retirement. Russell Osman, Paul Jewell, Frank Stapleton and John Byrne.

By then the shameful betrayal of the club was under way. The ransacking of a century of history and soul. The Goldstone was sold. I was drip-fed the story at much the same time as the fans. The local paper, the *Argus*, had to dig because the club was saying nothing. Then, when Bellotti and Archer eventually went public, the plan hardly sounded plausible. It was presented as an 'exciting new venture'. A brand-new 30,000-seater stadium would be built on the outskirts of the town on land owned by the council. The snag was we'd have to share Portsmouth's ground until it was built.

Archer rang me. What did I think? I told him as professionals we'd play wherever he wanted but the fans would need to see bricks on the ground at the new site. They'd have to be able to visualise a future. But the *Argus* soon made sure Archer was never trusted again. The front-page headline said it all. 'Offside!' It emerged there was no planning permission for a new stadium. The council had thrown it out weeks before. Worse, somebody discovered the club's Articles of Association had been amended to allow the owners and shareholders to profit from the sale of the ground.

It's an old story of greed and opportunism. Just a transaction to the owners, where millions were made. The Goldstone was knocked down and is now a retail park. The club would have to move, with nowhere to come home to. The owners didn't care.

Except the fans didn't take it lying down. We started the season terribly. I demanded Archer come down and tell the players what was going on, to give them some assurances, but his supposed pep talk was dreadful. Waffle. Nobody came out of it any the wiser as to where this was going. Morale was shot.

A group of supporters staged a protest on the pitch at half-time during a home game with Notts County. I had to go out and plead with them to come off. Archer and Bellotti hoped I'd continue to sweeten things with the fans, pacify them. But I was in agreement with the fans and said as much in the press conference afterwards. I admitted nobody knew what was happening with the club and that I was on the fans' side. The protest was a peaceful way of having their voice heard.

Bellotti was furious and phoned me to ban any more TV interviews. I just laughed at him. He was petrified the fans would get hold of him. It got so bad our kitman Jock was looking under Bellotti's car to check for a bomb. I told Bellotti he and Archer were running the club like a *Carry On* film. This situation, with the board and manager singing different tunes, wasn't going to last.

Along came our FA Cup tie, away at Canvey Island. Even though they were non-league, I was actually quite pleased with the result. We got away with a 2–2 draw and I thought we'd be OK at home in the replay. But a week later, a 3–0 home defeat to Walsall was the end for me. It came as no surprise. It was a horrible time for everyone who was working hard for the club.

Archer didn't often ring me at home so when he called on the Monday I knew what was coming. He was very disappointed with recent performances. 'It sounds like you want to sack me?' I said. He confirmed that. This time, I didn't walk away without a severance package. It was the principle rather than the money. Celtic gave me an opportunity and I didn't deliver. This time, in my view, I'd upheld my end. After 23 months, I left a club I'd grown to love. But I wasn't going to go quietly.

The ground saga ran and ran. There were more protests and pitch invasions. The FA threatened to expel the club if it moved to Portsmouth with no concrete plans for a return. The team was relegated that season with Jimmy as manager. He had no chance. The latest plan was to ground-share with Gillingham. Fans were in despair. It was heartbreaking to see so much history and passion just dismantled and disregarded.

A friend of mine, John Keehan, who'd helped me fundraise for the youth team, introduced me to his brother-in-law, Dick Knight, a successful local businessman and huge Brighton fan. Dick is an inspiring man and it was his vision and leadership that began the rebirth of Brighton and Hove Albion. He dreamed big and he had the drive and business experience to make things happen. A few like-minded business people formed a consortium and so many rallied around with offers of help. We called Archer and Stanley out publicly. The great BBC presenter Des Lynam lent a hand and his profile helped too.

The developers who had bought the stadium wanted £40,000 rent to let the club stay another season and in our first public move the consortium offered to pay it. The media was all over it. The campaign was only starting. It took years of persistence and persuasion and negotiation by Dick to finally get Archer out and people back in charge who cared about the club. Dick moved mountains to get planning permission for a beautiful stadium in the Sussex area about 10 miles outside Brighton. Finally the club was going to get the home it deserved. The Albion climbed out of the lower leagues over the next 20 years. It's a story well told by now, and I am proud to have played a small part in it.

Along the way there was an important landmark, the final game at the Goldstone. The week before the match, Dick and his group finally came to an agreement, thanks to the intervention of professional mediators, to take over the club. But with the club at the bottom of Division 3, a revival would be so much more difficult following relegation from the Football League.

On that emotional final afternoon, when many tears were shed, Stuart Storer got the only goal against Doncaster Rovers to lift the club off the bottom of the league. Stuart was the one player Bill Archer gave me money for. He cost £15,000. There are all kinds of irony wrapped up in that one.

Dick Knight's journey was long. Two seasons trekking to Gillingham for the fans. The club made the best of things on its return to Sussex at the Withdean athletics stadium for a decade, before finally enjoying home comforts at the superb Falmer Stadium, now the Amex. Dick stepped aside to allow the wealthy local businessman Tony Bloom to take the club to the next level and secure the building of the ground. It remains one of my favourite days in football, going there to watch Arsenal in a cup match at the spanking new stadium in front of 29,000 fans.

I live in Hove and it still annoys me sometimes when I drive past the retail park and remember how the club was betrayed. But it reminds me too that I was wrong, that first afternoon, when I stepped through the doors of the Goldstone. A club isn't defined by the state of its ground, it's measured in the love and pride of its supporters. The fans persevered and never gave up, not by a long shot.

16

Back to My Roots

WAS MANAGEMENT FOR ME? After nearly five years, what had happened at Celtic or Brighton to convince me I was really cut out for this line of work? Or that I particularly enjoyed it? I had enough contacts around the game if I wanted a way back but I knew in my heart of hearts that I didn't. Some aspects were satisfying but on the whole it was constant hassle. Win and the pressure lessened but not for long. I made my mind up it wasn't for me and I hadn't much appetite, truth be told, for getting back on the managerial merry-go-round.

Picking teams and organising training sessions, no problem. Scouting players, great. But there was plenty about management I could manage without. You never feel entirely in control, or at least I didn't. There's the politics of directors and owners, keeping your board onside. Placating the man who controls the purse strings, the one who decides if you get the help you need to improve the team.

Players can be difficult too. You inherit some who are unprofessional and some who can't take being left out of the team and cause trouble. Too many sleepless nights, kept awake by the responsibility of getting results. You had to be a certain type of character to handle it and I suspected I wasn't.

So at 40, I found myself looking around to see what else I might do. I rang Arsenal vice-chairman David Dein with an idea. There were so many players from my time, and earlier, still fond of the club, who were popular with the fans and considered themselves Arsenal men, wherever else their footballing lives had taken them. Wouldn't it be a good idea if the club ran a proper ex-players' association? Like Man United, Liverpool and Leeds were doing. Get former stars filling roles around the stadium on match days or helping to raise money for the club's charities. I have always been nostalgic about football and helping former players would give me satisfaction as well as a focus in my life. I fancied running this kind of operation, if Arsenal would agree and we could get it off the ground.

The lunch with David was going well and he seemed enthusiastic about my suggestion until he changed tack. 'Liam, this all makes sense and I think we will look at your idea, but I think there might be a better job for you back at the club.' Arsenal were having a complete rethink about their youth policy. Something wasn't working like it used to. The best Arsenal teams had always been built around players who had been educated and developed at the club. The foundations of the '71 double-winning side were built in the youth team. Bob Wilson, Pat Rice, Sammy Nelson, Peter Simpson, Charlie George, Ray Kennedy, Eddie Kelly and George Armstrong. Then came the 1970s influx from Dublin, along with English lads like Graham Rix, Richie Powling and David Price. Later, Don Howe's fingerprints were all over the crop that George Graham grew into champions. Tony Adams, Martin Keown, Paul Merson, David Rocastle, Paul Davis and Michael Thomas. But not many youngsters had made an impact since. The

production lines at clubs like Manchester United were outper-
forming Arsenal in a big way.

David wanted someone to head up a new youth structure,
completely independent of the first team manager. That's not
how it had usually worked. The manager was nearly always
responsible for picking all his football staff. So if the manager
got sacked, the youth team boss often followed him out the door.
But Arsenal wanted full separation of powers, with the manager
focusing on the present while the Head of Youth Development
would be playing the longer game.

There were plenty interested in taking it on, but David
encouraged me to apply. And I didn't need much convincing.
I prepared well for an extensive interview in front of the
directors and laid out my vision. Better facilities, bigger scouting
network, wider recruitment base. Develop young players
capable of winning trophies for the club.

I got the job and was thrilled to be back at Arsenal. It felt
more than a job. There was a romance to the prospect of
steering kids on the road I'd taken. I knew the pitfalls and the
right direction to take if you were going to have a career as a
professional footballer.

I'd be dealing again with Ken Friar all those years after we
discussed my contract. And dealing with Ken was always a
pleasure. My only concern was word on the grapevine that first
team manager Bruce Rioch, who'd been in the job a year, wasn't
impressed with my arrival and felt he should have made that
kind of call.

I arrived back at Highbury in August 1996 for my first full
day at work, with the new season dawning. I met Ken and
Richard Carr, the director responsible for youth development,
to agree budgets and shape strategy. I wanted to discuss facilities. We had the training ground at London Colney – mainly

for the first team – and the indoor JVC centre behind the Clock End at Highbury. It wasn't enough for a club the size of Arsenal. The idea for our own purpose-built youth training centre was born at that meeting.

I wanted to nip the Rioch issue in the bud too. The first team were back from a pre-season tour of Italy and I knew Bruce would be at the training ground preparing for the new season. I emphasised the importance of a good relationship with the first team manager. What did he want from me? Was there a style of play that needed to run through the club?

They sat listening, but I could tell they were not totally with me. They were distracted. Eventually, he stopped me in full flow. 'Liam, would you mind stepping outside for five or ten minutes?'

I paced the Highbury halls, thinking this is all very strange. Something is going on. Ken called me back in and was straight to the point. 'Liam, what we're going to tell you is very confidential. At around two o'clock this afternoon it is going to be announced that Bruce Rioch is no longer the Arsenal manager.'

It was turning into an eventful first day back at the club.

'So who is the new manager?' I asked.

'We don't know yet. All we know is that it's not going to be Bruce.'

Rioch was about to experience the sort of unpredictability that made me glad I'd chosen a new way of life. Youth development was pressurised too, in its own way, except the fruits of your work might not be seen for five years or more, rather than in 90 minutes.

Ken reckoned I'd be better off going home for the day.

It was two months before the new manager was appointed. My old teammate Pat Rice first held the job for three games and banked a unique 100% winning record. Names like Johan Cruyff and Terry Venables and David O'Leary had been linked.

So Arsène Wenger came from left field and there was some bafflement and scepticism around the club and English football in general, which still wasn't sure 'foreigners' had much to teach it. Everyone knew it was David Dein's idea. I wasn't among the 'Arsène Who' brigade. I knew about his work at Monaco, while Glenn Hoddle, who I respected greatly, spoke very highly of him. I won't pretend I felt he was a sure thing, but I was open-minded about his prospects.

We first met in one of the hospitality boxes at Highbury's Clock End, an introduction that included Ken, Richard and chief scout Steve Rowley. Arsène was charming, confident and straight down to business. He wanted to expand our scouting. We'd be no longer just about finding English talent, but developing kids from all over Europe and beyond. 'We have to think worldwide,' I recall him saying. It was a message that transformed Arsenal. The first team would change from fielding predominantly English playing staff into a European outfit. It was helpful that Dennis Bergkamp was already a great example of continental sophistication in the team. And the tremendous impact of Wenger's first signing, Patrick Vieira, opened everyone's eyes to Arsène's touch as a talent spotter.

We didn't differ that often over the years on the potential of players. And on a broader level, there was very little I could ever disagree with him on. His idea of football played well was right up my street. What he was undoubtedly right about was that players have to be dedicated and disciplined. My experiences in Italy meant I was already intent on introducing good habits around diet, preparation and recovery to the young players. He became convinced, in a short period of time, that English players were not really looking after themselves and

212

needed to change their ways to get the most out of their football careers.

When I was in Italy players constantly talked about longevity in their profession. In England, the only future many players worried about was the next good night out. Arsène changed that culture at Arsenal. He demanded the highest standards. And if you didn't buy into it you were on your way. Paul Merson and John Hartson are probably the best examples. Two extremely talented players who weren't prepared to buy into this new regime didn't last long. It made my job easier too when I spoke to our young players. You have got to be be 100% dedicated. 'Good better best . . .'

What's he like? It's up there among the questions I'm most often asked. I hardly knew any Frenchmen, Michel Platini was one but I didn't know him that well. Pick one thing that defines Arsène, I would say it is his curiosity. He is interested in everything. Science, economics, languages. How things work and how they can be improved. He wanted to know all about Arsenal as a club, its culture and its history of bringing young players through.

He is totally obsessed with football. He loved players who had technique and football intelligence. He wanted to win playing attractive football and he succeeded. He loved building a player, layering on the game intelligence once he was confident the foundations were there. And the foundations, for Arsène, were always technique, which had to be honed early, and attitude. He knew you couldn't teach desire.

As demanding as he was, there was tolerance too, an occasional extra mile for those who were worth it. Sometimes I'd be telling him about a kid with an edge. 'He's good, Arsène, but can be trouble.' He'd say, 'Liam, all the best players give a little trouble.' He maintained that the top players were driven by a dissatisfaction with themselves that sometimes spilled over in ways that meant they didn't always behave perfectly.

He went out of his way to help with recruitment, especially for young lads who had a choice of clubs to join. If the kid needed a little extra persuasion to come to us, Arsène could be relied upon to meet him and his family, join in the tour of the facilities. It was always impressive how he spoke to the player and his parents.

In his first decade in the job, what he did at the club was magnificent. He totally changed the style of football. Players who hardly ever played out from the back through midfield were now instructed and encouraged to do it. Adams, Bould, Keown, Dixon and Winterburn loved that he trusted them in possession of the ball. He transformed Arsenal from a long-ball team into an attractive team that won.

That job consumed 18 years of my life, longer than my time as a first-team footballer. I loved it. It was pressurised without being stressful. There weren't the same manic highs and crushing lows compared to playing or managing. The rewards didn't come along so swiftly but they were worth waiting for. Whether it was Jack Wilshere winning his first England cap or a kid you first saw at 10 running out for the reserves. Sometimes it might be a player who had gone elsewhere unlocking the ability you knew was in there. It was great to see a lovely kid like Fabrice Muamba play in the Premier League for Bolton and Birmingham. Sebastian Larsson and Kristoffer Olsson were two lads I often disagreed with Arsène about. I felt they should have had more of a chance at Arsenal. It was brilliant to see the two of them play together for Sweden many times, long after we'd said goodbye to them.

Richard Carr was a fantastic boss. David Court, a former Arsenal player, was my right-hand man. A brilliant organiser and a really good judge of a player. My old Ireland mate Don Givens came in and was an excellent coach. Neil Banfield too. Roy Massey came from Norwich to recruit boys at the younger age groups. So many guys who made a career in football, at Arsenal or elsewhere, were identified by Roy at seven or eight. Bob Arber was my main scout. We would travel to international underage tournaments together and invite prospects to spend time at the club.

There are things we achieved that made me just as proud as anything I did as a player. Bringing Don Howe back to Arsenal in 1997 – his fifth and final spell – was among my best moves. Don taught the other coaches as much as the kids. Much like me, the job was a change of pace for Don and he took great satisfaction in producing fine players and people.

And one day, Richard and I were driving around North London looking at options for a new youth centre when we came across this sports ground in Hale End, smack in the middle of West Ham and Tottenham territory. There were a couple of football pitches, a big cricket pitch and a few tennis courts, all owned by London University. We were like a couple on *Grand Designs* who saw an old cathedral they wanted to turn into a restaurant. This could be perfect.

We did the deal and within two years it had been refitted as Arsenal's youth academy. The place began another revamp in 2012 that was completed after I left. And now it's a state-of-the-art training centre, a world-class centre of excellence renowned for turning out the likes of Bukayo Saka and Emile Smith Rowe and Eddie Nketiah. I think Arsenal's two-base structure works on another level too. You make it at Hale End, you're halfway to where you really want to be, London Colney,

215

the first team training centre. It gives these youngsters, who get a lot of plaudits thrown at them early in life, another leap to strive for.

By the way, there's a guy I often disagreed with, when it came to his football philosophy as a manager, but he made academy life much more productive, even if he doesn't always get the credit he deserves. As FA technical director, Howard Wilkinson broke down the old barriers between clubs and schools that allowed football clubs to train kids much earlier. Why did England gain a reputation for failing to produce technical players? Why were skill levels constantly compared unfavourably to players in Spain or France or Holland or Italy? I'm certain it was down to the rules in place that stopped us coaching players younger than 13. In Holland, they had them at seven.

Wilkinson was up against the FA blazers on the schools committees, who wanted to keep the kids for their county and schoolboy sides. It was a bitter fight at times and I admire his persistence. His changes reshaped English football and the symbols of that revolution are talents like Phil Foden and Bukayo Saka, who compare unfavourably technically to very few of the world's top players.

Saka was with us at seven. A humble lad who was never late, forever hungry to learn and who enjoyed great support from his family. Which always helps. It's thrilling to watch him fulfil the potential we knew he had pretty early. Smith Rowe was a quiet kid, who, strangely for someone with his skill, seemed to lack a little confidence. I remember taking him aside and telling him he should be showing everyone watching that he is the best player on that pitch. He's a lad who really found himself away from Arsenal, in Germany, a perfect example of the loan system working as it should.

The first real breakthrough to the first team was Ashley Cole. We didn't all see it at first. He played as a forward in the underage teams, but wasn't really making an impact and was close to being let go. It helped his case that he was a humble kid who really wanted it. But it was youth coach Tom Walley who twigged his potential as a left back. We offered him a YTS place that had no guarantee of a professional contract when he turned 17. That landscape changed completely during my time. The coveted youngsters now demand guarantees before signing up to a scholarship. Or at least their agents do – there are agents sniffing around by the time these lads are 12, working their angles.

The problem for Ashley was Arsène had just taken a young left back from France called David Grondin. And as we'd seen with Vieira, Emmanuel Petit and Nicolas Anelka, this source of talent wasn't exactly letting him down. I made Ashley's case with the boss more than once, but it took a loan spell at Crystal Palace to convince him. The reviews coming back were gushing and offers were starting to arrive. Arsène brought him back for a closer look and Ashley grabbed his chance with both hands.

Cole's case underlined how difficult it was for young players from the academy to break through, particularly during that first decade, mainly because the standards set by the first team were so high. You had to be an exceptional talent. Like Cesc Fàbregas, who didn't stay with us long in the youth teams, but still followed the traditional Arsenal apprenticeship when he joined at 16 from Barcelona. We looked after his lodgings and placed him with a lovely Irish landlady in North London, Noreen Davies. Noreen got the Spanish TV in, made the food he liked and drove him everywhere. I remember having a chat with Gerard Piqué and his grandfather about making the same move as Cesc, but Gerard ended up going to Manchester United, where it didn't work out for him, for some reason.

There was another 16-year-old we were certain about. Niccolò Galli, son of Giovanni Galli, the famous AC Milan and Italy goalkeeper. A pal in Italy, Kevin Hughes, had tipped me off about this young centre back. He had the lot – physicality, skill and speed. When he came over to London he impressed everybody with his ability and attitude. There was just a maturity and intelligence about the lad, on and off the field. He was part of our Youth Cup-winning team in 2000 and was a kid on a mission to emulate his father's greatness. Arsène loved him and he was on the fast track to the first team squad except he missed home so much. I knew well how that felt, so after discussions with Arsène we decided to loan him back to Bologna for a year, to continue his development and finish his studies.

He was progressing as rapidly as we expected and had made his Serie A debut at the age of 17. Then came the darkest morning of my time back at Arsenal, when news arrived that Niccolò had been killed in an accident the night before when riding his moped on the outskirts of Bologna. Everyone at Arsenal was devastated for his lovely family and mourned a colleague who had become extremely popular during his short stay in London. Arsène and I are convinced he would have gone to the very top of the game and would have captained Arsenal and Italy. The training centre used by Bologna is now named after Niccolò. He left an equally lasting impression at ours.

At any one time, we were overseeing the development of up to 120 players across the different age groups. That meant mistakes were inevitable. As is often highlighted, Harry Kane was once one of our own. He was at Arsenal for a couple of years until he was nine or 10. Truth is, he was a late developer and didn't compare well with some lads who were rated better at the same age. Later on, when Harry began to make headlines, I was told the reason we let him go was a lack of athleticism. I wasn't responsible for letting him leave, but you know where the buck stops! I was told that he wasn't very athletic. In our defence, it took Tottenham a while to realise how good he was too, sending him on loan to the lower divisions several times, where he didn't pull up many trees either.

Sometimes in football you need a lucky break and it came Kane's way when Tim Sherwood became the new Spurs manager. Sherwood had worked with Kane in Tottenham's under 21s, believed in him, and gave him his big chance. He never looked back. Nothing came easy for Kane. He has achieved his remarkable success through utter determination in the face of setbacks and it is thoroughly deserved. He worked tirelessly on his game and became an outstanding player and professional. He didn't make his Premier League debut until he was nearly 21. Michael Owen and Wayne Rooney, the top English strikers of their generation, had started at 17. When you see what Kane has done in becoming England's record goalscorer it is really remarkable and a credit to him.

Mark Noble, a West Ham legend, was another we had around that age. He was a natural footballer with a great attitude and winning mentality. A fantastic lad who loved his training. Trouble was, his family were devoted Hammers and wanted him to play for West Ham. He had the great career I hoped for and knew was in him.

Serge Gnabry is now a German international and serial winner in the Bundesliga with Bayern Munich. We had him at Arsenal from the age of 16. He progressed early and made his first team debut at the age of 17. He stalled for the next two years and eventually Arsène gave up on him. We sent him to West Bromwich Albion in the Championship on loan. Tony Pulis, West Brom's manager, played him once as a substitute in the time he spent there. Pulis, an established and successful manager, said 'he wasn't at the required level for West Brom'. Arsène sold him to Werder Bremen for £5 million. Judging young players is not an exact science.

We analysed all these kids in so many ways. We measured them, weighed them, put the stopwatch on them, plotted them on charts, crunched their numbers. Yet for all this data, youth development will always have a place for instinct. Often it's your gut tells you a kid has it. Sometimes the problem is in a player's make-up and it might be a move, a different club, a coach who believes in a kid, and everything clicks into place.

Ultimately, there's no formula for moulding people. David Bentley should have played 500 games in the Premier League based on his talent. But he never really took football seriously enough. I don't think he ever loved the game. We sold him to Blackburn for £2 million and had a 50% sell-on clause when he went to Tottenham for £15 million. So he made us a packet. But it didn't surprise me when he effectively retired before he was 30.

I've heard people say Jermaine Pennant is another who wasted his talent, but I would see it differently. He didn't reach the heights we hoped for at Arsenal, having splashed a lot of money for him at 15 from Notts County. But considering his difficult childhood and the lack of support around him, he should be proud of how far his ability took him, including to a Champions League final.

Youngsters are going to make mistakes, and some learn from them quicker than others. Some may not appreciate what they have. Jay Bothroyd was a promising striker, a local lad from

Islington who also played in that 2000 Youth Cup side. We were playing West Ham in the Premier League Youth Cup final when Don Givens subbed him. He lost it and as he walked past the dugout, pulled off his shirt and threw it at Don Howe. Watching in the stands, I'd made up my mind before I'd reached the dressing room or spoken to Don. There were standards and lines you didn't cross. He'd never play for us again. I knew Arsène would back me. We sold him to Coventry for £1 million a week later. It turned out Jay had a good career and late on he won an England cap. Maybe it was a lesson worth learning.

Then you had a character like Nicklas Bendtner, who arrived from Denmark with a lot going for him. A skilful forward with a powerful physique. But unfortunately, he'd probably be able to describe still the decor in my office, so often was he in there. He just didn't have the mentality to handle the early fame that can ruin you as a player. He ended up doing time in a Danish prison even though he won 81 caps for his country.

The great flaw Jack Wilshere had – the second-best English player the academy produced in my time, after Ashley – is that he was just too brave for his own good. I watched him play for England at 20 alongside Frank Lampard and Steven Gerrard and was sure he'd be a fixture in the team for years. But Jack went into tackles I'd never have attempted. He just wasn't streetwise. And injuries cruelly ruined his career.

There was a contradiction in the job. You mould footballers as people and then they become products. Making money out of them was important. At a rough guess, we brought in £250 million to £300 million from the sale of players developed while I was at Arsenal. Funds we could reinvest in the academy and use in the transfer market for the first team. Moving a player on at the right time, at whatever age, was vital. Even if it's just to free up space in the younger teams for a better prospect. That part of my job was the only downside in my position as Academy Manager.

It was the hardest part of the job. Especially with the youngest kids. Every January I had to steel myself mentally. There are support services for youngsters and parents. It's not just goodbye and thanks. The club will do everything to make sure the kid gets a new start somewhere else and a spell at a club like Arsenal is still a great experience even if it ends in disappointment.

But that disappointment can be crushing for a young man. I decided early it had to be me breaking bad news. It wouldn't have been fair for me to put that onto other coaches. Roy Massey took care of the very young boys, but at under 14, 16, 18, I let them know their fate.

Some of the boys know what's coming. They've worked it out over the season. But he and his parents are sitting there, unable to look at you, begging the words not to come out of your mouth. You try to be strong and decisive, but also kind, compassionate and understanding. To give the kid and his parents something. It's not the end.

I changed my mind once, in my last year. I buckled. The January ritual was taking place at Hale End. An Under 14 kid called Danny Ballard was next up and we had decided there were just too many boys ahead of him. Danny broke down in the office. He was sobbing uncontrollably, and he was such a smashing kid that I started to well up too. For some reason, I just couldn't go through with this one. 'OK, Danny, forget what I said, you can stay.' It was of my final decisions before I stepped down from my role after nearly 20 years. Happily, Danny made the most of his reprieve, stayed with Arsenal until his early 20s before moving on to Millwall and Sunderland. He is a Northern Ireland international and is building a fine career in the game.

Maybe it was a sign the job had worn me down a little too. I had told the club I would be stepping down at the end of that season. I'd begun to enjoy it a little less every year, with every added layer of bureaucracy. At first, decisions got made quickly. You chatted with a lad and his parents, showed them around the club and they made the call. Over the years, negotiations with agents became more protracted. And much like Arsène with the first team, we didn't have the money to throw at players that the likes of Chelsea and Manchester City could. Parents and the boys often expected too much.

As soon as the Premier League began to categorise academies, the workload also multiplied. Of course, Arsenal has to be a Category 1 academy because of the club's standing. But that meant huge numbers of staff, forests of paperwork, thousands of boxes to be ticked. It wasn't the job I came into.

I know it was something that bothered Arsène too. He often mentioned how Arsenal had around 70 employees when he joined, but it was closer to 500 by the time he left. Many of these employees didn't have the foggiest idea about Arsenal or its history and it felt like the soul of the place was being lost. Of course it had become more a business than a club.

The change of ownership was a factor. The fallout among the board that lead to Stan Kroenke coming in was felt in two ways. Arsène was already hamstrung in the market because of the money borrowed and spent in building the Emirates Stadium. Now he'd lost his chief ally David Dein, who he was very close to. David was his buffer between the football and operational side of the club. Ivan Gazidis came in as Kroenke's man to run the show. To be fair to Ivan, a business growing so quickly and with so many different revenue streams needed more structure. But there no longer seemed to be much of a buffer between the business and the football. Before long those of us on the football side of the operation, which some would still consider to be a pretty essential part, found ourselves running virtually every decision past the Human Resources department. Before, if you had a problem with a player or a coach, it would get sorted by having a meeting with Ken Friar or Arsène, who would essentially knock a few heads together. But nothing got resolved quickly any more. There was always another meeting.

The club was very kind when I told them I'd decided to step away. They made me an ambassador. Representing Arsenal on pre-season trips, helping with the charitable foundations, keeping an eye on the players out on loan. The kind of thing I had had in mind, I suppose, when I phoned David Dein many years earlier. It was a thank you, really, by the board, and was appreciated. I had three years in that very enjoyable role. I thoroughly enjoyed being part of the club again and it was a privilege to work there at such an exciting time in Arsenal's history. With huge respect to men like Herbert Chapman and Bertie Mee and George Graham, I believe Arsène has been Arsenal's greatest manager, for the way he revolution-ised the club and the style with which he achieved success. The Invincibles team stands as his proud legacy.

Possibly my favourite souvenir from the entire experience wasn't a medal or a cup or a jersey. It arrived one evening, a few years ago, via a ding on WhatsApp. A message from Kieran Gibbs, a lad I signed at 16 from Wimbledon when the club disbanded in 2004 and became Milton Keynes Dons. He was small and weak physically but had a good football brain and a lovely left foot. I gave him a chance. He played 137 times for Arsenal before moving to West Brom, where he played another 100-odd. He was about to leave England for Major League Soccer in Miami when the text arrived. He doesn't mind me sharing it.

'Dear Liam. I hope you don't mind me messaging. As my time playing in the UK comes to an end, I sit with the family and discuss all the amazing memories we've been able to have over the last 20 years. When we stripped everything back we came to an important question, how did a lot of this become possible? Your name came up almost instantly as it was you who brought me to Arsenal and gave me the opportunity to fulfil my dream. I remember the day you offered me a scholarship like it was yesterday and I remember all the other times I got a chance to speak to you and get little lessons and bits of advice that have helped guide me through my career to this day. You believing in me and giving me a chance has enabled me to give my family a life we've never dreamed of and for that I am forever grateful.'

The vast majority of footballers are good people who thoroughly appreciate what the game has given them. It was marvellous to be a small part of so many of their lives.

17

Stuck in the Middle With You

THE CALL FROM RTÉ's Head of Sport was a surprise. Big Jack was gone, Mick McCarthy's first term as Ireland boss had disappointed and we weren't going to the 1998 World Cup in France. But Niall Cogley wanted me to be part of it on RTÉ's punditry panel, where my great friend John Giles had been a fixture for more than a decade. The conversation didn't proceed far before I was explaining exactly why this could never happen. Because of the man who had been on the panel even longer. Eamon Dunphy. 'I don't think I could work with Dunphy, Niall. Too much bad blood down the years.'

The former international Eamon Dunphy was by now almost as big a draw as the football for his trenchant analysis, delivered in colourful terms with great certainty, even if there was a reasonable chance he'd be changing his mind before too long. Rarely, it seemed, did a broadcast finish without him declaring somebody shameful or a disgrace, or identifying a cancer in the game that had to be eradicated. He seemed to instinctively go against the grain, and famously doubted Michel Platini's quality all the way through his nine goals en route to France winning Euro '84. He certainly wasn't a fence sitter, as was often the case among pundits at the time. In many quarters, he was almost regarded as an enemy of the state during Italia '90, after he was savagely critical of Jack Charlton and his style of play. Before that, he'd been even more critical of me, often in his other job as a Sunday newspaper columnist. He wrote a lot of stuff that was below the belt and very upsetting to my family and friends.

To understate things, I didn't like him. An impression that had been shared widely in the Ireland dressing room. When our fortunes faded under Eoin Hand, Eamon was harsh on the team and never missed a chance to take aim at me. I was arrogant and self-indulgent. I chose money over football when I went to Italy. I had too much influence in the Irish dressing room and picked the team. It was total garbage. Later, I'm certain Eamon bad-mouthed me to Jack, before he'd even arrived in Dublin. So I told Niall Cogley that, no, I wouldn't be working with Eamon Dunphy.

Thing is, myself, Eamon and John might have had our first outing together in the Maracanã rather than the Montrose studio of RTÉ if Bertie Mee had allowed me to go on Ireland's South American tour in 1974. Because Dunphy was on that tour, in the squad selected by new boss Giles for the games against Chile, Brazil and Uruguay.

Eamon had always been well-versed on political matters. He wore a black armband playing for Millwall after Bloody Sunday in 1972. He had spoken out against the apartheid regime in South Africa. In Santiago, he was haunted by walking out in a stadium where Pinochet's junta had tortured and executed thousands of socialist activists. When he came home Eamon told a newspaper that Ireland should never have gone. The FAI was outraged at the negative publicity his protests attracted and banned him, aged 29, from ever representing the country again. A very FAI way of handling things! So we never found out if the three of us could have made up a functional midfield.

I enjoyed the punditry game. My first venture as an analyst came at Euro '88. Though injured, Jack had invited me to travel to Germany to help around training and the team hotel. And ITV wanted me on their commentary team for Ireland's games with England and the Soviet Union. On that great afternoon in Stuttgart, I was beside the brilliant commentator Brian Moore in the Neckarstadion gantry. Brian was a lovely man, friendly and welcoming, and I was instantly comfortable in his company. Back on punditry duty in England, Brian Clough was giving Ireland no chance, scoffing at the lack of pace between Kevin Moran and Mick McCarthy at the back. Knowing Kevin was a lot faster than he got credit for, I said I'd rather have our two than your two – Mark Wright and Tony Adams, who was still raw then. Brian had told me not to be reluctant to give my opinions. He was full of encouragement.

I sensed even Brian was probably getting a bit frustrated as our defence and Packie Bonner held firm following Ray Houghton's early goal. This had been billed in some of the poorer quarters of the English media as England v England B, given the number of English-born lads in our team. At one stage Brian reheated the joke that was doing the rounds, that the initials of the FAI stand for Find Another Irishman, so I pointed out that John Barnes, out there in front of us playing for England, was born in Jamaica. Which was a bit unfair on John, who'd lived in England since he was a kid. But I knew most of the English-born lads playing for us were proud to wear the Irish shirt. Their parents or grandparents had come from Ireland, so that sort of stuff bugged me.

The exchange with Cloughie went down well at home. The consensus was I'd handled myself OK. Brian Moore was great to work with and my first time in the punditry role had gone very well. That was far from my thoughts back at the hotel, where the mother of all parties kicked off. To beat England in the Euros was the greatest result Ireland had ever had, and it was well after midnight when Jack beckoned me over to the bar. 'Get the lads to bed, Liam. We have the Soviets in three days' time.' I looked at him in amazement. 'Jack, I'm grateful you brought me along but I don't do miracles. You fucking tell them!'

It's the biggest regret of my football life, not playing in one of those tournaments Ireland reached. From that first afternoon in the Dalymount dressing room, suddenly crippled by anxiety, this was always the dream. Over the years, so many dodgy offside flags had pushed the prospect further away but you could never fully give up on it. The Dublin football communities I grew up in cherished the fact that we had arrived on this stage. It would have meant the world to my family to see me out there. It would have meant the world to me. So it was gutting to miss out. I didn't know whether to accept Jack's invitation to accompany the squad, but I was delighted I went. It was on opportunity of a lifetime to be around it, to get a taste of it, to almost feel part of it. We went so close to making it to the semis in Germany, and when Italia '90 came around and I wasn't in the squad the prospect of working in TV sport came along again.

This time I was with the BBC. I had met the head of sport, Brian Barwick, with his football producer Niall Sloane, and we got on well. I'd be working with John Motson and Barry Davies as a co-commentator. Both were great commentators, but contrasting characters. Davies was a little aloof and had a schoolmasterly air about him. I felt, at first, that he almost resented having a footballer with him in the commentary box. He had his views on football and how it should work and he didn't necessarily welcome anyone else's contribution getting in the way of his chance to share them. John Motson was entirely different. Motty, as everyone called him, couldn't have been more welcoming. He didn't come across nearly as confident as Davies. In fact, before we'd go to air, he was invariably a bag of nerves. A little panicky as he rummaged through his stats and notes. Yet when the game kicked off, he clicked into gear and the words flowed. And he was constantly inviting me in, encouraging me to say my piece. In the end, I got on fine with Barry too, but whenever those big BBC decisions had to be made, around who to choose for a major final, I suppose for his warmth and openness, I was always pleased when Motty got the gig.

Returning to Italy was also a chance to properly explore a country I'd spent nearly seven years in but mainly seen from inside hotel rooms or football stadiums. And Ireland's assignment in Sardinia and Sicily was an invitation to enjoy the sea, beaches, food and wine. Again I was grateful to Jack for allowing me to mix freely with the lads around the team hotel. There was trust that I hadn't entirely jumped the fence into media.

Just as is the case with any Irish person I've talked to about Italia '90, those weeks seared all these vivid memories. Those long seconds after Van Breukelen spilled it, before Niall Quinn slid in to get us out of the group. A packed Marassi Stadium back in my former home of Genoa. Packie's save from Romania's Timofte and Dave O'Leary stepping up, out of Jack's doghouse and into Irish sporting history. On RTÉ, 'a nation held its breath'. On BBC, I just remember slipping into friendship mode. 'Come on, Dave. You can do it. Keep it on target.'

My sister Breda had jumped on a plane, caught up in the madness at home, and was there that evening at the magnificent meal laid on by a few of my Italian friends at one of the best restaurants in the city. The place was full of Irish supporters, many of the accents from Dublin's leafy southside. Half the country might have been emptying the credit unions to get out here, but Irish football was moving in new circles too. The rugby boys were on board.

On to Rome to play Italy, and more treats. My old Ireland teammate Gerry Ryan made it out and I got him a game in a charity fundraising match. Europe versus South America. Zico, Falcão and Junior were in their ranks, but Gerry gave their full back a chasing and made a goal for Paolo Rossi.

And then a poster from my bedroom wall in Glenshesk Road come alive. A meeting with an all-time hero, Bobby Charlton. The BBC flew him in because Ireland were in the quarter-finals. We did an interview with him about his brother. It was easy to see why they might have had difficulty getting on. Bobby was quietly spoken, shy almost. You would get through a thesaurus or two before landing on shy to describe Jack.

I even got down to Naples to watch my old Inter teammates Zenga, Ferri and Bergomi go out on penalties to Maradona and Argentina. The whole experience was a thrill. I was retired only a few months from playing, so the BBC gave me a great way to experience a competition of this magnitude. I was spoiled really with that early media work and got a taste for it. Jack and the lads did me another favour by qualifying for the '94 World Cup, so I got to tour the USA with the BBC. New York, Orlando, Dallas, Washington.

And I got to work on one of the best team performances I've seen – beside Barry Davies in the gantry for AC Milan's 4–0 win over Barcelona in the 1994 European Cup final. An exhibition of utter control and class and a privilege to witness. Italian football was booming. Serie A was the best league in the world. It had become big in England as well, an interest that accelerated after Paul Gascoigne's move from Spurs to Lazio. I got work too alongside the late Peter Brackley on Channel 4's *Football*

Italia live matches. A gentleman and a funny guy. Mainly we recorded from a booth in London on Sunday afternoons, but for the bigger games, we might fly to Rome or Milan.

After nearly seven years in Italian football, Channel 4 wanted me on for my knowledge of the Italian game. You could know the Italian game a little too well, however. One of my final matches for Channel 4 was an infamous meeting of AC Milan and Brescia in 1993. This was the Milan of van Basten, Rijkaard, Gullit, Maldini and Baresi, while Brescia were in relegation trouble, so the outcome should have been a foregone conclusion. Well it was, but in a very Italian sense. A draw would make Milan champions and would be of assistance to Brescia's plight too. I was convinced a draw was an absolute certainty.

Peter was of the same view, though we skirted around this likelihood for the first half, which involved no attacking action of note. To say it was two boxers barely laying a glove on each other would be overselling it. These boxers hardly got off their stools. Getting bored, as the second half followed the same pattern, I said to Peter that this is what happens, in Italy, when a draw suits both teams. 'It's a foregone conclusion, Peter. The match will finish in a draw.'

Cue Milan youngster Demetrio Albertini showing his inexperience by firing, out of the blue, into the top corner of Brescia's goal from 20 yards. Although the Milan celebrations appeared suitably sheepish, I could see the smug look on the face of our producer, an Anglo-Italian, who didn't favour criticism of the product. Though his smile dissolved around two minutes later when the Milan defence inexplicably parted, including a comedy collapse from Baresi, allowing Luca Brunetti to saunter in for the equaliser.

Peter: 'That's amazing, 1–1 . . .' A chuckle in his voice.

'I don't think it's amazing at all, Peter. I think Milan have actually let them score there. Baresi didn't seem too bothered about them coming forward . . .

'Our viewers are certainly getting an insight into the Italian way of playing football. I think there will be a stewards' enquiry after this match.'

Of course there was no such thing. Nobody in Italy batted an eyelid. But there was an immediate enquiry after the game in the Channel 4 studio. The producer was incandescent. 'You can't say things like that. You will alienate our viewers.' From there, matters escalated until our Anglo-Italian friend was on the receiving end of a crude invitation to stick *Football Italia* up his arse. I thought they wanted my opinion. I didn't do many more Sunday afternoon games for them.

Because BBC mainly called for tournaments with Ireland involved, failure to reach Euro '96 meant I didn't get a place in the squad for the finals. Jack Charlton also lost his job on the back of that. Instead I took on my most unusual punditry assignment: analysing the games in Italian for a TV station in Ticino, the Italian speaking Canton of Switzerland. My Italian could stand up reasonably in a dressing room or a night out in a trattoria, but I'm not sure it was satisfactory to talk the people of southern Switzerland through the games. Though the programme director seemed happy enough. In any case, I enjoyed a great tournament immensely. England went so close with Alan Shearer and Paul Gascoigne at their best throughout the tournament.

Then, a few months before France '98, Niall Cogley from RTÉ called. He was well prepared for my reluctance. 'Meet me,' he requested. 'Eamon wants you on board.' When we sat down, he made the case that I'd be well able to hold my own on air with Eamon. And he made me a financial offer that was better than I expected. What did I do? I did what I'd invariably done down the years whenever a tricky situation presented itself – I rang John Giles.

It had always sort of baffled me, the relationship John and Eamon had. In my eyes, John was a fount of wisdom, a rock of sense. Eamon didn't fall under any of those categories, as far as I was concerned. Yet the two of them had been great friends since their teenage years in Dublin. They were at Manchester United as young men, played together in the Irish team, came home from England and worked together at Shamrock Rovers. They were on TV as a duo and often out together socialising and enjoying themselves. I'd never spoken to John about this before and I asked him bluntly about their relationship. I'm not sure how I put it, but it probably amounted to 'What exactly do you see in Eamon?'

John, as he nearly always manages to do, captured a multitude in a sentence or two. 'Put it this way, Liam, you'll never be bored in his company.' He encouraged me to come on board for the World Cup, and pack it in then if I wasn't happy. So it began, a quarter of a century on Irish TV, myself between John and Eamon.

John was right. It wasn't dull. Things were a touch frosty at the outset. But a night out or two broke down a few defences. And when the cameras were rolling, it just seemed to work between us. John was very relaxed and hardly seemed to notice he was on television. He sees the game so clearly. He is brilliant at spotting the two or three things that are going right for a team, and the two or three things going wrong, that determine how a game might pan out.

I realised quickly too that I had been unfair in regarding Eamon as someone who just said controversial things for the sake of it. Maybe he did, at times, but he was much more serious about the work than I'd imagined he'd be. He brought a journalistic outlook, a different way of looking at things, and often set the agenda for us, like a producer. John might nail the details of a match, but Eamon was always looking to place the match in a bigger picture. So he could turn a routine Champions League night into a referendum on the very future of football. How the game was being destroyed by cheating, or money, or conservative coaches, or whatever.

Thankfully, we had the best master of ceremonies around, either stirring or keeping a lid on things, whatever was needed, in the late Bill O'Herlihy, a great presenter. Despite having worked as a soccer journalist for years, who read everything written about the game, Bill would give the impression that he was utterly naive and needed the simplest things explained. But of course it was his way of working for the viewer.

And if things were plodding along on a humdrum night, Bill had a masterful way of sparking a row. Of throwing a grenade. 'Liam, I saw you wrote in your *Examiner* column a few weeks ago that . . . but now you're saying . . .' And you couldn't help yourself but be sucked in. 'Hold on a second, Bill . . .' And he'd lean back in his chair, delighted.

There were plenty of rows over the years. It all kicked off between me and Eamon the night he mocked Arsène Wenger and likened him to John Cleese in *Fawlty Towers*. And of course he accused me of letting club loyalties cloud my judgement. 'You've jumped the fence, baby.' In many cases, we were all more or less in agreement, but Eamon had this knack of exaggerating the core of an argument and turning it into a performance. There was a Champions League night with Manchester United where we all agreed Cristiano Ronaldo had behaved pretty petulantly but Eamon told us during the commercial break he was going in two-footed. 'Liam doesn't want me to say this, but Ronaldo is a disgrace to football.' Now

Cristiano had probably already scored 35 goals that season, but as far as Eamon was concerned, 'this fella Ronaldo is a cod'.

Graeme Souness, on the occasions he came over to work with us, loved all this, and constantly told us he couldn't believe what you were allowed to say on RTÉ compared to when he worked on TV in England. I think it opened his eyes and he probably brought some of that back home with him when he started on Sky. On RTÉ, Graeme contributed just like the rest of us. There is that brilliant moment when Eamon was haranguing him about something and eventually he turns, exasperated, and asks 'Where did you manage?'

'I managed to stay alive for 63 and a half years, baby.'

Certainly never boring.

Invariably the biggest rows happened on international nights, with Ireland playing, when the temperature rose and everybody was much more passionate. Things would be heated from the start, with Eamon convinced, for example, that Mick McCarthy wasn't up the task as Ireland manager, and only had the job because he was one of Jack's most loyal disciples. When Ireland blew qualification for the 2000 Euros by conceding from a late corner in Macedonia, Eamon wanted Mick sacked. While me and John were more supportive, citing his introduction of youngsters like Shay Given and Robbie Keane.

This division set the tone for the World Cup campaign that followed, which I still regard as the finest achievement by an Ireland manager, surpassing even Jack's three qualifications. We survived a group with Portugal and the Netherlands, beating the Dutch in Dublin and progressing via a playoff with Iran. Roy Keane was playing his best football for Ireland and Eamon was nibbling at small portions of humble pie over McCarthy.

I was attending a conference for academy managers at a hotel in the north of England in May 2002 when I looked at my phone, which had been on silent, and noticed a pile of messages from RTÉ and BBC and various newspapers requesting my opinion. Roy Keane had been sent home from the pre-tournament training camp in Saipan after a row with Mick over facilities and equipment. This became a debate, no, a civil war, that divided the country.

It wasn't cut and dried. Of course anybody who had played for Ireland and encountered the FAI's often amateurish approach to preparations had to have sympathy for Keane, but there's a time for taking a stand and surely this wasn't it. It might have been better for everyone if he had been given special treatment, been left at home for another week after a tough season with Manchester United. Putting that to one side, I figured he was still out of order when I got to know the circumstances. He had given the manager no option but to send him home.

John, who did more than anyone to demand better standards from the FAI, was of a similar view, and we both expressed that in the media. But Eamon, who also hosted a radio show, thought Keane a god and could only see things from his point of view. As was his style, Eamon inflated this into something much bigger than a dispute between two men who had never been that fond of each other. This was Roy demanding more than Irish football had historically expected. And McCarthy tolerating mediocrity and lack of ambition.

It became a crusade for Eamon. By now, he and I had been getting on pretty well, but he stopped speaking to me. Worse, he fell out with John, his pal for ever. You could cut the tension with a knife when the three of us convened in the studio for Ireland's first World Cup match, with Eamon dressed in the colours of our opponents, Cameroon. Even the unflappable Bill was feeling the pressure. He wasn't comfortable and certainly couldn't risk his usual gambit of sparking a row. What a weird few weeks it was. Sad thing is, our relationship breakdown was replicated in arguments among people across the country.

In the end, Ireland played well, Mick did well, taking us to a last 16 exit, very unluckily on penalties to Spain. Qualifying for the World Cup and performing so well in the group is something we can only dream about nowadays. But the overriding emotion around 2002 is regret. With Roy Keane there, I think we could have bettered Jack's quarter-final finish in 1990.

As for the panel, it all blew over between us eventually. One day John and Eamon just started talking again, and I followed suit. I've no doubt Bill was the most relieved man in Dublin when he reported for duty and found us chatting outside the studio.

Eamon and I will never entirely see eye to eye. Anyway, if you agreed with him today, he might have changed his mind by tomorrow. But we're pals. He didn't hold back in his criticism of me but I take solace I'm in among the likes of Platini, Cantona and Ronaldo. Eamon didn't rate them either.

We had another 14 years together, always enjoyable, never boring. And plenty of other ex-players kept things interesting along the way, especially German international Didi Hamann. I'm still a regular guest on Eamon's podcast too, with John, the band getting back together.

John left RTÉ in 2016, then Eamon in 2018. This year it was my turn to call it a day, after 25 years, 35 altogether in punditry, paid to talk about the game I loved. There's a new generation of Irish internationals having their say now, the likes of Damien Duff, Shay Given, Kevin Doyle and Richie Sadlier. It was a privilege and a pleasure to be asked to give my views, and just another of the many blessings football brought me.

18

Trap

GIOVANNI TRAPATTONI IS A revered football legend in his
native Italy and regarded as a coaching giant far beyond. He
is among a handful of managers to win league championships
in four different countries, Italy, Germany, Portugal and
Austria. I was with him for two of the six Serie A titles he won
as manager of Juventus, where he also added a European Cup,
two UEFA Cups and two European Cup Winners' Cups.

The call came from Don Givens, my former Ireland teammate, who had worked with me for a few years in the Arsenal
academy. Don now worked for the FAI as Ireland U21 manager.

'Liam, do you think you could give Trapattoni a ring? John
Delaney has heard through an agent that he might be interested
in the Irish job. Could you find out for certain?'

I was astonished.

There are awkward moments when you jump that fence
from player and manager to pundit. I found it really uncomfortable on RTÉ during Steve Staunton's term as Ireland
manager. Steve was an old teammate who I liked, but the job
worked out badly for him. Bobby Robson, who was meant to
work alongside him and guide him, got sick. John Delaney

was the FAI chief executive and I think he came up with the idea of the Robson–Staunton ticket. But after some promising early results, things went downhill for Steve and criticism was fierce. A lot of people were upset that the previous manager, Brian Kerr, had been dismissed by Delaney, and that didn't help Steve's situation.

Steve had been a friend and I'm glad to say still is. But I had a job to do too as a pundit. At least it wasn't hard to come across as measured when you were sitting beside Eamon Dunphy, who was typically candid in his appraisal. I hope I was fair, but there was not much that was positive to be said. It got to the stage where I was thankful some of Ireland's games were now being screened on the other channel, TV3, including one of Steve's lowest moments and one of the country's worst results, a 5–2 defeat in Cyprus. I really felt for the guy and knew well his anguish on that touchline as things spun out of control.

Steve lost his job and soon the talk around the game had it that Delaney was ringing every agent he knew to see who might be interested in taking the job. While that was the way of the football world, it also suggested a certain desperation. So I was amazed when Don phoned me one day to say my old Juve boss might be tempted.

My endorsement was instant. 'If you can get him, get him.'

Behind the scenes, the telecoms billionaire Denis O'Brien had agreed to fund the salary for a new manager, so money wasn't going to be a stumbling block. Don wanted me to ring Trap to gauge his thinking. So I did. 'Hello, Mister.' There was never any animosity between us, despite how things had ended in Turin. His immediate enthusiasm convinced me this might just work. '*Si, si, si, si. Sono interessato.*'

Delaney was delighted. He had slipped back into the anonymity of 'the committee' when Steve was sacked, but was now front and centre again, making it clear he was driving this ambitious recruitment by the association.

I took a couple of days off from Arsenal and agreed to travel with Don to meet Giovanni in Salzburg, where he had just won the Austrian Bundesliga the previous season. He was the same warm, expressive character I had said goodbye to 16 years earlier. The hands going, rattling questions at us in his charming mix of colourful Italian phrases and random English words, me keeping Don relatively up to speed. He brought us out for a nice meal, we shared pleasantries and memories, then it was back to his place to talk business.

Not money. That was for a meeting with Delaney and the FAI. He wanted to talk football. He wanted to know what he would be getting into. Was this a hopeless case? He'd seen the Cyprus game and noticed our narrow escape against San Marino. Were there any prospects here? I assured him we had some top-class players. Robbie Keane, Damien Duff, Shay Given, Richard Dunne. Plenty of talented lads who were good pros backing those players up and a few prospects coming through. And that with his ability to motivate and organise a team, I felt we had a genuine chance of doing well.

I was back home when he rang a few weeks later. He was taking it. My great friend Marco Tardelli would be his assistant and Fausto Rossi his fitness coach. 'I want you too.' He needed someone who knew the lie of the land, who knew the players. I told him I already had a full-time job with Arsenal and it might be difficult for me to get permission to take him up on his offer. I did feel a certain obligation, having played a part in getting Giovanni this far. And the thought of working with the Irish team and Giovanni and Marco was very appealing.

Ken Friar, part of Arsenal's furniture, was still around, and another of our many meetings followed in his office. He had no problem with me doing the Ireland job as long as Arsène Wenger was happy. Far from having reservations, Arsène was adamant I should do it. It would be good for me and for the club, he reasoned. I'd get to watch plenty of players on our radar. I had a contract with RTÉ Sport which I had to give up as it would have been a complete conflict of interest. I was spending enough time away from Arsenal anyway. RTÉ understood the situation.

So I rang Trap back and said yes. And there was huge excitement at the prospect of returning to a place I thought I'd left behind – the dressing room.

One of the first things on the agenda was to try to bring back into the fold players who had retired from international football, for one reason or another. The truth was, in that difficult period, we inherited some players who weren't all that keen to play for their country. Call-ups were suddenly not so attractive. Even in my day, club managers were forever pressuring players to skip internationals. But back then, as well as the honour of representing Ireland, the few quid that came our way was useful. By now, players earned so much it meant little financially. You were either committed or not. Players were increasingly mindful of their responsibilities to their clubs and going away with Ireland wasn't going to help them earn a new contract.

I wasn't naive about this part of the job. All footballers are different. There are players who desperately want to turn out for their country and some who can take it or leave it. Most are honoured and wouldn't dream of opting out if selected. A handful are so passionate about their countries they lift themselves to another level. For a small few, the whole thing is a bit of a chore they probably went along with at first to further their careers. Flights, hotels, anything that involved being away from their families could be difficult for some players.

However, we needed everyone on board. To start with, I told Trap there were three worth making a real effort with. Steve Finnan had retired to focus on his Liverpool career. A great lad, his injuries were making life difficult for him. Trap didn't need any convincing we needed Steve. He knew all about him, saw him win the Champions League with Liverpool in 2005.

Andy O'Brien was another who'd decided he'd had enough. He was among those who copped plenty of stick in the media following the Cyprus defeat and was sick of the hassle.

While Stephen Ireland was a player we definitely wanted. He had announced himself as an international with the first goal at Croke Park against Wales. I told Trap this kid might be a little difficult but would be worth it. A good passer of the ball, he made intelligent runs from midfield into the penalty area and could take a chance when it came his way.

We set up meetings in a Manchester hotel. Finnan was first and easiest. He wanted to play anyway but was genuinely conflicted, injuries plaguing him. With me interpreting, Trap assured him he was really important to us. Steve was on board straight away.

Andy had brought along his father, who did most of the talking. 'Why does my son get all the blame when things go wrong?' he wanted to know. We explained this was a new campaign and assured him we valued him. The past was the past, clean slate, all that jazz. But he couldn't be talked round. He had no beef with us but the Cyprus fallout meant he was done.

Then we met Stephen. Just 22, he hadn't played since an unfortunate episode when he left an Ireland squad with the excuse that his grandmother had died, when she hadn't, as it soon became clear.

I'd also heard that he didn't get on with some of the other players, that he was a sensitive lad who might have found the usual dressing room carry-on hard going. I just stressed to Stephen that we all rated him highly and wanted him to return. Nothing that had gone before mattered to us.

'So, what do you reckon?'

'I'll think about it,' Stephen said.

'Right.'

'What did he say?' Trap wanted to know.

'He'll think about it.'

'OK.'

I wasn't sure where to take things after that.

'Oh, if I do come back, I want the number 10 shirt.'

I was taken aback. 'Ah well, we'll see about that.'

'What did he say?' asked Trap again.

'Oh, nothing, it's nothing . . .'

I knew then we were fighting a losing battle. We shipped a lot of unfair criticism for being unable to convince Stephen to return. I kept my counsel. But can you imagine us meeting the players who were really committed to the national team and telling them Stephen Ireland is coming back but Robbie, you have to give him your number 10 shirt? Stephen never took up the open invitation we left him with.

Don Givens and I picked Trap's first squad. We cast the net wide and selected a few newcomers, including the likes of Wes Hoolahan, Glenn Whelan and Damien Delaney, who weren't exactly youngsters but were getting their chance now. A week-long training camp in the Algarve was the perfect introduction to Trap's methods for the players, and a reminder to me. In those early months, the media made a lot of my punditry work, suggesting players stung by previous criticism of them wouldn't accept me. I honestly didn't detect animosity from anyone. I said to one or two of the senior lads that it would be their turn one day, and they'd have to call it as they saw it. It was never a problem.

In one of the first meetings, Trap addressed all the negative stuff in the media in his inimitable way. 'Today's newspapers, tomorrow's toilet paper.' He stressed in that first meeting that he didn't give a fuck about journalists' or pundits' opinions. Worry about what your manager and teammates think of you, forget the outside noise.

The lads were almost immediately treated to a display of the eccentricity I remembered well from my Juventus days. We had brought our own chef with us to Portugal, Dave Steele, who had served up breakfast in the room the hotel had organised. He was already feeling the pressure because he understood Italians and their knowledge of food. And Trap had been a strict preacher of good diet throughout his career. First morning, down came Trap to inspect the hot buffet trays. All was well until he lifted one lid. Mushrooms.

'Ahhhh, *funghi*, *funghi*, fucking *funghi*. For breakfast! Get it out. *Velenosa* [poisonous].'

He was going crazy, slamming stuff around, shouting. Dave didn't know what hit him. The players were baffled. But Trap was adamant mushrooms were bad for the liver, and they never reappeared under his watch.

He laid down his law plenty more times on the training ground that week. He was almost 70, but energy still crackled off him. The same old two-fingered whistle. Demanding attention. Drilling in habits. Constantly making small adjustments. He was a stickler for detail. And like John Giles, he wasn't slow to add another half hour of set-piece practice on the end of training when the lads were hanging to get back to the hotel.

The players were with him from the start, respected him, appreciated what he had achieved and responded to his methods. Marco was great around the lads too. Watching them

245

at close quarters work with a group stirred an old longing for the parts of this job that I did enjoy. Out on the grass, coaching a set of lads to make them into a functional team. Putting a shape on an ambition. From day one, I had a good feeling about this set-up.

It turned out to be an excellent World Cup qualifying campaign. We didn't lose a match in 10. Drew with Italy twice and should have beaten them twice. Our football was quite pragmatic. Trap had a reputation as a conservative coach. 'You want the show, you go to the opera,' was among his many sayings. But plenty of his teams entertained, when they had the right players to do so. He had a good look at what Ireland had available and decided our squad was better suited to keeping it tight in a straightforward 4-4-2 and minimising our mistakes. And could you disagree with someone who had won so many trophies and coached some of the best players in the world? We had good players in lots of areas but there was no Roy Keane or John Giles to run the midfield or impose order on a game.

When he decided on the formation, he wanted two holding midfielders and wide players who would attack and defend the flanks. A player like Andy Reid would not have a role. I liked Andy as a player and made his case to Trap more than once. But he just didn't see where he could fit him in. He wanted pace wide, while protecting the centre of the pitch was a basic requirement in every Trap team, and he settled quickly on Glenn Whelan and Keith Andrews in there.

Having dealt with the press in Italy, ours wasn't going to present a problem. He could predict a sticky question a mile off and had a regular knack of buying time by asking Manuela Spinelli, his interpreter, what that guy was saying, even though he could understand English pretty well. Then he'd answer a completely different question, throwing in a few quirky phrases and giving the media lads a handy headline.

Another trademark of all Trap's teams was a box player, a clinical finisher, from Rossi to Klinsmann. Robbie Keane was perfect for what he wanted in a striker and was great in that campaign. On our return to Nicosia, where Ireland had had a terrible result last time, the pressure was on. We knew it was a game we had to win. Kevin Doyle had put us ahead early but they levelled and we were labouring on a muggy, hot September evening. We needed to win this. Trap got Caleb Folen to warm up. He always liked the option of a big lad off the bench. 'What do you think?' he asked me. Robbie had looked tired in the second half, while Doyle was still bursting a gut chasing everything.

'Get Robbie off?' I said.

He gave me a bemused look.

'We take Doyle off!'

Within five minutes, Robbie got the winner. From a few yards down the touchline Trap treated me to another lift of the eyebrow. Another lesson.

But after the draw at home to Italy, the clouds burst on another Trap storm. When Sean St Ledger headed a goal in the 87th minute, the roof came off Croke Park. We had the world champions of Buffon and Pirlo by the throats. So how did we concede an equaliser to Gilardino in the last minute?

Trap was raging. Like a madman. He went bananas in the dressing room. It was one of his rules that he repeated over and over from that first week. If you're winning, take time over throws-ins and free kicks. Throw it backwards or throw it down the line. Never across the pitch. Make it difficult for the opposition to get possession. It came back to his insistence on protecting the centre of the field. Lose the ball there and you are exposed badly.

From a throw-in in their half we lost possession and the Italians had broken on us. We had been caught on a counter-attack when leading the game, which was sacrilege, an unforgivable mistake for any Italian coach, let alone Trap.

So he was fuming when we came in. Steaming. Gesticulating. Pointing at me. Screaming in Italian. 'You Irish, you're fucking crazy. What did I tell you? Never leave yourself open. Headless fucking chickens.' The lads were agog. Kevin Kilbane, who took the throw-in, keeps the head down. But Trap never singles someone out in any case, never personalises it. It's always group responsibility. Same after in the media. Never blames people, protects players. I know the lads appreciated that. Though I got the biggest bollocking I've ever had from Trap that night and I wasn't even playing.

That result put paid to our chances of automatic qualification ahead of the Italians, but there was still a playoff with France. It was France because of a late Sepp Blatter carve-up that decided, just before the draw, to seed the playoffs and keep the bigger nations apart and give them home advantage in the second legs. It was outrageous arrogance by FIFA that they felt it was acceptable to move the goalposts at the 11th hour. It was an attitude to smaller countries like Ireland I recognised from my playing days. Did we matter at all? That was our first warning sign of the obstacles we'd have to surmount to make it to South Africa.

Trap was very down after the first leg in Dublin, when we lost to a lucky Nicolas Anelka goal in front of another 70,000 full house at Croke Park. He felt he had let Ireland down. From my experience, that's the normal gloom every manager suffers the day after an important game is lost. I reminded him of the progress we'd made, told him he'd laid strong foundations for the coming Euros. And in any case, these lads wouldn't be frightened in the second leg. We were huge underdogs but I knew we had every chance of turning it round in Paris.

The great pity is we didn't make more of our dominance during a brilliant hour in the Stade de France, among the finest hours of football an Irish team has delivered. There's this strange theory out there that the players actually defied Trap that night, that they released the handbrake, as they say, to go at France. That's total nonsense. Trap set the team up well and he was thrilled with how we attacked in a controlled way without leaving ourselves open at the back. Truth is, we outplayed France because the lads displayed the huge character we knew they had.

We were winning one–nil when everything turned on an inexplicable decision, one I'll take to the grave. It's forever woven in Irish culture. The clear handball by Thierry Henry that led to the William Gallas goal. Missed by Swedish referee Martin Hansson.

Without delving too deep into conspiracies or self-pity, I think we can safely say, that if the shoe was on the other foot, the referee would have found a way to reverse the decision. There was no VAR, no screen, but someone would have got in his ear, somehow the message would have got through. Maybe one of those mysterious flags that denied us so often might have gone up. He should have known anyway and consulted somebody. Our outrage was too instinctive, too genuine. Our lads weren't good actors – not that good.

I never blamed Henry. I talked to him on the pitch that night and he just put his hands up in that Gallic way. 'What could I do?' But it was a normal football reaction. The ball bounces awkwardly, your arm goes out and if the referee doesn't see it, happy days. We've all done it, though usually when the stakes are a little lower. I never held it against him.

I told Trap a few weeks later that was it for me, and I resigned. There was no pressure from Arsenal, but it wasn't fair to the club and my full-time job. My media work had taken me away for a day, day and a half tops. But with Ireland I could be gone for five or six days, for a double-header. Plus there were players to watch at weekends.

I returned to the RTÉ panel, where I increasingly found myself defending Trap during his second and third campaigns, particularly from Eamon, who, not for the first time, was becoming savagely critical of a manager he'd once lauded.

Some of that was loyalty on my part, no doubt. But there was also this fantasy out there that we had the players to go toe to toe with the finest teams around, if only our tactics were more ambitious. It just wasn't the case. Trap took over a team when the very best players had seen their best days, and we just didn't have enough to dictate terms against the better sides. And if anyone deserved savage criticism it was the FAI for failing to put in place a structure for developing our young players. I often thought about the glory years with Jack, and how companies were lining up to be associated with the team. That goodwill and finance was never properly harnessed to build something sustainable. Indeed, during all the years I worked with Arsenal, nobody at the FAI once came to me and asked to see a modern youth development set-up. The Dublin Gaelic football team and Limerick hurling team came to take in whatever knowledge they could, but the FAI seemingly had nothing to learn.

In any case, I was delighted for Giovanni and Marco when they took us to the 2012 Euros, even if in their term in charge we struggled to recover from the defeats we took out in Poland. Defeats, by the way, against three of the strongest teams in Europe, Spain, the eventual winners, finalists Italy and Croatia, who were unfortunate to end up in this group of death.

I learned years later that the FAI received something between €5 million and €10 million for that wrong we suffered in Paris. The staff or players were never told about the hush-hush Blatter–Delaney deal. When you consider that and all the full houses we had, Trapattoni more than paid his way with points and money in the coffers. It had proved a great decision to hire him.

For me, it was another qualification near miss. Reaching that World Cup would have made up for a lot of hurt I'd experienced as a player. But again it wasn't to be. This time, for a change, it was down to a flag not going up.

But I loved those two years, representing my country again, feeling the hairs on the back of my neck lift during the anthem, returning to a dressing room. Doing it at Croke Park brought a special dimension. The atmosphere in there was incredible, better than I'd ever experienced with Ireland. When 70,000 saw us go within a minute of beating the world champions, there was noise that hadn't been generated at Lansdowne or even Dalymount.

The venue meant little to Trap or Marco, except the prospect of a bigger crowd. Lots of the players were used to Croke Park, after history was made in 2007, when the team played there for the first time, beating Wales. But there was a certain irony for me, representing Ireland at the headquarters of the GAA, all those years after I was expelled from school for playing soccer instead of Gaelic. How times had changed.

It brought back memories too of all the outings here with my dad and brothers, watching the Dubs. The Bradys were once a Gaelic family. Edward and Patrick, my great-grand-uncles, won their All-Ireland medals with Dublin. I was born to be a footballer, but maybe it was fitting to make this short detour back to Croker.

Epilogue: Thanks to Football

I AM BLESSED TO have had more than 50 years as a professional in a game I have loved since I was a little boy. Football has been my life.

Vivid memories stick with me. I'm around six or seven, watching *Grandstand* on Saturday afternoon with my mother and father, waiting for the football classifieds. Hanging on for the Millwall result. My brothers Ray and Pat are playing. It doesn't go well. 'Oh, those poor boys,' my mother says. It made her and my dad's weekend when they won.

One day, Ray comes home and has a friend with him. It's the day before an international match. So Charlie Hurley, a huge star at the time, calls round for dinner. He is spotted coming into the house and word spreads instantly around our cul-de-sac in Whitehall. The house is soon overrun with kids.

I'm on the bus to Athlone with my brother Frank and the rest of the Shamrock Rovers team. I must be around 10. We reach St Mel's Park, and Rovers officials look after me during the match. Frank is great, in my eyes anyway. Afterwards, I'm allowed into the dressing room. Rovers have won. It's loud and happy. I want to spend my life in rooms like this.

I was lucky to have heroes right up close. Family holidays were football trips. My father was a bullockman, employed by British Rail to mind cattle on the boat from Dublin to Holyhead. A tough job, but it got us free travel. Down to London on the train to watch my brothers. I just wanted to follow in their footsteps. There was no plan or charted course. Just a driving ambition to play professional football and give it my best shot.

All the times I played with a ball when I was young, all the skills I practised, all the hours on the street, in the park, on the way to the shops, all those hours added up to allow me to play at the highest level. My vision came to fruition and my dreams came true.

My schoolboy club St Kevin's laid the foundations. We had a great team over four or five years, thanks to our manager, Des Lawlor. The club was in its infancy then but has become one of the best in Ireland at teaching young footballers the game. I was proud to be Kevin's first senior international. That there have been so many since demonstrates what an outstanding part of the Whitehall community the club is.

Arsenal, Ireland, Wembley – I could picture how I wanted it to go when I got on that plane to London at 13. Sure I was scared, but my desire and passion to be a pro outweighed the fear.

It happened for me almost easily. An apprenticeship at 15, turning professional at 17, first team debut a few months later and at 18 my first cap for Ireland. A winner's medal at Wembley and PFA Player of the Year in 1979.

After Arsenal came the plan. Follow Keegan, play in Germany. A new life with my new wife. The plan didn't quite fall into place. Instead it was Turin and Juventus. Two league titles and the first time I encountered rejection in my football career.

I overcame that setback and played in Italy for seven seasons, which set me up financially better than most. Too many great players from my time weren't that fortunate. I returned to London to West Ham, where I had three very happy years. Qualifying for Euro '88 under Jack Charlton was so satisfying, even if I suffered more rejection shortly afterwards. I never got to play on the highest international stage. It's a huge regret, but then neither did the two greatest Irish players of all time, Johnny Giles and George Best. Such is football.

Management was not a success for me, but I had a go. I know what it entails. I could have ducked that experience but am glad I didn't. To manage Glasgow Celtic was an honour. To sit on the touchline at Parkhead and Ibrox Park as manager of Celtic was a privilege. To see Brighton and Hove Albion qualify for European football for the first time in a great new stadium is more satisfaction beyond words. I live in the city. I see how proud the people are of their team. I played a small part in that.

It was a dream job at Arsenal as Head of Youth Development, to look after so many young footballers. Some made it at Arsenal at the highest level. Some made it elsewhere and had great careers and some didn't make it at all. But my guess is most are proud to have been in the mix. I want to thank all the people at Arsenal who helped me do that job for 20 years. They know who they are.

Arsenal were generous to give me three years as an ambassador for the club. I travelled with the first team, got to see first-hand how much things have changed in the way today's players travel and prepare. It gave me the opportunity to have lunch with Alex Ferguson and Bobby Charlton up at Manchester United. Alex and I probably spent more time talking horse racing than football. When Arsenal faced Bayern Munich in the Champions League, it was a delight to meet my old friend Karl-Heinz Rummenigge again and hold another inquest into why we didn't win a Scudetto at Inter.

I love to go back to Arsenal now as a supporter. It feels like home. It was special to get together with the 1979 Cup Final winners 40 years on. It was a mark of the club's class how it embraced that anniversary and hosted a memorable day for us. They invited Arsenal supporters from various walks of life. The great jockey A.P. McCoy, boxing promoter Frank Warren, the comedian Alan Davies. The former Commons speaker John Bercow was there, but had no need to keep order. Two great Northern Irish actors, Adrian Dunbar and Stephen Rea. Stephen told us he first supported Arsenal because we were the nearest thing to a united Ireland team. He wasn't alone in that.

It was great Terry was there, the boss again for one night. We lost him in July 2022. That made it even more poignant when the seven Irish Gunners from '79 and '80 finally got back together later that year. David O'Leary and John Devine hadn't been at the 40-year reunion. So all seven of us had never been in the same room together since I left for Italy. We restaged a few old photographs and refought a lot of old battles. It was a lovely, long, emotional day. I hope we all make it back together again.

It gets harder to count on things like that. Anyone can get ill, but the football community of that era sees tragedy all around us. John Hollins, who joined us in the weeks after that cup final, died this year, after suffering with dementia. Big Gordon McQueen, who carried the fight against us at Wembley, the same. The double winner John Radford is suffering. Willie Young, the eighth Celt, is not well. We think of Big Jack and Bobby. Nobby Stiles and Martin Peters, also World Cup winners. Everybody who played then knows all the heading that was demanded. In training, more than games. We draw our conclusions and I'm sure lots of us worry.

Again, I'm lucky. I was typically the 'server', the guy knocking balls into the box so the big guys could head them away or head them in. But it's sad and scary and a reminder to take nothing for granted.

Friends for life is another of sport's most important gifts, and I have so many. In Ireland, England, Italy. And not just from soccer. Despite getting expelled from the place, I'm still on a WhatsApp group with the lads from St Aidan's, our Gaelic team that won the Leinster titles. Some of us play golf together. A few years after we left school, many of us had the thrill of being in Croke Park to watch our old teammate Tommy Drumm win the All-Ireland with Dublin. He lined up beside another great friend and teammate, Kevin Moran, who managed to have the best of both worlds and play for Dublin and Ireland.

I've seen a lot of the world through football. My formal education finished at 15 but football taught me much more about life than a classroom ever could. Europe, the Middle East, Asia, Africa, North America and South America – football has taken me everywhere and I've taken in the different cultures and history.

It hasn't only been football. Growing up, the dinner table in the Brady house buzzed with chat about every sport and I've been privileged to witness so many great sporting occasions. And football got me up close to many of my heroes.

Sea Pigeon and Monksfield battling it up the hill at Cheltenham. Istabraq winning three Champion Hurdles. Dunwoody, Francombe, Walsh and A.P. McCoy. Royal Ascot, Epsom and the Curragh. Vincent O'Brien and Aidan O'Brien. Nijinsky and Galileo. Frankel and Henry Cecil. Michael Kinane and Sea the Stars. Enable and Frankie Dettori.

I got to play golf with two Masters winners, Gary Player and Sandy Lyle. And two Ryder Cup captains, Luke Donald and Paul McGinley. I witnessed Darren Clarke lift the Ryder Cup at the K Club. I went round with Christy O'Connor Sr at my beloved Royal Dublin. My great mate Keith Maxwell gave me the opportunity to play at Sunningdale when he was the pro there.

I'd never make it as a pro, but music has been a huge part of my life too. It has been in my house for as long as I can remember. My sister Breda bopping to Buddy Holly on the wireless. Eamonn, who was in the Irish Merchant Navy, bringing home a record player and our first vinyl – 'The Last Time' by the Rolling Stones. I was hooked for ever. Frank loved Frank Sinatra. He thought he *was* Frank Sinatra. In 1978, Alan Ball asked me if I wanted to go and see Sinatra at the Royal Festival Hall. I jumped at the chance. He treated me. What a night.

Living in London was a ticket to the music world. I saw Rod Stewart and the Faces at the Wembley Arena. The Eagles on their tour to promote *Hotel California*. The Who. Eric Clapton in Genoa. Bruce Springsteen at the San Siro. Elton John with a piano and Ray Cooper at the Theatre Royal Drury Lane. Roger Walters playing *The Wall* in Twickenham. The Stones in Hyde Park. Neil Young in Rotterdam. Paul Simon in the RDS.

Again, football allowed me to meet many of them. Though not yet my idol and ultimate hero, Bob Dylan. I can't tell you how many hours I have spent listening to this man. I've been to many of his shows. If there's anyone out there who could help me I'd be forever grateful. I just want to shake his hand, I don't want to dissect 'Mr Tambourine Man'.

I did meet Bono, at the cinema. Jack would let the Irish squad go to the pictures in Dublin on the evening before an international match. This time, the rest of them went to one of the *Beverly Hills Cop* films, but I wanted to see *Superman*.

Their movie finished early and as I'm coming out on my own, there was Bono standing beside me. I'd never met him before but couldn't resist. 'Hey, Bono.' 'Ah, hi, Liam.' 'You wouldn't do me a favour . . .'

He obliged, fair play to him, and stepped up onto the Ireland coach parked outside and wished the lads all the best for the game the next day.

Andy Townsend, a massive U2 fan, was star-struck. 'I can't believe you know Bono.'

'Ah yeah, we've been friends all my life.'

We're all dreamers and sometimes we're all spoofers.

I thank football for my life. It is the greatest game, and I will be forever grateful I played it. I've had a ball.

Acknowledgements

I want to thank some people who made this book possible:

The journalist Nick Callow, firstly for his persistence in persuading me to attempt this memoir and then his hard work with the research and writing involved.

The journalist Larry Ryan, for his ability and talent in putting my memories and stories on to the pages of this book.

Arsenal Football Club, for developing me into a professional footballer and giving me the foundation to have more than 50 years in one way or another in this great game.

To my literary agent Tim Bates, for his help in finding me the right publisher.

Finally, to my publishers Eriu/Bonnier Books UK, for giving me the time and support to complete the book in the way I wanted it.